Mathematics Beginning Math

Visual Multiplication

ISBN-13: 978-1981443833
ISBN-10: 1981443835

Congratulations on choosing Home Workbookfor your child! Parents and teachers agree that Home Workbooks help children learn the skills that they need to be successful in school. Each book offers educational practice pages that are based on academic standards. They are perfect for practice at home, when traveling, and during school breaks.

CONTENTS

Page

Beginning Math

Visual Multiplication

Visual Multiplication

☞ Use the dots to help you fill in the blanks to each of the multiplication problems.

(1)

____ rows and ____ columns makes a total of ____.

(2)

____ rows and ____ columns makes a total of ____.

(3)

____ rows and ____ columns makes a total of ____.

(4)

____ rows and ____ columns makes a total of ____.

(5)

____ rows and ____ columns makes a total of ____.

(6)

____ rows and ____ columns makes a total of ____.

(7)

____ rows and ____ columns makes a total of ____.

(8)

____ rows and ____ columns makes a total of ____.

(9)

____ rows and ____ columns makes a total of ____.

Visual Multiplication

☞ Use the dots to help you fill in the blanks to each of the multiplication problems.

(1) ____ rows and ____ columns makes a total of ____.

(2) ____ rows and ____ columns makes a total of ____.

(3) ____ rows and ____ columns makes a total of ____.

(4) ____ rows and ____ columns makes a total of ____.

(5) ____ rows and ____ columns makes a total of ____.

(6) ____ rows and ____ columns makes a total of ____.

(7) ____ rows and ____ columns makes a total of ____.

(8) ____ rows and ____ columns makes a total of ____.

(9) ____ rows and ____ columns makes a total of ____.

(10) ____ rows and ____ columns makes a total of ____.

Visual Multiplication

☞ Use the dots to help you fill in the blanks to each of the multiplication problems.

(1)  ____ rows and ____ columns makes a total of ____.

(2) 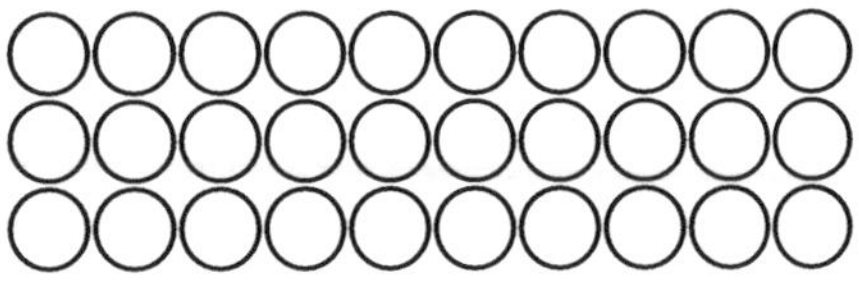 ____ rows and ____ columns makes a total of ____.

(3) 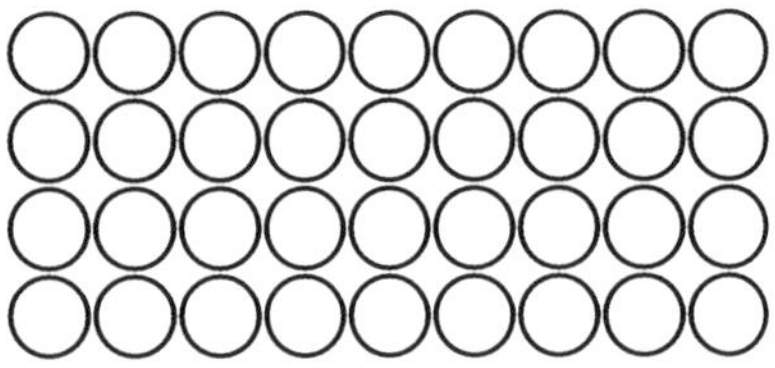 ____ rows and ____ columns makes a total of ____.

(4) 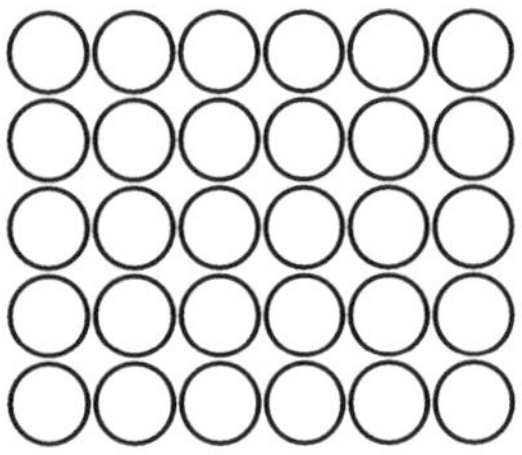 ____ rows and ____ columns makes a total of ____.

(5) 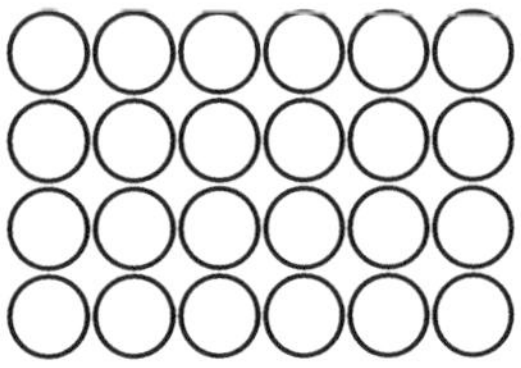 ____ rows and ____ columns makes a total of ____.

(6)  ____ rows and ____ columns makes a total of ____.

(7)  ____ rows and ____ columns makes a total of ____.

(8) 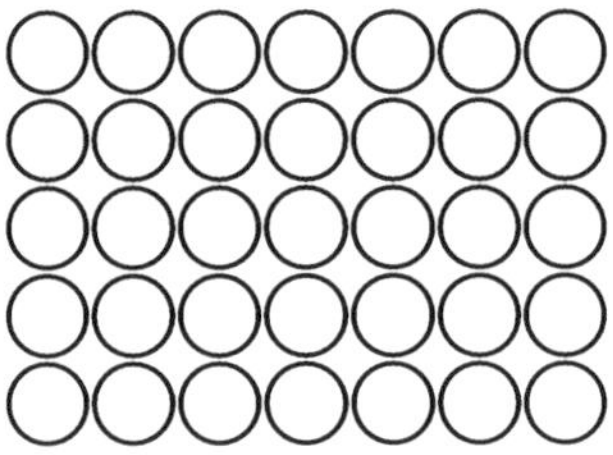 ____ rows and ____ columns makes a total of ____.

(9) 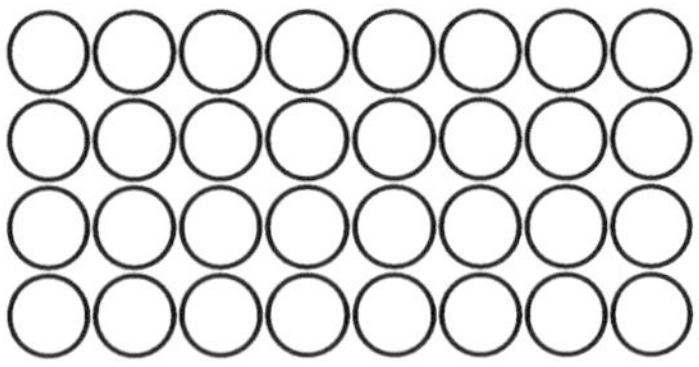 ____ rows and ____ columns makes a total of ____.

(10) 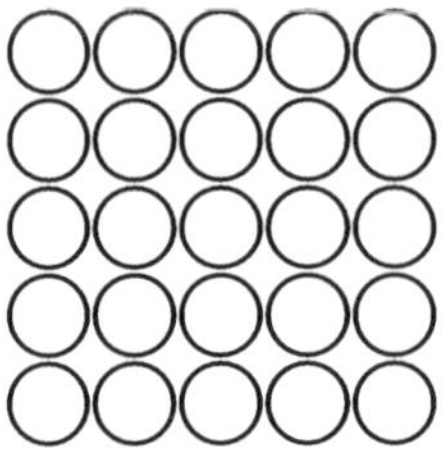 ____ rows and ____ columns makes a total of ____.

Visual Multiplication

☞ Use the dots to help you fill in the blanks to each of the multiplication problems.

(1) 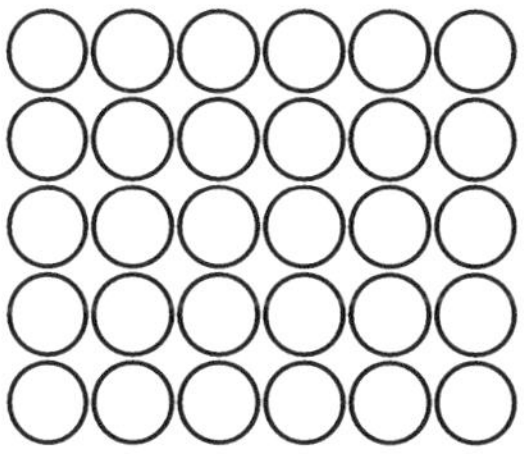 ____ rows and ____ columns makes a total of ____.

(2)  ____ rows and ____ columns makes a total of ____.

(3)  ____ rows and ____ columns makes a total of ____.

(4)  ____ rows and ____ columns makes a total of ____.

(5)  ____ rows and ____ columns makes a total of ____.

(6) 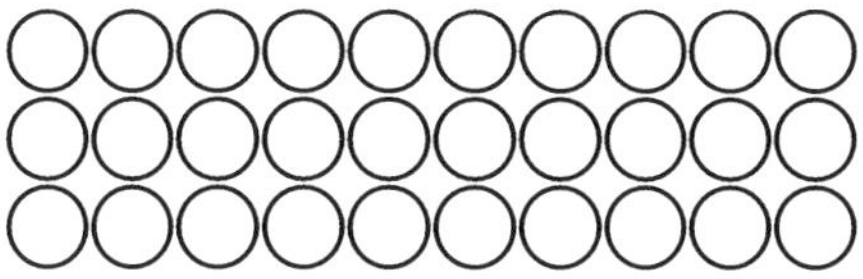 ____ rows and ____ columns makes a total of ____.

(7)  ____ rows and ____ columns makes a total of ____.

(8) 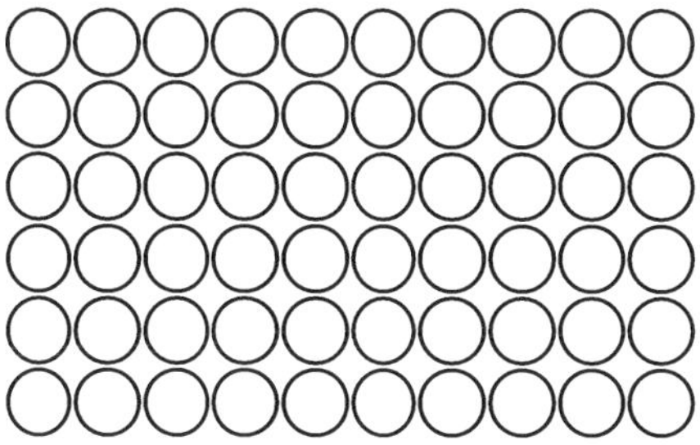 ____ rows and ____ columns makes a total of ____.

(9) 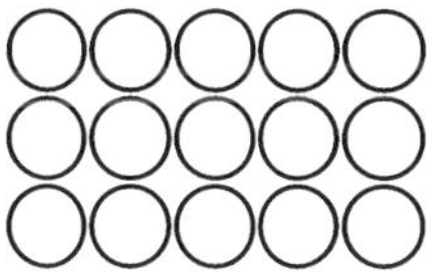 ____ rows and ____ columns makes a total of ____.

(10) 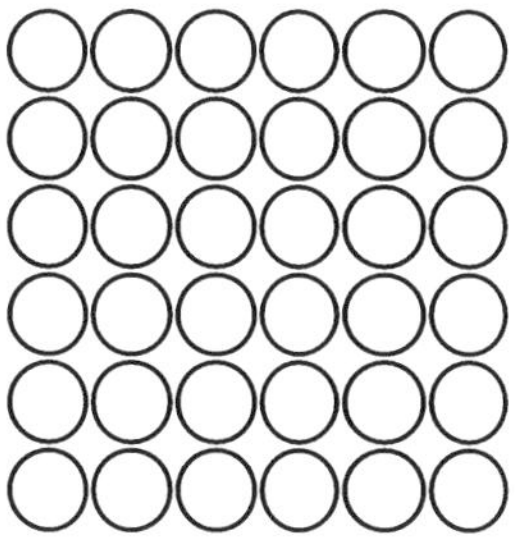 ____ rows and ____ columns makes a total of ____.

(11)  ____ rows and ____ columns makes a total of ____.

Visual Multiplication

☞ Use the dots to help you fill in the blanks to each of the multiplication problems.

(1)

____ rows and ____ columns makes a total of ____.

(2)

____ rows and ____ columns makes a total of ____.

(3)

____ rows and ____ columns makes a total of ____.

(4)

____ rows and ____ columns makes a total of ____.

(5)

____ rows and ____ columns makes a total of ____.

(6)

____ rows and ____ columns makes a total of ____.

(7)

____ rows and ____ columns makes a total of ____.

(8)

____ rows and ____ columns makes a total of ____.

(9)

____ rows and ____ columns makes a total of ____.

Visual Multiplication

Use the dots to help you fill in the blanks to each of the multiplication problems.

(1)

____ rows and ____ columns makes a total of ____.

(2)

____ rows and ____ columns makes a total of ____.

(3)

____ rows and ____ columns makes a total of ____.

(4)

____ rows and ____ columns makes a total of ____.

(5)

____ rows and ____ columns makes a total of ____.

(6)

____ rows and ____ columns makes a total of ____.

(7)

____ rows and ____ columns makes a total of ____.

(8)

____ rows and ____ columns makes a total of ____.

(9)

____ rows and ____ columns makes a total of ____.

(10)

____ rows and ____ columns makes a total of ____.

(11)

____ rows and ____ columns makes a total of ____.

Visual Multiplication

Name: ______________________ **Date:** ______________________

☞ Use the dots to help you fill in the blanks to each of the multiplication problems.

(1) ____ rows and ____ columns makes a total of ____.

(2) ____ rows and ____ columns makes a total of ____.

(3) ____ rows and ____ columns makes a total of ____.

(4) ____ rows and ____ columns makes a total of ____.

(5) ____ rows and ____ columns makes a total of ____.

(6) ____ rows and ____ columns makes a total of ____.

(7) ____ rows and ____ columns makes a total of ____.

(8) ____ rows and ____ columns makes a total of ____.

(9) ____ rows and ____ columns makes a total of ____.

(10) ____ rows and ____ columns makes a total of ____.

Visual Multiplication

Use the dots to help you fill in the blanks to oach of the multiplication problems.

(1)

____ rows and ____ columns makes a total of ____.

(2)

____ rows and ____ columns makes a total of ____.

(3)

____ rows and ____ columns makes a total of ____.

(4)

____ rows and ____ columns makes a total of ____.

(5)

____ rows and ____ columns makes a total of ____.

(6)

____ rows and ____ columns makes a total of ____.

(7)

____ rows and ____ columns makes a total of ____.

(8)

____ rows and ____ columns makes a total of ____.

(9)

____ rows and ____ columns makes a total of ____.

(10)

____ rows and ____ columns makes a total of ____.

(11)

____ rows and ____ columns makes a total of ____.

Visual Multiplication

☞ Use the dots to help you fill in the blanks to each of the multiplication problems.

(1)  ____ rows and ____ columns makes a total of ____.

(2) 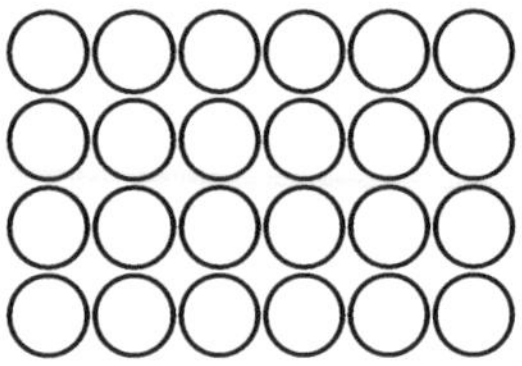 ____ rows and ____ columns makes a total of ____.

(3)  ____ rows and ____ columns makes a total of ____.

(4)  ____ rows and ____ columns makes a total of ____.

(5)  ____ rows and ____ columns makes a total of ____.

(6) 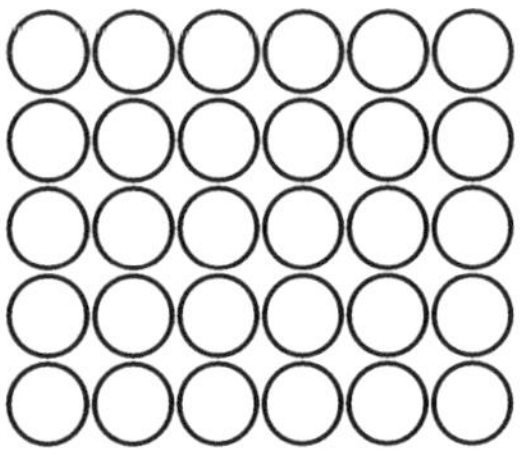 ____ rows and ____ columns makes a total of ____.

(7) 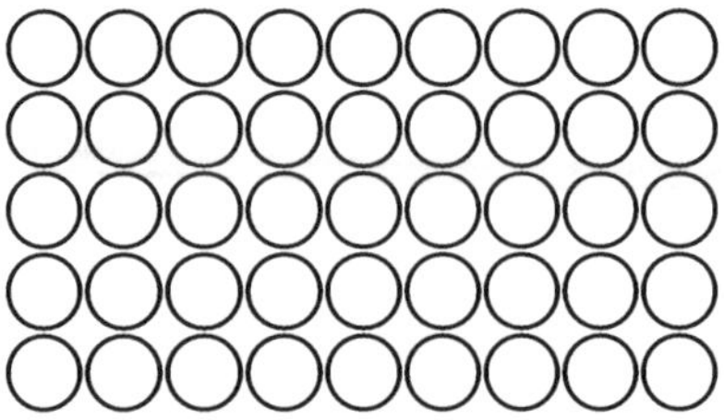 ____ rows and ____ columns makes a total of ____.

(8) 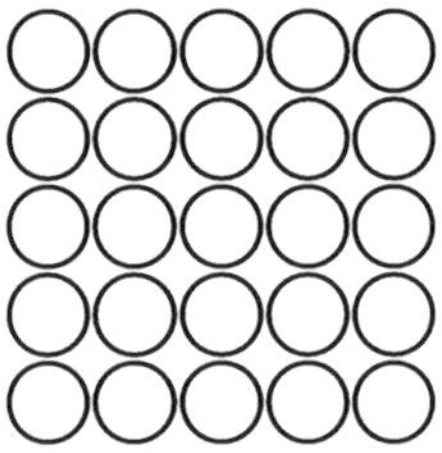 ____ rows and ____ columns makes a total of ____.

(9) 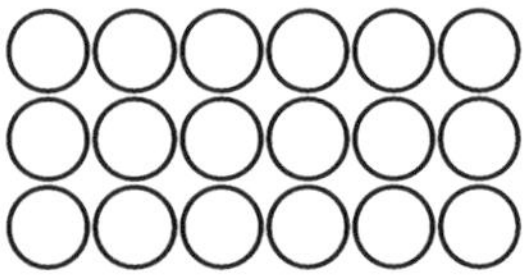 ____ rows and ____ columns makes a total of ____.

(10)  ____ rows and ____ columns makes a total of ____.

(11)  ____ rows and ____ columns makes a total of ____.

Visual Multiplication

Use the dots to help you fill in the blanks to each of the multiplication problems.

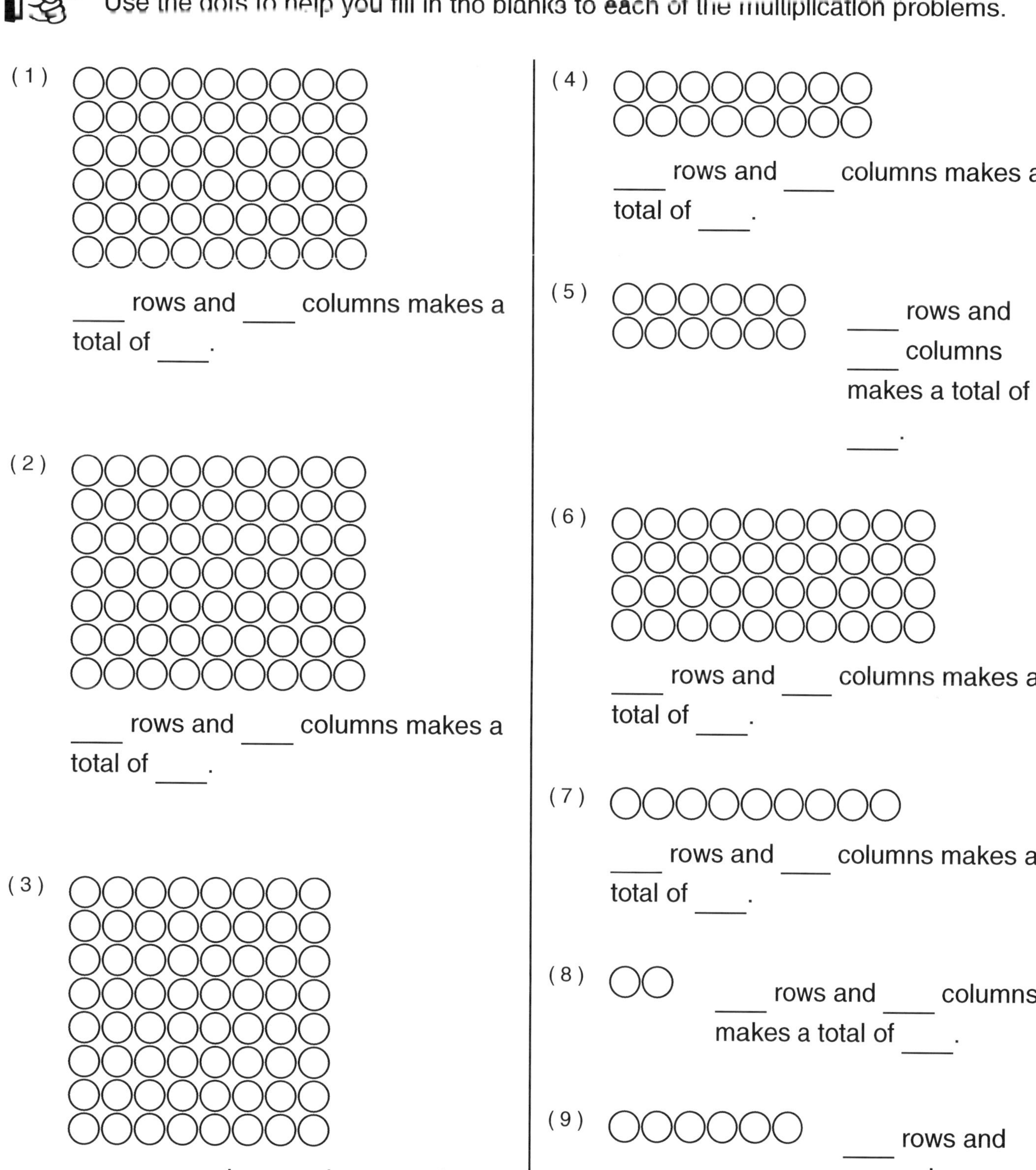

(1) ____ rows and ____ columns makes a total of ____.

(2) ____ rows and ____ columns makes a total of ____.

(3) ____ rows and ____ columns makes a total of ____.

(4) ____ rows and ____ columns makes a total of ____.

(5) ____ rows and ____ columns makes a total of ____.

(6) ____ rows and ____ columns makes a total of ____.

(7) ____ rows and ____ columns makes a total of ____.

(8) ____ rows and ____ columns makes a total of ____.

(9) ____ rows and ____ columns makes a total of ____.

Visual Multiplication

☞ Use the dots to help you fill in the blanks to each of the multiplication problems.

(1) ____ rows and ____ columns makes a total of ____.

(2) ____ rows and ____ columns makes a total of ____.

(3) ____ rows and ____ columns makes a total of ____.

(4) ____ rows and ____ columns makes a total of ____.

(5) ____ rows and ____ columns makes a total of ____.

(6) ____ rows and ____ columns makes a total of ____.

(7) ____ rows and ____ columns makes a total of ____.

(8) ____ rows and ____ columns makes a total of ____.

(9) ____ rows and ____ columns makes a total of ____.

(10) ____ rows and ____ columns makes a total of ____.

Visual Multiplication

☞ Use the dots to help you fill in the blanks to each of the multiplication problems.

(1) ○○○○○○○

____ rows and ____ columns makes a total of ____.

(2) ○○○○○○○○○○

____ rows and ____ columns makes a total of ____.

(3) ○○○○○

____ rows and ____ columns makes a total of ____.

(4)

____ rows and ____ columns makes a total of ____.

(5)

____ rows and ____ columns makes a total of ____.

(6)

____ rows and ____ columns makes a total of ____.

(7)

____ rows and ____ columns makes a total of ____.

(8)

____ rows and ____ columns makes a total of ____.

(9)

____ rows and ____ columns makes a total of ____.

Visual Multiplication

☞ Use the dots to help you fill in the blanks to each of the multiplication problems.

(1)  ____ rows and ____ columns makes a total of ____.

(2) 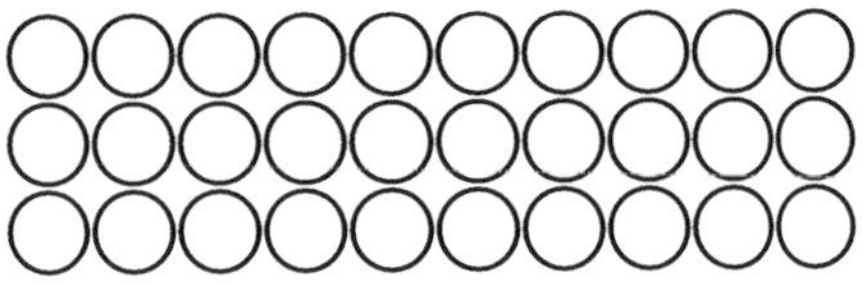 ____ rows and ____ columns makes a total of ____.

(3) 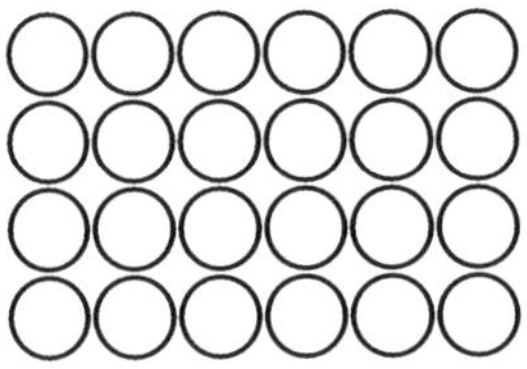 ____ rows and ____ columns makes a total of ____.

(4) 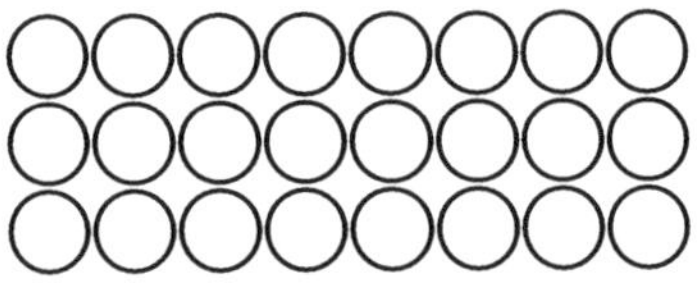 ____ rows and ____ columns makes a total of ____.

(5) 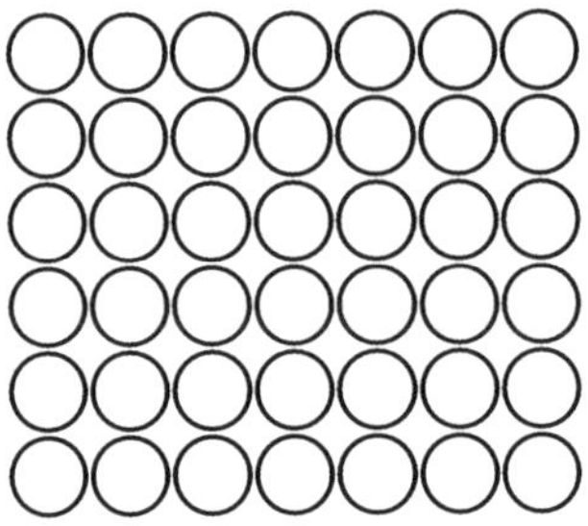 ____ rows and ____ columns makes a total of ____.

(6) 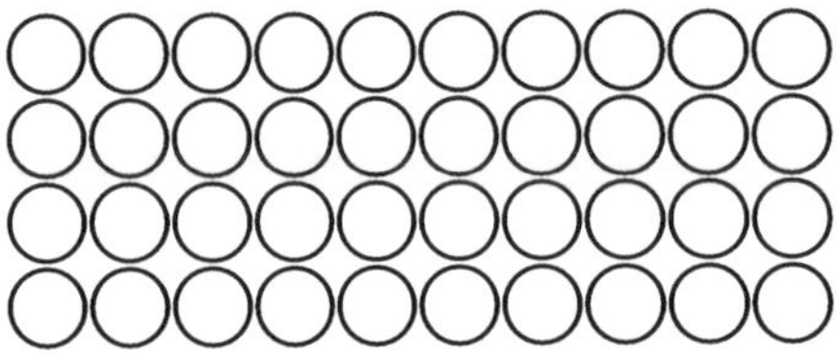 ____ rows and ____ columns makes a total of ____.

(7) 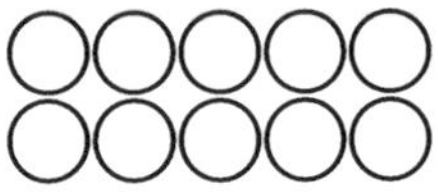 ____ rows and ____ columns makes a total of ____.

(8)  ____ rows and ____ columns makes a total of ____.

(9)  ____ rows and ____ columns makes a total of ____.

(10) 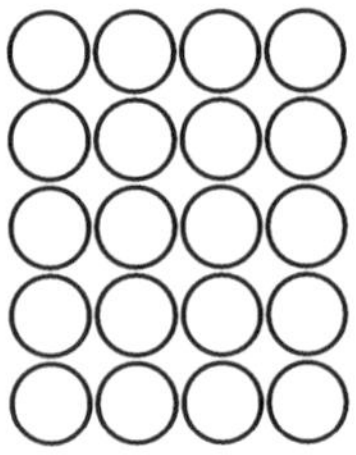 ____ rows and ____ columns makes a total of ____.

(11)  ____ rows and ____ columns makes a total of ____.

Visual Multiplication

☞ Use the dots to help you fill in the blanks to each of the multiplication problems.

(1) 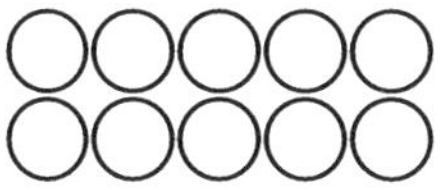 ____ rows and ____ columns makes a total of ____.

(2) 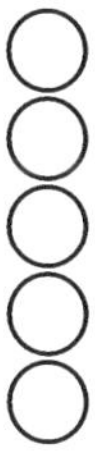 ____ rows and ____ columns makes a total of ____.

(3)  ____ rows and ____ columns makes a total of ____.

(4)  ____ rows and ____ columns makes a total of ____.

(5) 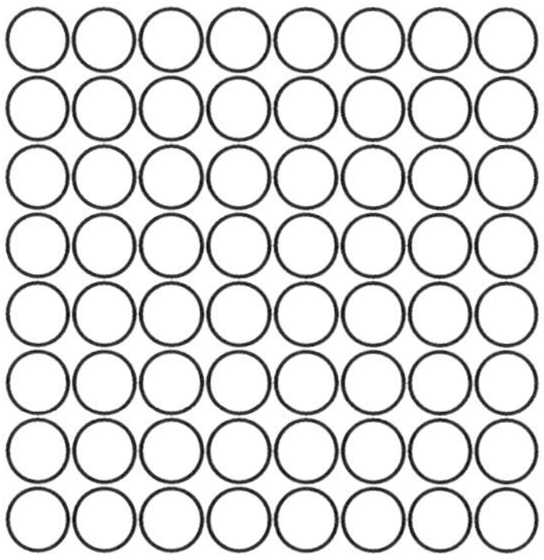 ____ rows and ____ columns makes a total of ____.

(6) 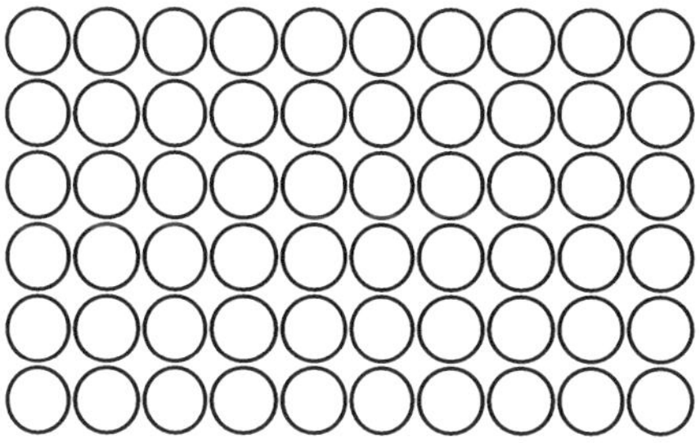 ____ rows and ____ columns makes a total of ____.

(7) 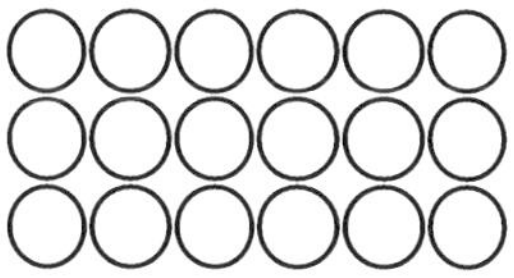 ____ rows and ____ columns makes a total of ____.

(8)  ____ rows and ____ columns makes a total of ____.

(9) 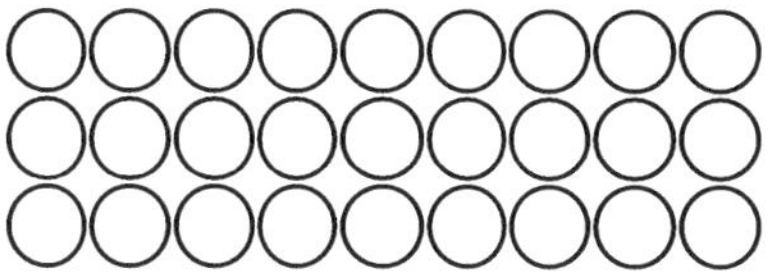 ____ rows and ____ columns makes a total of ____.

(10)  ____ rows and ____ columns makes a total of ____.

(11)  ____ rows and ____ columns makes a total of ____.

Visual Multiplication

☞ Use the dots to help you fill in the blanks to each of the multiplication problems.

(1)

____ rows and ____ columns makes a total of ____.

(2)

____ rows and ____ columns makes a total of ____.

(3)

____ rows and ____ columns makes a total of ____.

(4)

____ rows and ____ columns makes a total of ____.

(5)

____ rows and ____ columns makes a total of ____.

(6)

____ rows and ____ columns makes a total of ____.

(7)

____ rows and ____ columns makes a total of ____.

(8)

____ rows and ____ columns makes a total of ____.

(9)

____ rows and ____ columns makes a total of ____.

(10)

____ rows and ____ columns makes a total of ____.

Visual Multiplication

Date: ______________________

Use the dots to help you fill in the blanks to each of the multiplication problems.

(1)

____ rows and ____ columns makes a total of ____.

(2)

____ rows and ____ columns makes a total of ____.

(3)

____ rows and ____ columns makes a total of ____.

(4)

____ rows and ____ columns makes a total of ____.

(5)

____ rows and ____ columns makes a total of ____.

(6)

____ rows and ____ columns makes a total of ____.

(7)

____ rows and ____ columns makes a total of ____.

(8)

____ rows and ____ columns makes a total of ____.

(9)

____ rows and ____ columns makes a total of ____.

Visual Multiplication

☞ Use the dots to help you fill in the blanks to each of the multiplication problems.

(1)

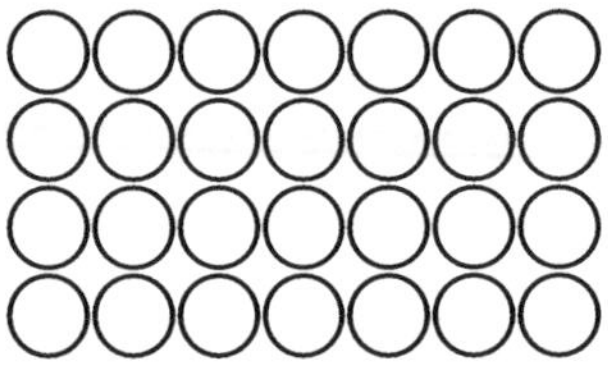

____ rows and ____ columns makes a total of ____.

(2)  ____ rows and ____ columns makes a total of ____.

(3)

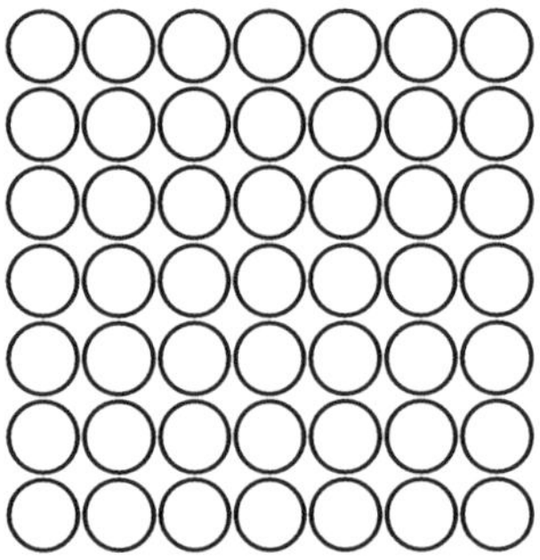

____ rows and ____ columns makes a total of ____.

(4)  ____ rows and ____ columns makes a total of ____.

(5) 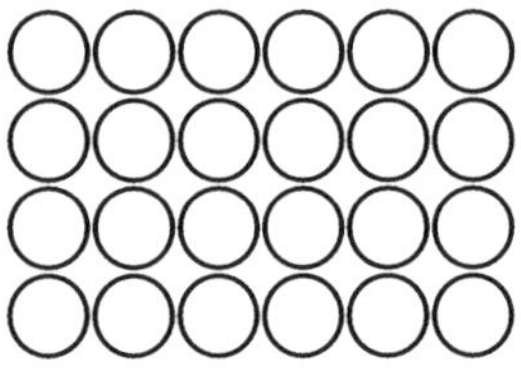 ____ rows and ____ columns makes a total of ____.

(6)

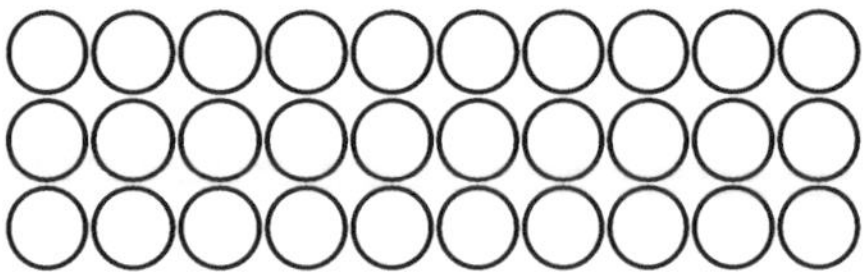

____ rows and ____ columns makes a total of ____.

(7)

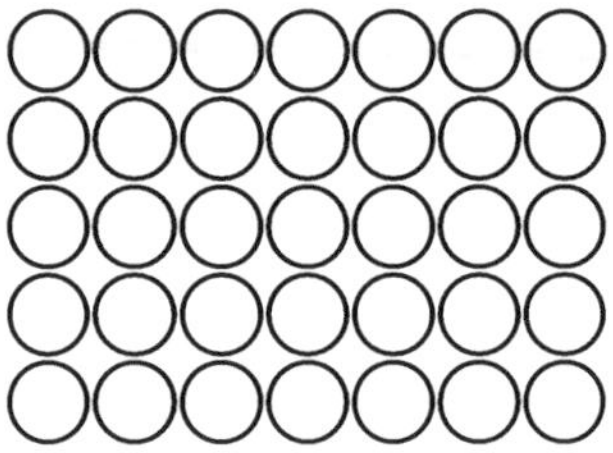

____ rows and ____ columns makes a total of ____.

(8)  ____ rows and ____ columns makes a total of ____.

(9)

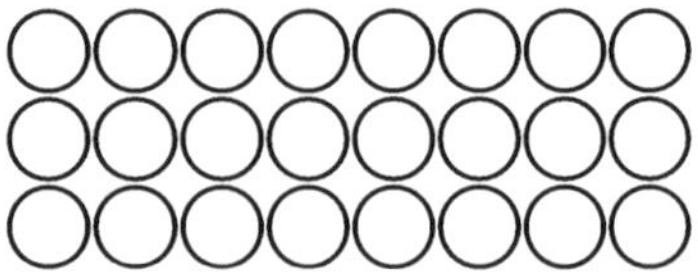

____ rows and ____ columns makes a total of ____.

(10)  ____ rows and ____ columns makes a total of ____.

Visual Multiplication

Use the dots to help you fill in the blanks to each of the multiplication problems.

(1) ___ rows and ___ columns makes a total of ___.

(2) ___ rows and ___ columns makes a total of ___.

(3) ___ rows and ___ columns makes a total of ___.

(4) ___ rows and ___ columns makes a total of ___.

(5) ___ rows and ___ columns makes a total of ___.

(6) ___ rows and ___ columns makes a total of ___.

(7) ___ rows and ___ columns makes a total of ___.

(8) ___ rows and ___ columns makes a total of ___.

(9) ___ rows and ___ columns makes a total of ___.

(10) ___ rows and ___ columns makes a total of ___.

Visual Multiplication

Use the dots to help you fill in the blanks to each of the multiplication problems.

(1) ___ rows and ___ columns makes a total of ___.

(2) ___ rows and ___ columns makes a total of ___.

(3) ___ rows and ___ columns makes a total of ___.

(4) ___ rows and ___ columns makes a total of ___.

(5) ___ rows and ___ columns makes a total of ___.

(6) ___ rows and ___ columns makes a total of ___.

(7) ___ rows and ___ columns makes a total of ___.

(8) ___ rows and ___ columns makes a total of ___.

(9) ___ rows and ___ columns makes a total of ___.

(10) ___ rows and ___ columns makes a total of ___.

Visual Multiplication

Use the dots to help you fill in the blanks to each of the multiplication problems.

(1)

____ rows and ____ columns makes a total of ____.

(2)

____ rows and ____ columns makes a total of ____.

(3)

____ rows and ____ columns makes a total of ____.

(4)

____ rows and ____ columns makes a total of ____.

(5)

____ rows and ____ columns makes a total of ____.

(6)

____ rows and ____ columns makes a total of ____.

(7)

____ rows and ____ columns makes a total of ____.

(8)

____ rows and ____ columns makes a total of ____.

(9)

____ rows and ____ columns makes a total of ____.

(10)

____ rows and ____ columns makes a total of ____.

(11)

____ rows and ____ columns makes a total of ____.

Visual Multiplication

☞ Use the dots to help you fill in the blanks to each of the multiplication problems.

(1) ○○○○○○○

____ rows and ____ columns makes a total of ____.

(2) ○○ ○○ ○○ ○○ ○○

____ rows and ____ columns makes a total of ____.

(3) ○○○○○○ ○○○○○○

____ rows and ____ columns makes a total of ____.

(4) ○○○○○

____ rows and ____ columns makes a total of ____.

(5) ○○○○○○○○○ (5 rows of 9)

____ rows and ____ columns makes a total of ____.

(6) ○○○○○○○○○○ (7 rows of 10)

____ rows and ____ columns makes a total of ____.

(7) ○○○○

____ rows and ____ columns makes a total of ____.

(8) ○○○○○○○ (3 rows of 7)

____ rows and ____ columns makes a total of ____.

(9) ○○○○○○○○○○ (4 rows of 10)

____ rows and ____ columns makes a total of ____.

(10) ○○ ○○

____ rows and ____ columns makes a total of ____.

Visual Multiplication

Use the dots to help you fill in the blanks to oaoh of the multiplication problems.

(1)

____ rows and ____ columns makes a total of ____.

(2)

____ rows and ____ columns makes a total of ____.

(3)

____ rows and ____ columns makes a total of ____.

(4)

____ rows and ____ columns makes a total of ____.

(5)

____ rows and ____ columns makes a total of ____.

(6)

____ rows and ____ columns makes a total of ____.

(7)

____ rows and ____ columns makes a total of ____.

(8)

____ rows and ____ columns makes a total of ____.

(9)

____ rows and ____ columns makes a total of ____.

(10)

____ rows and ____ columns makes a total of ____.

(11)

____ rows and ____ columns makes a total of ____.

Visual Multiplication

☞ Use the dots to help you fill in the blanks to each of the multiplication problems.

(1) ___ rows and ___ columns makes a total of ___.

(2) ___ rows and ___ columns makes a total of ___.

(3) ___ rows and ___ columns makes a total of ___.

(4) ___ rows and ___ columns makes a total of ___.

(5) ___ rows and ___ columns makes a total of ___.

(6) ___ rows and ___ columns makes a total of ___.

(7) ___ rows and ___ columns makes a total of ___.

(8) ___ rows and ___ columns makes a total of ___.

(9) ___ rows and ___ columns makes a total of ___.

(10) ___ rows and ___ columns makes a total of ___.

Visual Multiplication

☞ Use the dots to help you fill in the blanks to each of the multiplication problems.

(1) ____ rows and ____ columns makes a total of ____.

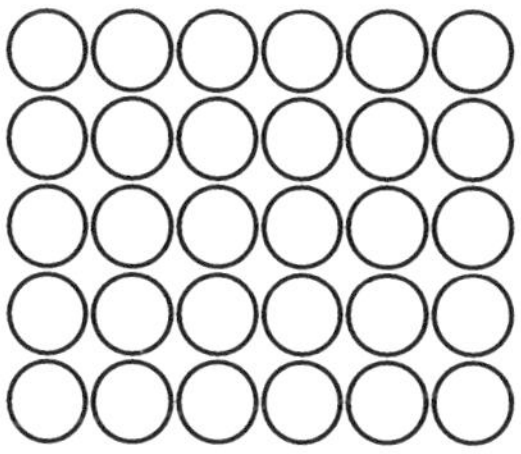

(2) ____ rows and ____ columns makes a total of ____.

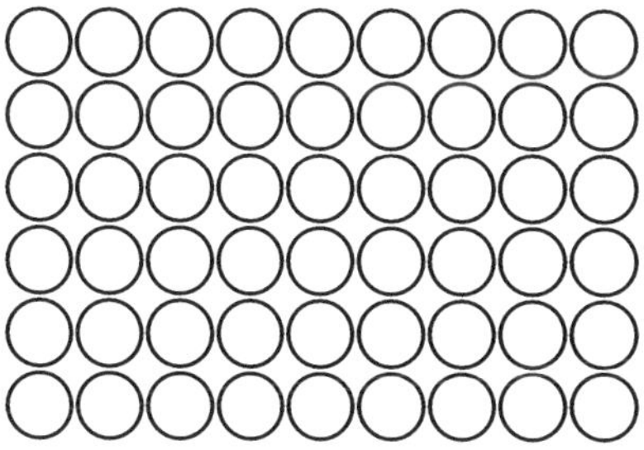

(3) ____ rows and ____ columns makes a total of ____.

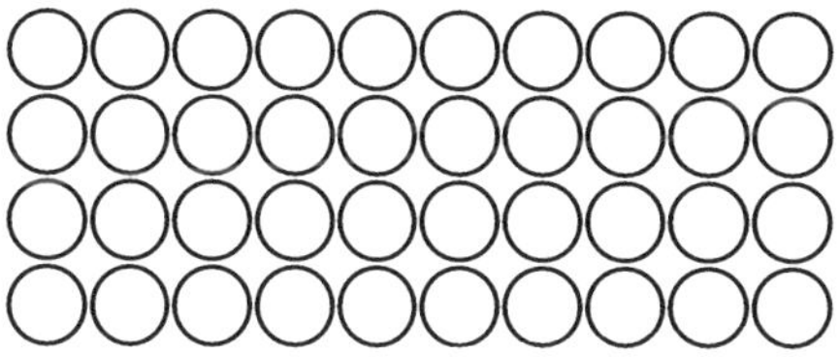

(4) ____ rows and ____ columns makes a total of ____.

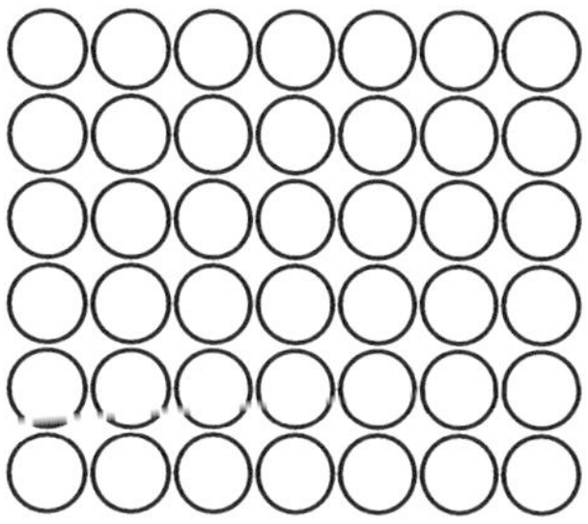

(5) ____ rows and ____ columns makes a total of ____.

(6) ____ rows and ____ columns makes a total of ____.

(7) ____ rows and ____ columns makes a total of ____.

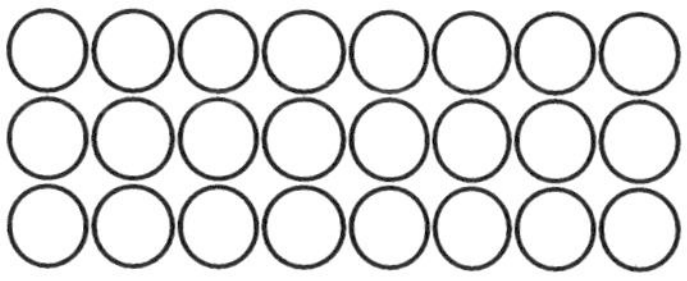

(8) ____ rows and ____ columns makes a total of ____.

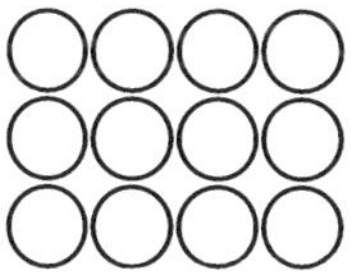

(9) ____ rows and ____ columns makes a total of ____.

(10) ____ rows and ____ columns makes a total of ____.

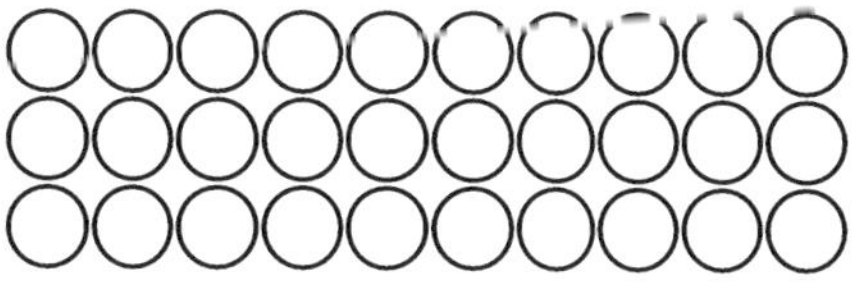

Visual Multiplication

☞ Use the dots to help you fill in the blanks to each of the multiplication problems.

(1)

____ rows and ____ columns makes a total of ____.

(2)

____ rows and ____ columns makes a total of ____.

(3)

____ rows and ____ columns makes a total of ____.

(4)

____ rows and ____ columns makes a total of ____.

(5)

____ rows and ____ columns makes a total of ____.

(6)

____ rows and ____ columns makes a total of ____.

(7)

____ rows and ____ columns makes a total of ____.

(8)

____ rows and ____ columns makes a total of ____.

(9)

____ rows and ____ columns makes a total of ____.

Visual Multiplication

Use the dots to help you fill in the blanks to each of the multiplication problems.

(1) ____ rows and ____ columns makes a total of ____.

(2) ____ rows and ____ columns makes a total of ____.

(3) ____ rows and ____ columns makes a total of ____.

(4) ____ rows and ____ columns makes a total of ____.

(5) ____ rows and ____ columns makes a total of ____.

(6) ____ rows and ____ columns makes a total of ____.

(7) ____ rows and ____ columns makes a total of ____.

(8) ____ rows and ____ columns makes a total of ____.

(9) ____ rows and ____ columns makes a total of ____.

Visual Multiplication

☞ Use the dots to help you fill in the blanks to each of the multiplication problems.

(1)

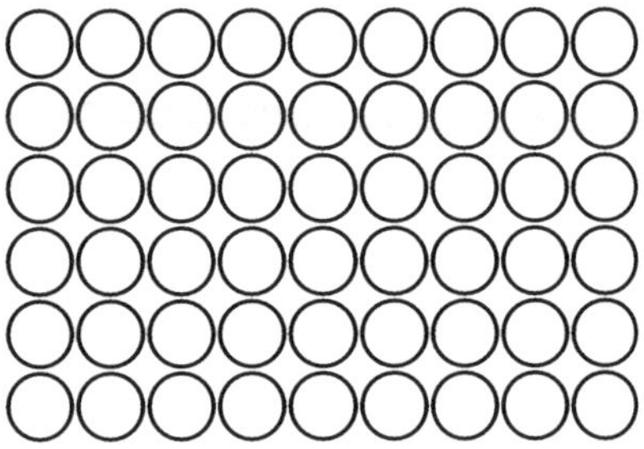

____ rows and ____ columns makes a total of ____.

(2)

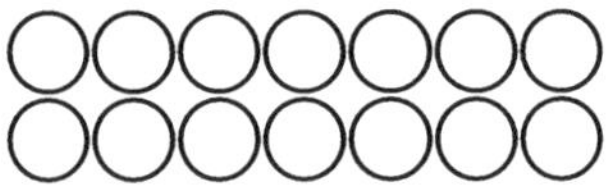

____ rows and ____ columns makes a total of ____.

(3)

____ rows and ____ columns makes a total of ____.

(4)

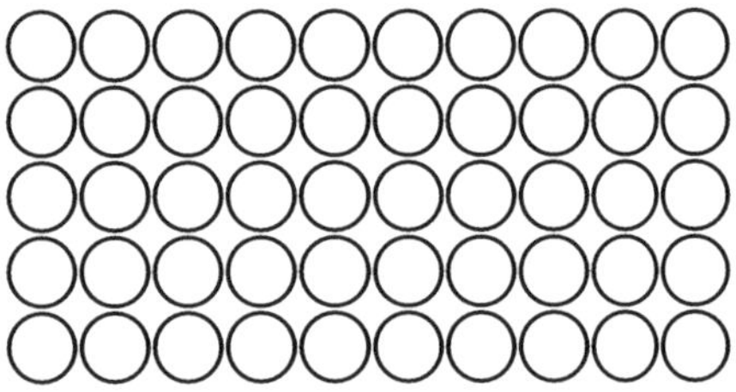

____ rows and ____ columns makes a total of ____.

(5)

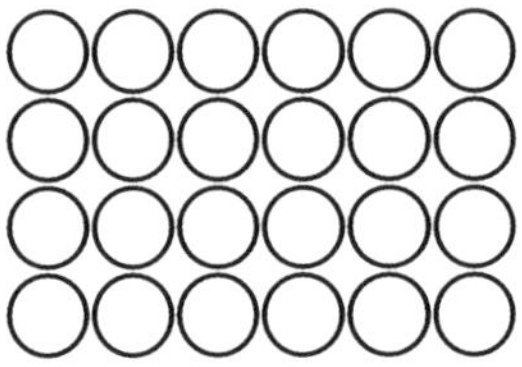

____ rows and ____ columns makes a total of ____.

(6)

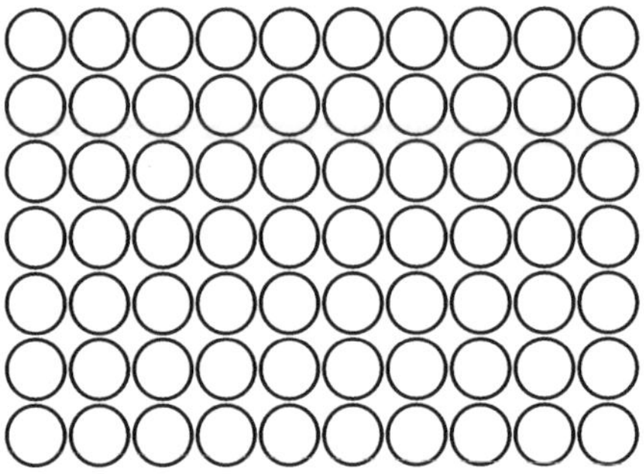

____ rows and ____ columns makes a total of ____.

(7)

____ rows and ____ columns makes a total of ____.

(8)

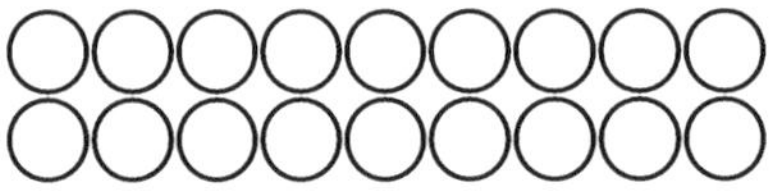

____ rows and ____ columns makes a total of ____.

(9)

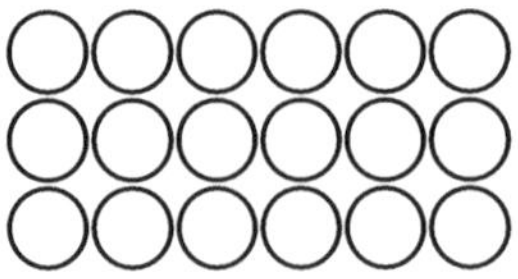

____ rows and ____ columns makes a total of ____.

(10)

____ rows and ____ columns makes a total of ____.

Visual Multiplication

☞ Use the dots to help you fill in the blanks to each of the multiplication problems.

(1) ____ rows and ____ columns makes a total of ____.

(2) ____ rows and ____ columns makes a total of ____.

(3) ____ rows and ____ columns makes a total of ____.

(4) ____ rows and ____ columns makes a total of ____.

(5) ____ rows and ____ columns makes a total of ____.

(6) ____ rows and ____ columns makes a total of ____.

(7) ____ rows and ____ columns makes a total of ____.

(8) ____ rows and ____ columns makes a total of ____.

(9) ____ rows and ____ columns makes a total of ____.

(10) ____ rows and ____ columns makes a total of ____.

Visual Multiplication

☞ Use the dots to help you fill in the blanks to each of the multiplication problems.

(1) 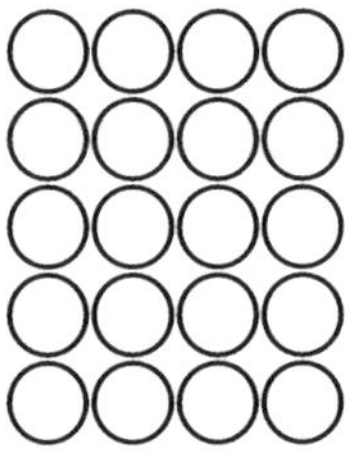 ____ rows and ____ columns makes a total of ____.

(2)  ____ rows and ____ columns makes a total of ____.

(3)  ____ rows and ____ columns makes a total of ____.

(4) 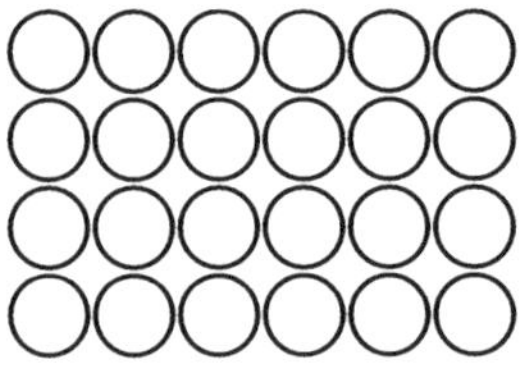 ____ rows and ____ columns makes a total of ____.

(5) 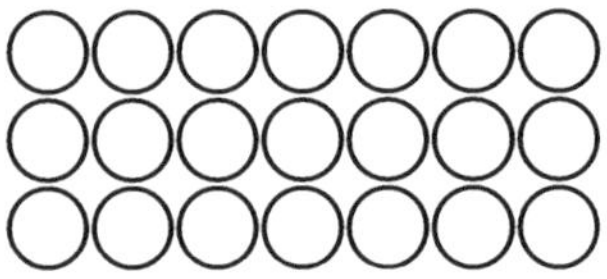 ____ rows and ____ columns makes a total of ____.

(6) 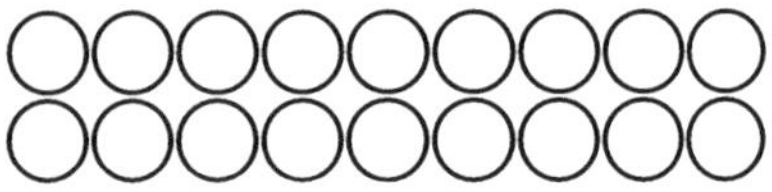 ____ rows and ____ columns makes a total of ____.

(7) 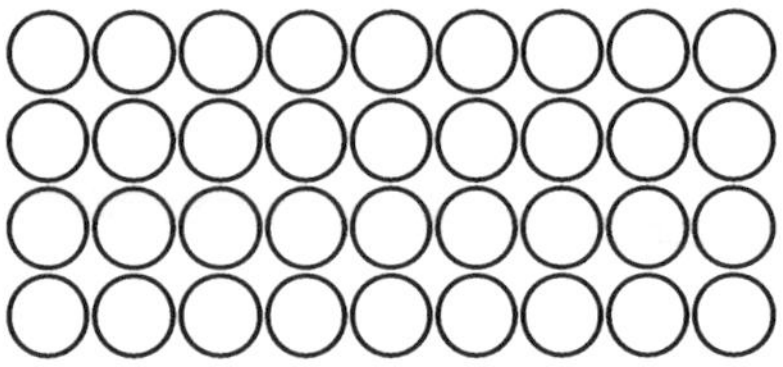 ____ rows and ____ columns makes a total of ____.

(8) 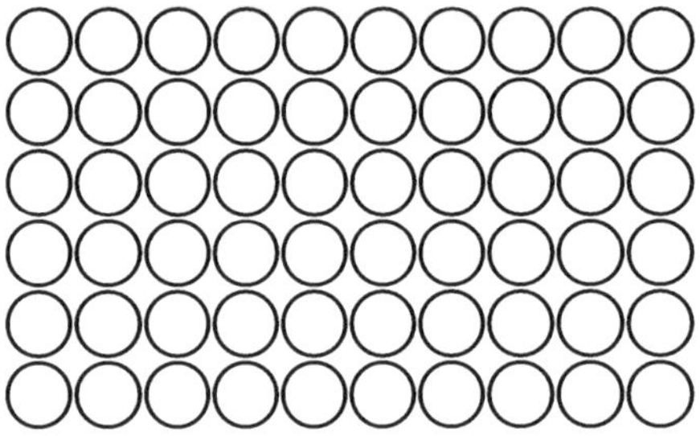 ____ rows and ____ columns makes a total of ____.

(9)  ____ rows and ____ columns makes a total of ____.

(10)  ____ rows and ____ columns makes a total of ____.

(11)  ____ rows and ____ columns makes a total of ____.

Visual Multiplication

☞ Use the dots to help you fill in the blanks to each of the multiplication problems.

(1) ____ rows and ____ columns makes a total of ____.

(2) ____ rows and ____ columns makes a total of ____.

(3) ____ rows and ____ columns makes a total of ____.

(4) ____ rows and ____ columns makes a total of ____.

(5) ____ rows and ____ columns makes a total of ____.

(6) ____ rows and ____ columns makes a total of ____.

(7) ____ rows and ____ columns makes a total of ____.

(8) ____ rows and ____ columns makes a total of ____.

(9) ____ rows and ____ columns makes a total of ____.

(10) ____ rows and ____ columns makes a total of ____.

Visual Multiplication

☞ Use the dots to help you fill in the blanks to each of the multiplication problems.

(1)

____ rows and ____ columns makes a total of ____.

(2)

____ rows and ____ columns makes a total of ____.

(3)

____ rows and ____ columns makes a total of ____.

(4)

____ rows and ____ columns makes a total of ____.

(5)

____ rows and ____ columns makes a total of ____.

(6)

____ rows and ____ columns makes a total of ____.

(7)

____ rows and ____ columns makes a total of ____.

(8)

____ rows and ____ columns makes a total of ____.

(9)

____ rows and ____ columns makes a total of ____.

Visual Multiplication

☞ Use the dots to help you fill in the blanks to each of the multiplication problems.

(1) ___ rows and ___ columns makes a total of ___.

(2) ___ rows and ___ columns makes a total of ___.

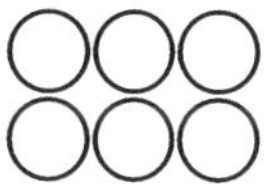

(3) ___ rows and ___ columns makes a total of ___.

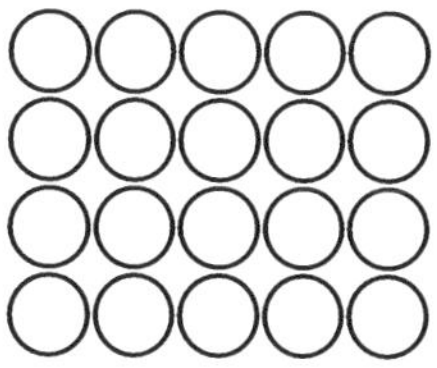

(4) ___ rows and ___ columns makes a total of ___.

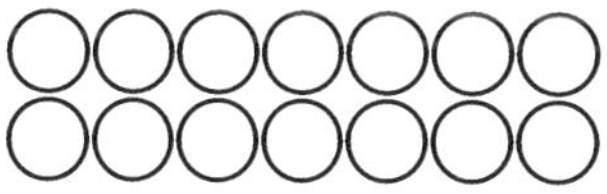

(5) ___ rows and ___ columns makes a total of ___.

(6) ___ rows and ___ columns makes a total of ___.

(7) ___ rows and ___ columns makes a total of ___.

(8) ___ rows and ___ columns makes a total of ___.

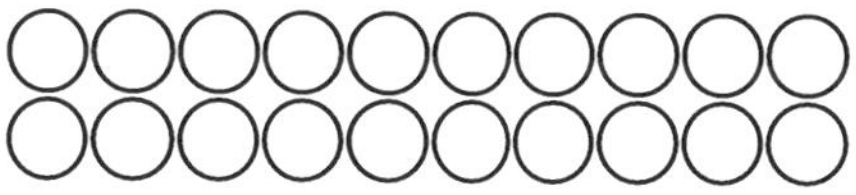

(9) ___ rows and ___ columns makes a total of ___.

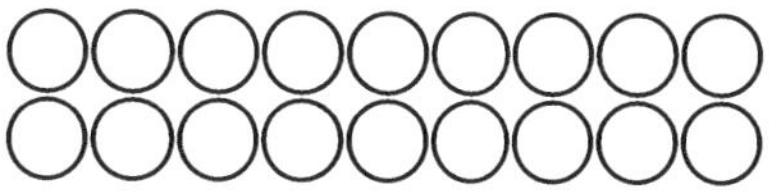

(10) ___ rows and ___ columns makes a total of ___.

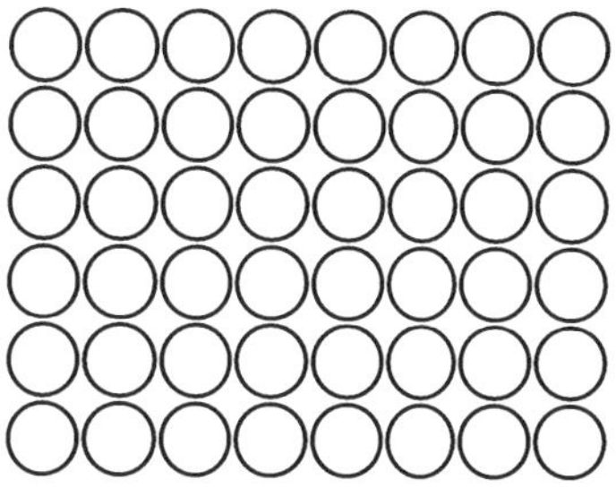

(11) ___ rows and ___ columns makes a total of ___.

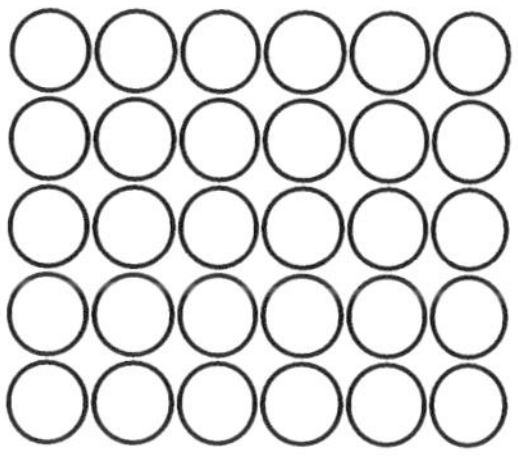

Visual Multiplication

☞ Use the dots to help you fill in the blanks to each of the multiplication problems.

(1) ____ rows and ____ columns makes a total of ____.

(2) ____ rows and ____ columns makes a total of ____.

(3) ____ rows and ____ columns makes a total of ____.

(4) ____ rows and ____ columns makes a total of ____.

(5) ____ rows and ____ columns makes a total of ____.

(6) ____ rows and ____ columns makes a total of ____.

(7) ____ rows and ____ columns makes a total of ____.

(8) ____ rows and ____ columns makes a total of ____.

(9) ____ rows and ____ columns makes a total of ____.

Visual Multiplication

☞ Use the dots to help you fill in the blanks to each of the multiplication problems.

(1) ____ rows and ____ columns makes a total of ____.

(2) ____ rows and ____ columns makes a total of ____.

(3) ____ rows and ____ columns makes a total of ____.

(4) ____ rows and ____ columns makes a total of ____.

(5) ____ rows and ____ columns makes a total of ____.

(6) ____ rows and ____ columns makes a total of ____.

(7) ____ rows and ____ columns makes a total of ____.

(8) ____ rows and ____ columns makes a total of ____.

(9) ____ rows and ____ columns makes a total of ____.

(10) ____ rows and ____ columns makes a total of ____.

Visual Multiplication

☞ Use the dots to help you fill in the blanks to each of the multiplication problems.

(1)

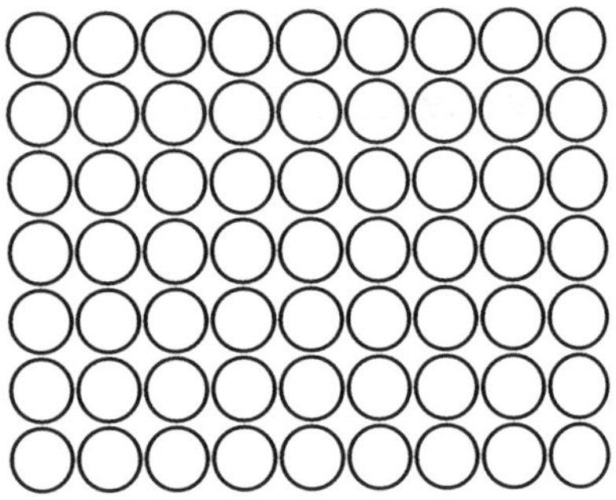

____ rows and ____ columns makes a total of ____.

(2)

____ rows and ____ columns makes a total of ____.

(3)

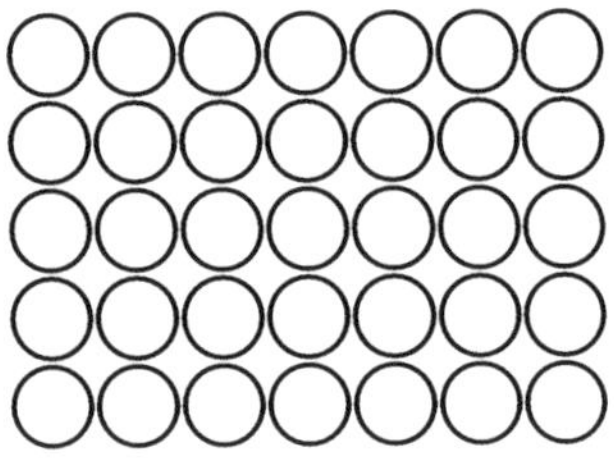

____ rows and ____ columns makes a total of ____.

(4)

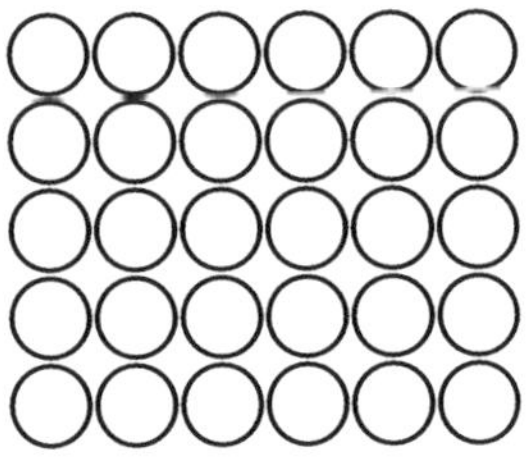

____ rows and ____ columns makes a total of ____.

(5)

____ rows and ____ columns makes a total of ____.

(6)

____ rows and ____ columns makes a total of ____.

(7)

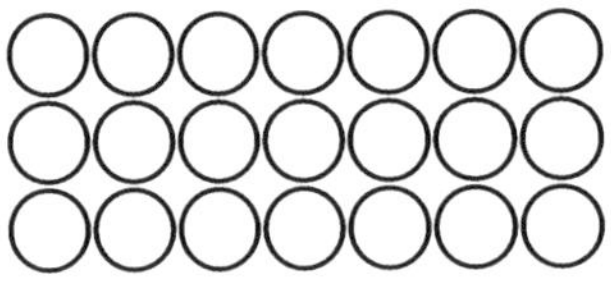

____ rows and ____ columns makes a total of ____.

(8)

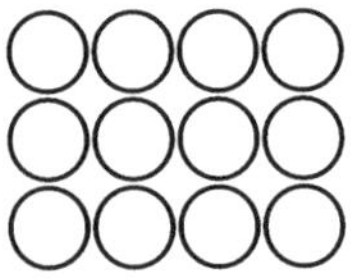

____ rows and ____ columns makes a total of ____.

(9)

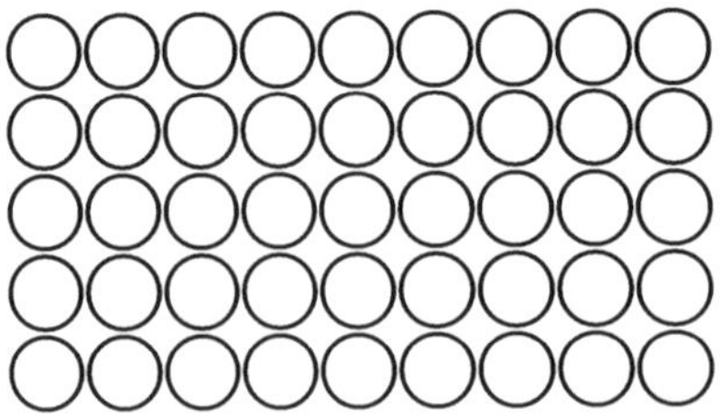

____ rows and ____ columns makes a total of ____.

(10)

____ rows and ____ columns makes a total of ____.

Visual Multiplication

 Use the dots to help you fill in the blanks to each of the multiplication problems.

(1)

____ rows and ____ columns makes a total of ____.

(2)

____ rows and ____ columns makes a total of ____.

(3)

____ rows and ____ columns makes a total of ____.

(4)

____ rows and ____ columns makes a total of ____.

(5)

____ rows and ____ columns makes a total of ____.

(6)

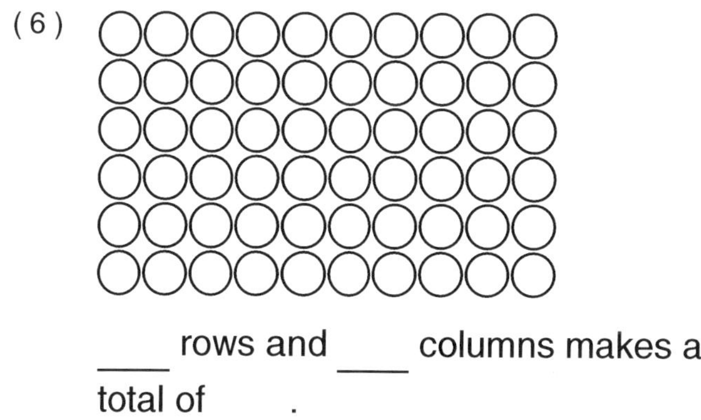

____ rows and ____ columns makes a total of ____.

(7)

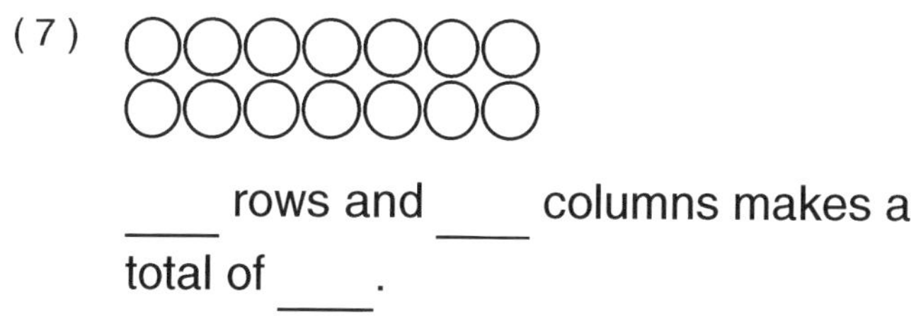

____ rows and ____ columns makes a total of ____.

(8)

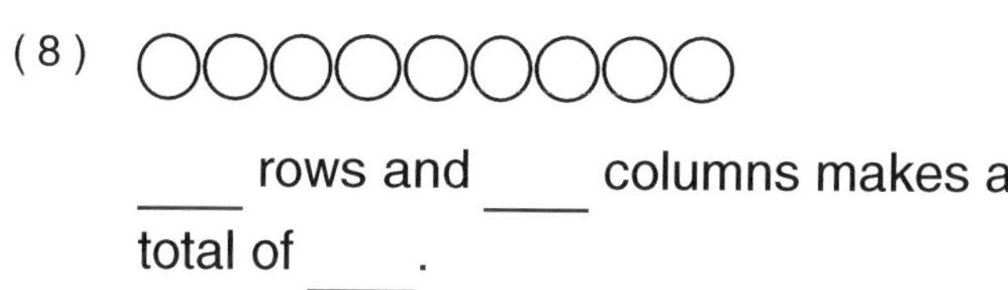

____ rows and ____ columns makes a total of ____.

Visual Multiplication

☞ Use the dots to help you fill in the blanks to each of the multiplication problems.

(1)

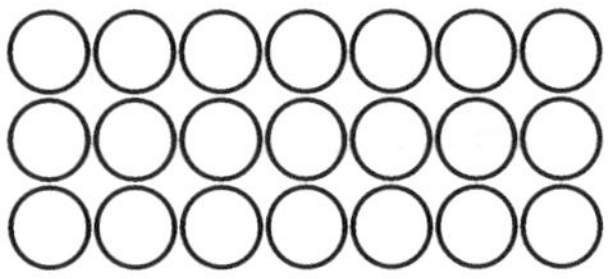

____ rows and ____ columns makes a total of ____.

(2)

____ rows and ____ columns makes a total of ____.

(3)

____ rows and ____ columns makes a total of ____.

(4)

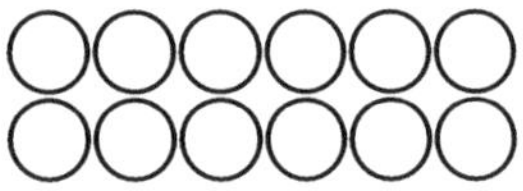

____ rows and ____ columns makes a total of ____.

(5)

____ rows and ____ columns makes a total of ____.

(6)

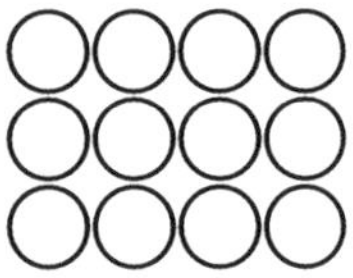

____ rows and ____ columns makes a total of ____.

(7)

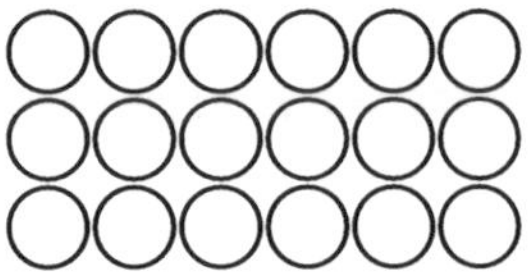

____ rows and ____ columns makes a total of ____.

(8)

____ rows and ____ columns makes a total of ____.

(9)

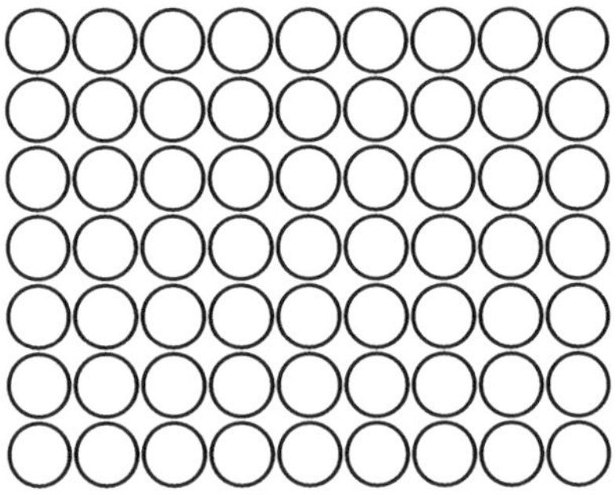

____ rows and ____ columns makes a total of ____.

(10)

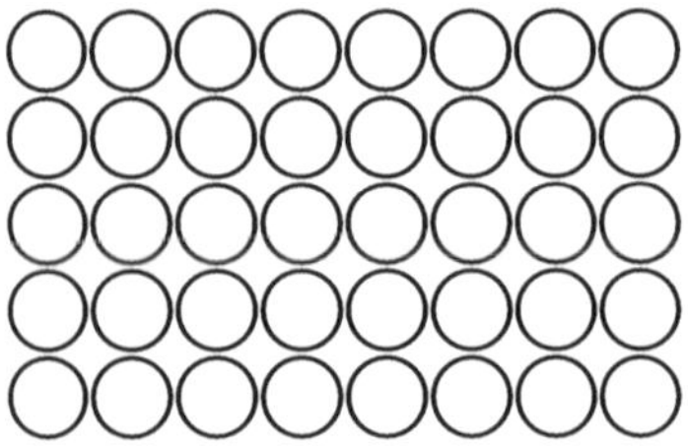

____ rows and ____ columns makes a total of ____.

Visual Multiplication

☞ Use the dots to help you fill in the blanks to each of the multiplication problems.

(1)  ____ rows and ____ columns makes a total of ____.

(2)  ____ rows and ____ columns makes a total of ____.

(3) 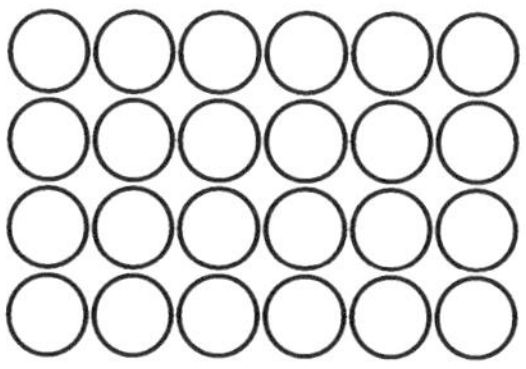 ____ rows and ____ columns makes a total of ____.

(4)  ____ rows and ____ columns makes a total of ____.

(5) 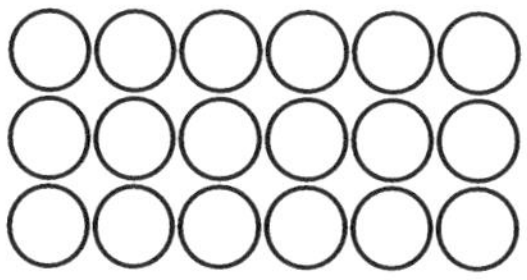 ____ rows and ____ columns makes a total of ____.

(6) 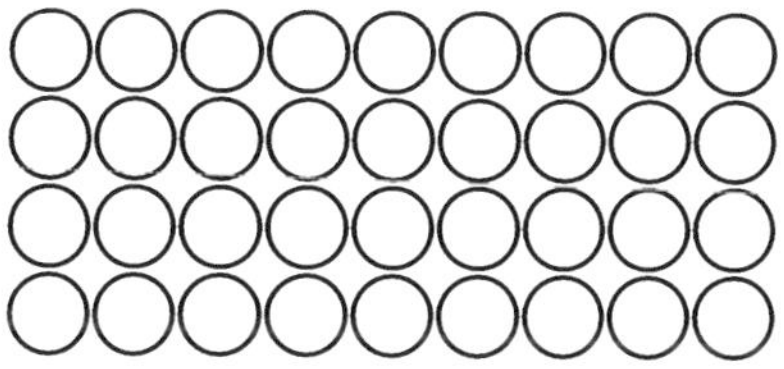 ____ rows and ____ columns makes a total of ____.

(7) 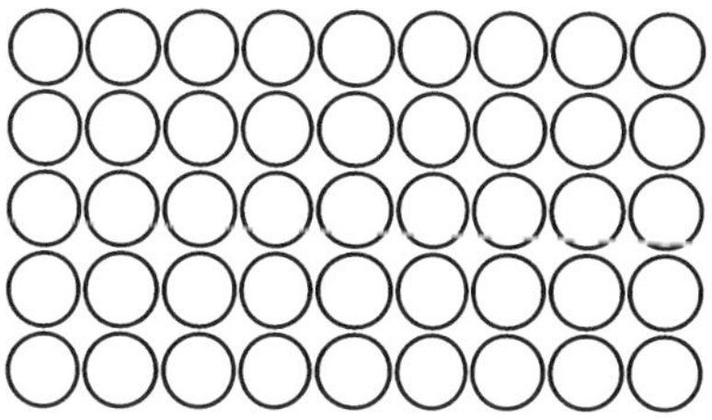 ____ rows and ____ columns makes a total of ____.

(8) 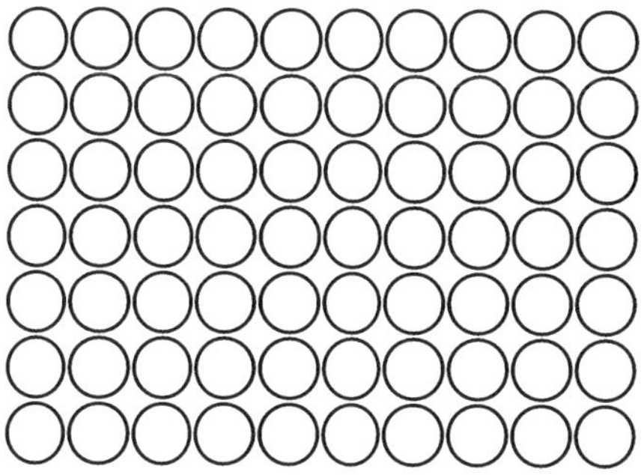 ____ rows and ____ columns makes a total of ____.

(9)  ____ rows and ____ columns makes a total of ____.

(10) 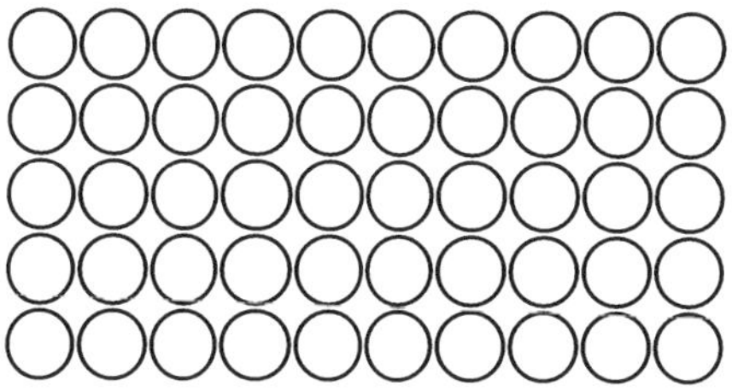 ____ rows and ____ columns makes a total of ____.

Visual Multiplication

☞ Use the dots to help you fill in the blanks to each of the multiplication problems.

(1) 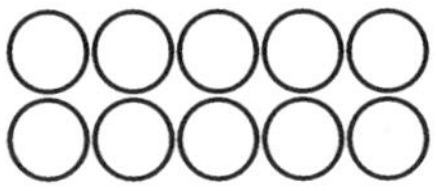 ____ rows and ____ columns makes a total of ____.

(2)  ____ rows and ____ columns makes a total of ____.

(3)  ____ rows and ____ columns makes a total of ____.

(4)  ____ rows and ____ columns makes a total of ____.

(5) 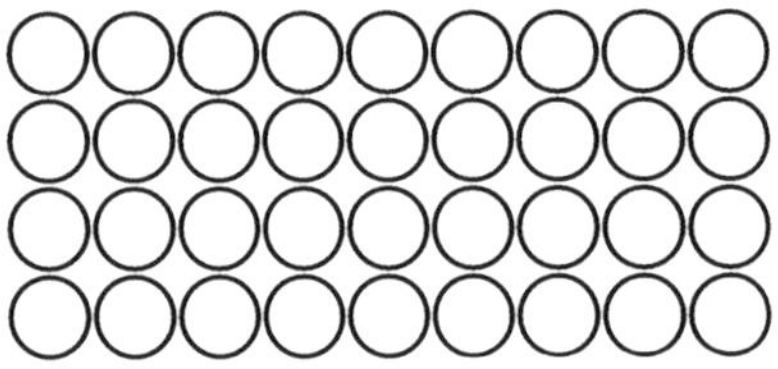 ____ rows and ____ columns makes a total of ____.

(6)  ____ rows and ____ columns makes a total of ____.

(7) 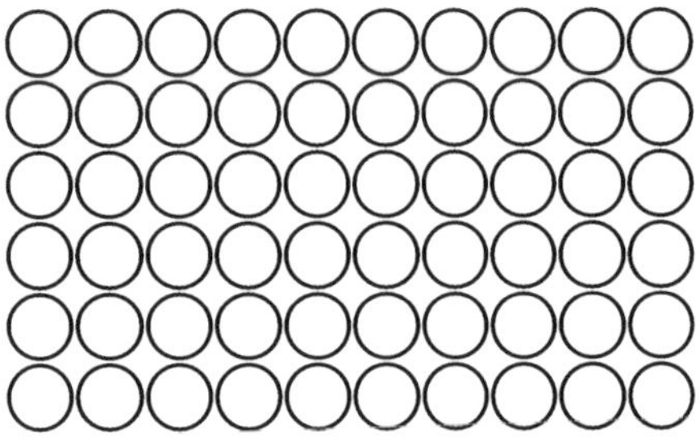 ____ rows and ____ columns makes a total of ____.

(8) 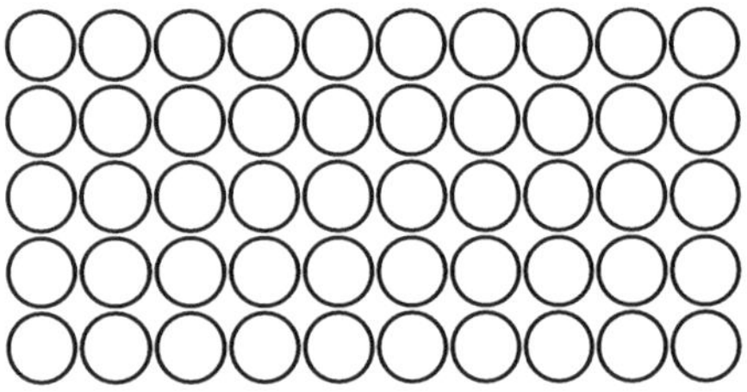 ____ rows and ____ columns makes a total of ____.

(9)  ____ rows and ____ columns makes a total of ____.

(10) 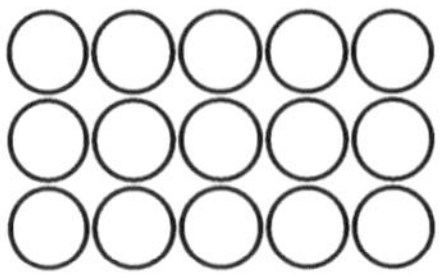 ____ rows and ____ columns makes a total of ____.

(11)  ____ rows and ____ columns makes a total of ____.

Visual Multiplication

Use the dots to help you fill in the blanks to each of the multiplication problems.

(1)  ____ rows and ____ columns makes a total of ____.

(2) 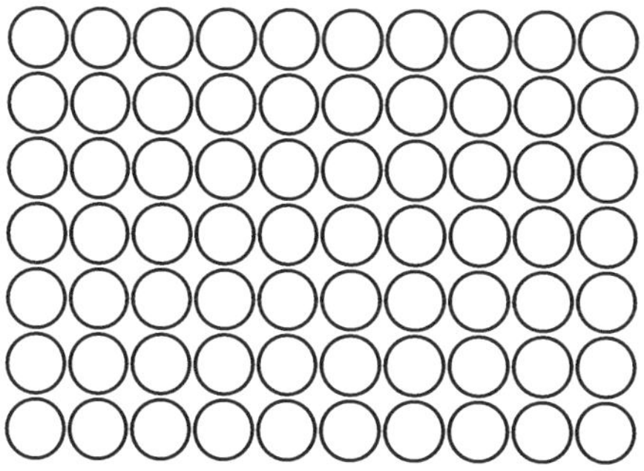 ____ rows and ____ columns makes a total of ____.

(3)  ____ rows and ____ columns makes a total of ____.

(4)  ____ rows and ____ columns makes a total of ____.

(5) 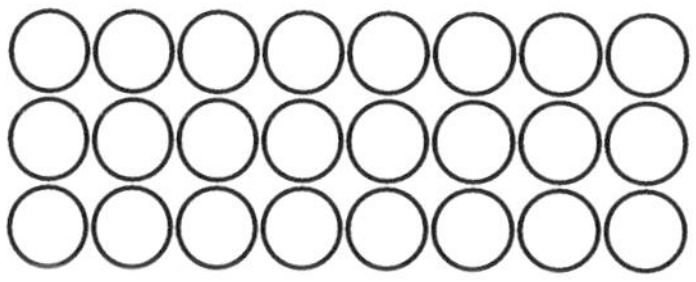 ____ rows and ____ columns makes a total of ____.

(6)  ____ rows and ____ columns makes a total of ____.

(7)  ____ rows and ____ columns makes a total of ____.

(8) 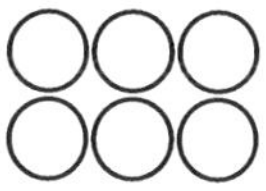 ____ rows and ____ columns makes a total of ____.

(9) 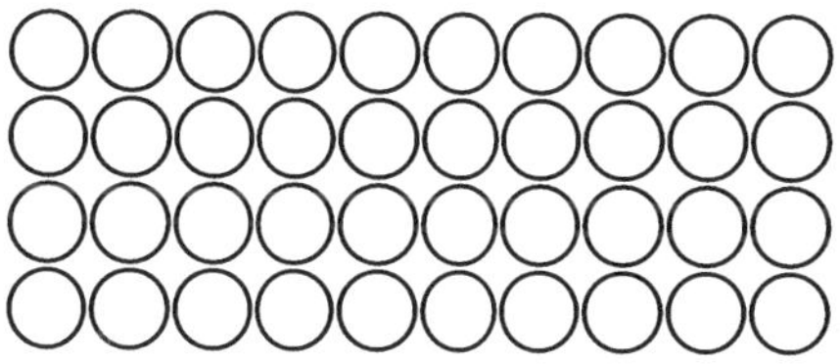 ____ rows and ____ columns makes a total of ____.

(10) 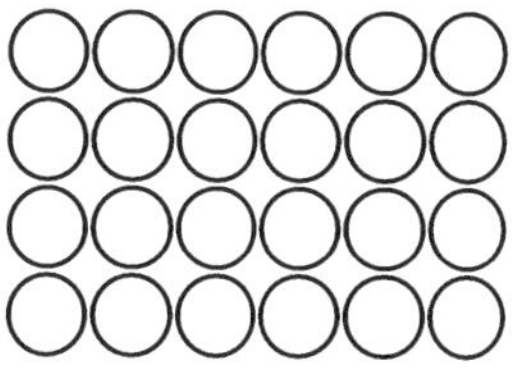 ____ rows and ____ columns makes a total of ____.

(11) 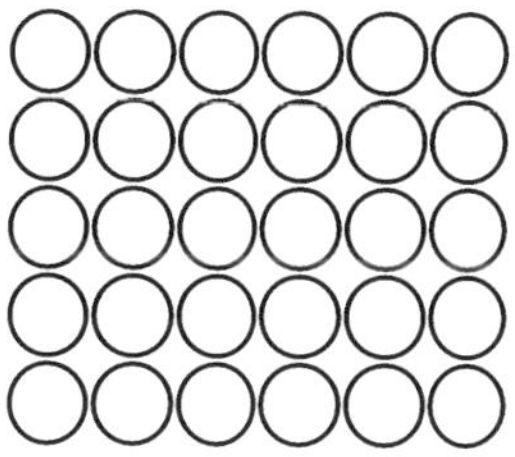 ____ rows and ____ columns makes a total of ____.

Visual Multiplication

☞ Use the dots to help you fill in the blanks to each of the multiplication problems.

(1) ____ rows and ____ columns makes a total of ____.

(2) ____ rows and ____ columns makes a total of ____.

(3) ____ rows and ____ columns makes a total of ____.

(4) ____ rows and ____ columns makes a total of ____.

(5) ____ rows and ____ columns makes a total of ____.

(6) ____ rows and ____ columns makes a total of ____.

(7) ____ rows and ____ columns makes a total of ____.

(8) ____ rows and ____ columns makes a total of ____.

(9) ____ rows and ____ columns makes a total of ____.

(10) ____ rows and ____ columns makes a total of ____.

Visual Multiplication

Use the dots to help you fill in the blanks to each of the multiplication problems.

(1)

____ rows and ____ columns makes a total of ____.

(2)

____ rows and ____ columns makes a total of ____.

(3)

____ rows and ____ columns makes a total of ____.

(4)

____ rows and ____ columns makes a total of ____.

(5)

____ rows and ____ columns makes a total of ____.

(6)

____ rows and ____ columns makes a total of ____.

(7)

____ rows and ____ columns makes a total of ____.

(8)

____ rows and ____ columns makes a total of ____.

(9)

____ rows and ____ columns makes a total of ____.

(10)

____ rows and ____ columns makes a total of ____.

Visual Multiplication

☞ Use the dots to help you fill in the blanks to each of the multiplication problems.

(1) ○○○○○○○○○○

___ rows and ___ columns makes a total of ___.

(2)

___ rows and ___ columns makes a total of ___.

(3)

___ rows and ___ columns makes a total of ___.

(4)

___ rows and ___ columns makes a total of ___.

(5) ○○

___ rows and ___ columns makes a total of ___.

(6) ○○○○○○○

___ rows and ___ columns makes a total of ___.

(7)

___ rows and ___ columns makes a total of ___.

(8)

___ rows and ___ columns makes a total of ___.

(9)

___ rows and ___ columns makes a total of ___.

(10)

___ rows and ___ columns makes a total of ___.

Visual Multiplication

Use the dots to help you fill in the blanks to each of the multiplication problems.

(1)  ____ rows and ____ columns makes a total of ____.

(2)  ____ rows and ____ columns makes a total of ____.

(3)  ____ rows and ____ columns makes a total of ____.

(4) 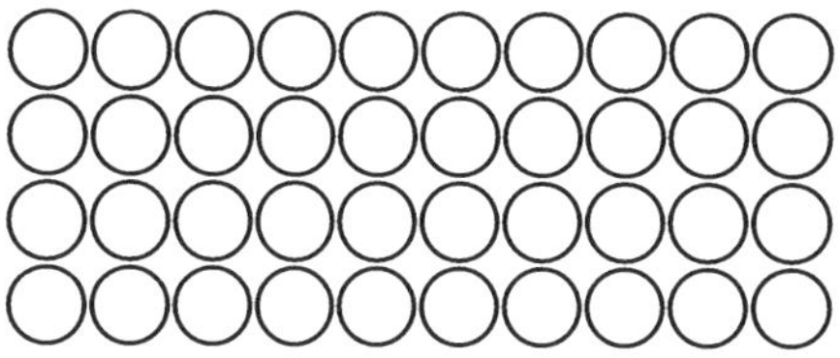 ____ rows and ____ columns makes a total of ____.

(5) 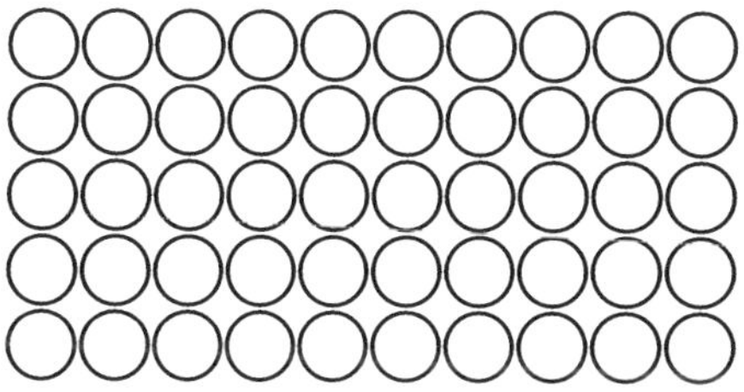 ____ rows and ____ columns makes a total of ____.

(6) 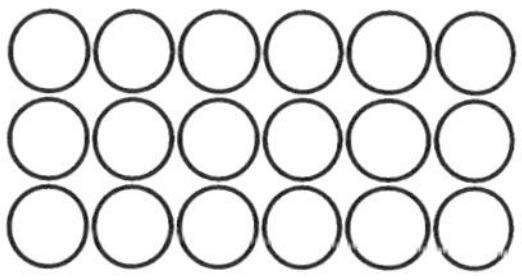 ____ rows and ____ columns makes a total of ____.

(7) 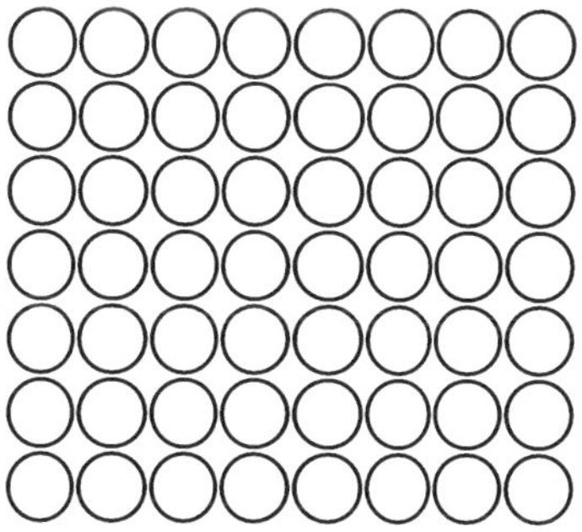 ____ rows and ____ columns makes a total of ____.

(8)  ____ rows and ____ columns makes a total of ____.

(9) 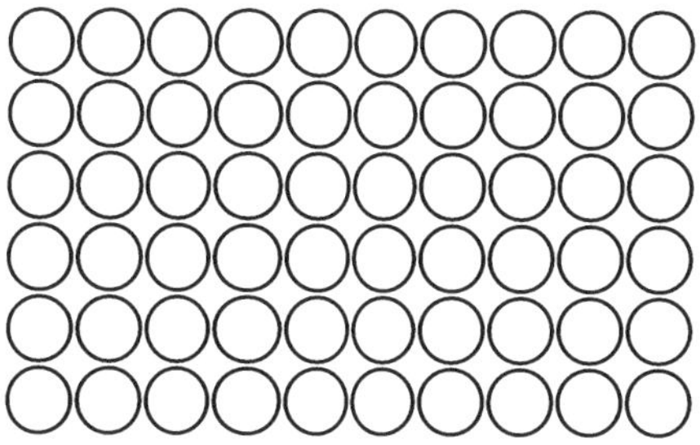 ____ rows and ____ columns makes a total of ____.

(10)  ____ rows and ____ columns makes a total of ____.

Visual Multiplication

☞ Use the dots to help you fill in the blanks to each of the multiplication problems.

(1) ____ rows and ____ columns makes a total of ____.

(2) ____ rows and ____ columns makes a total of ____.

(3) ____ rows and ____ columns makes a total of ____.

(4) ____ rows and ____ columns makes a total of ____.

(5) ____ rows and ____ columns makes a total of ____.

(6) ____ rows and ____ columns makes a total of ____.

(7) ____ rows and ____ columns makes a total of ____.

(8) ____ rows and ____ columns makes a total of ____.

(9) ____ rows and ____ columns makes a total of ____.

(10) ____ rows and ____ columns makes a total of ____.

Visual Multiplication

☞ Use the dots to help you fill in the blanks to each of the multiplication problems.

(1) ____ rows and ____ columns makes a total of ____.

(2) ____ rows and ____ columns makes a total of ____.

(3) ____ rows and ____ columns makes a total of ____.

(4) ____ rows and ____ columns makes a total of ____.

(5) ____ rows and ____ columns makes a total of ____.

(6) ____ rows and ____ columns makes a total of ____.

(7) ____ rows and ____ columns makes a total of ____.

(8) ____ rows and ____ columns makes a total of ____.

(9) ____ rows and ____ columns makes a total of ____.

(10) ____ rows and ____ columns makes a total of ____.

(11) ____ rows and ____ columns makes a total of ____.

(12) ____ rows and ____ columns makes a total of ____.

(13) ____ rows and ____ columns makes a total of ____.

Visual Multiplication

Use the dots to help you fill in the blanks to each of the multiplication problems.

(1) ___ rows and ___ columns makes a total of ___.

(2) ___ rows and ___ columns makes a total of ___.

(3) ___ rows and ___ columns makes a total of ___.

(4) ___ rows and ___ columns makes a total of ___.

(5) ___ rows and ___ columns makes a total of ___.

(6) ___ rows and ___ columns makes a total of ___.

(7) ___ rows and ___ columns makes a total of ___.

(8) ___ rows and ___ columns makes a total of ___.

(9) ___ rows and ___ columns makes a total of ___.

(10) ___ rows and ___ columns makes a total of ___.

(11) ___ rows and ___ columns makes a total of ___.

(12) ___ rows and ___ columns makes a total of ___.

Visual Multiplication

☞ Use the dots to help you fill in the blanks to each of the multiplication problems.

(1) ____ rows and ____ columns makes a total of ____.

(2) ____ rows and ____ columns makes a total of ____.

(3) ____ rows and ____ columns makes a total of ____.

(4) ____ rows and ____ columns makes a total of ____.

(5) ____ rows and ____ columns makes a total of ____.

(6) ____ rows and ____ columns makes a total of ____.

(7) ____ rows and ____ columns makes a total of ____.

(8) ____ rows and ____ columns makes a total of ____.

(9) ____ rows and ____ columns makes a total of ____.

(10) ____ rows and ____ columns makes a total of ____.

Visual Multiplication

☞ Use the dots to help you fill in the blanks to each of the multiplication problems.

(1)

____ rows and ____ columns makes a total of ____.

(2)

____ rows and ____ columns makes a total of ____.

(3)

____ rows and ____ columns makes a total of ____.

(4)

____ rows and ____ columns makes a total of ____.

(5)

____ rows and ____ columns makes a total of ____.

(6)

____ rows and ____ columns makes a total of ____.

(7)

____ rows and ____ columns makes a total of ____.

(8)

____ rows and ____ columns makes a total of ____.

(9)

____ rows and ____ columns makes a total of ____.

Visual Multiplication

 Use the dots to help you fill in the blanks to each of the multiplication problems.

(1)

____ rows and ____ columns makes a total of ____.

(2)

____ rows and ____ columns makes a total of ____.

(3)

____ rows and ____ columns makes a total of ____.

(4)

____ rows and ____ columns makes a total of ____.

(5)

____ rows and ____ columns makes a total of ____.

(6)

____ rows and ____ columns makes a total of ____.

(7)

____ rows and ____ columns makes a total of ____.

(8)

____ rows and ____ columns makes a total of ____.

(9)

____ rows and ____ columns makes a total of ____.

ANSWER KEY

Visual Multiplication

Visual Multiplication
ANSWER KEY

 Use the dots to help you fill in the blanks to each of the multiplication problems.

(1) 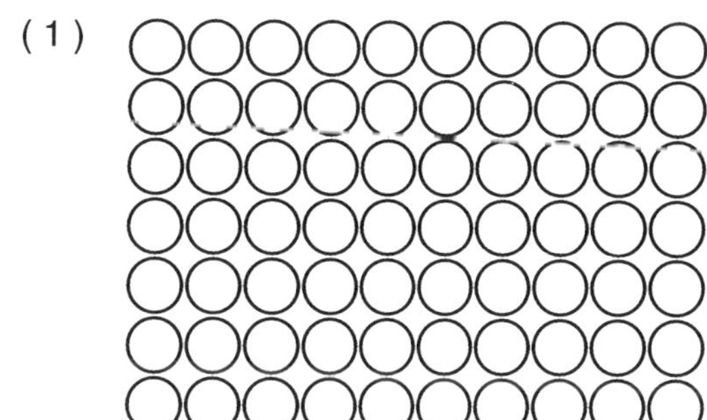

7 rows and 10 columns makes a total of 70.

(2) 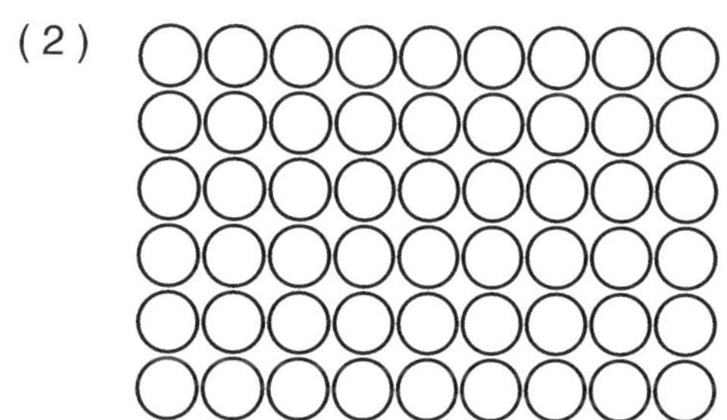

6 rows and 9 columns makes a total of 54.

(3) 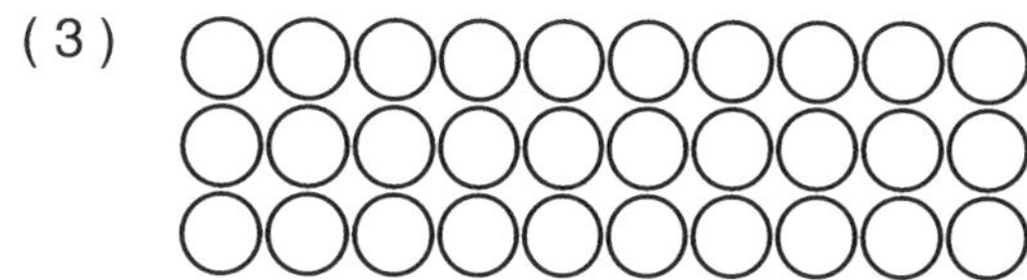

3 rows and 10 columns makes a total of 30.

(4) 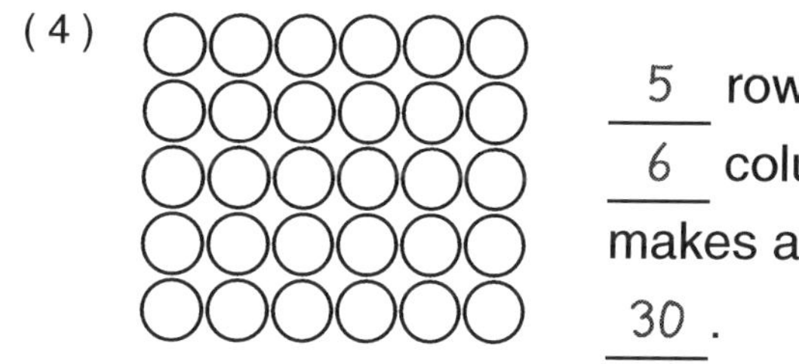

5 rows and 6 columns makes a total of 30.

(5) 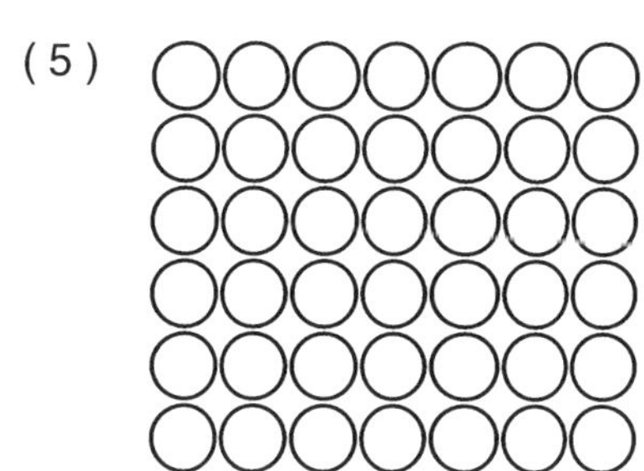

6 rows and 7 columns makes a total of 42.

(6) 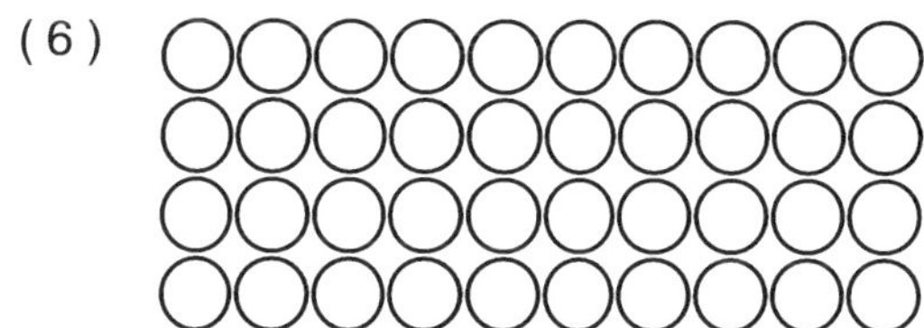

4 rows and 10 columns makes a total of 40.

(7) 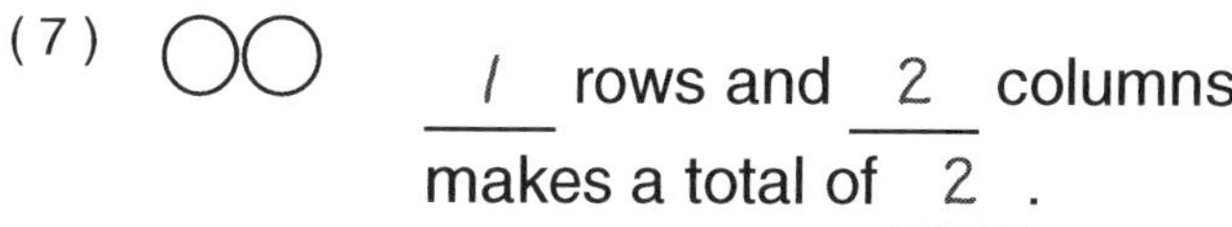

1 rows and 2 columns makes a total of 2.

(8) 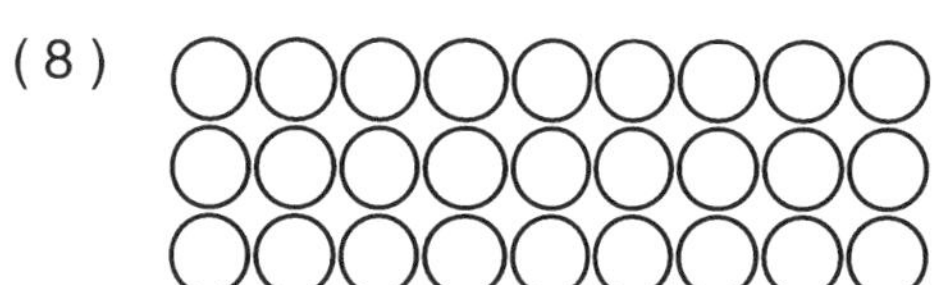

3 rows and 9 columns makes a total of 27.

(9) 

2 rows and 7 columns makes a total of 14.

Visual Multiplication
ANSWER KEY

 Use the dots to help you fill in the blanks to each of the multiplication problems.

(1) 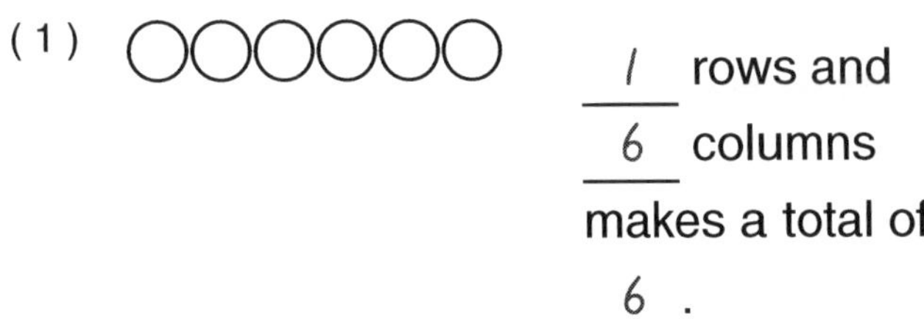

1 rows and 6 columns makes a total of 6.

(2) 1 rows and 8 columns makes a total of 8.

(3) 2 rows and 7 columns makes a total of 14.

(4) 5 rows and 3 columns makes a total of 15.

(5) 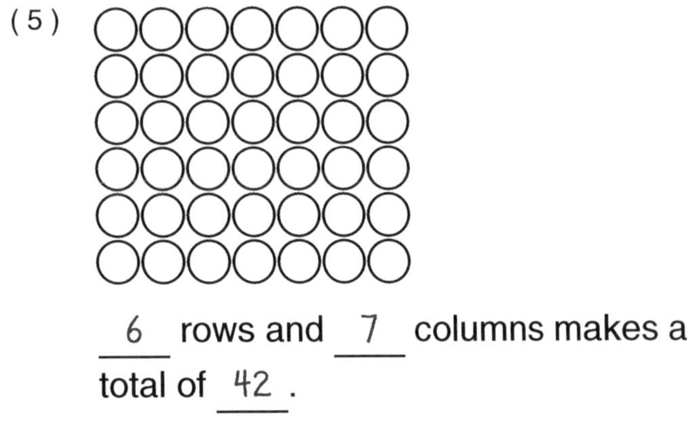

6 rows and 7 columns makes a total of 42.

(6) 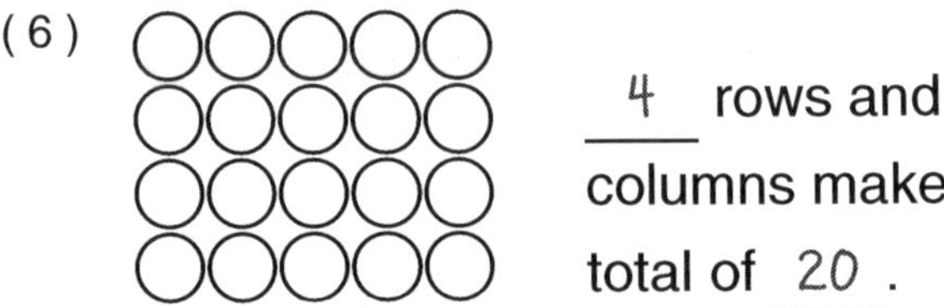

4 rows and 5 columns makes a total of 20.

(7) 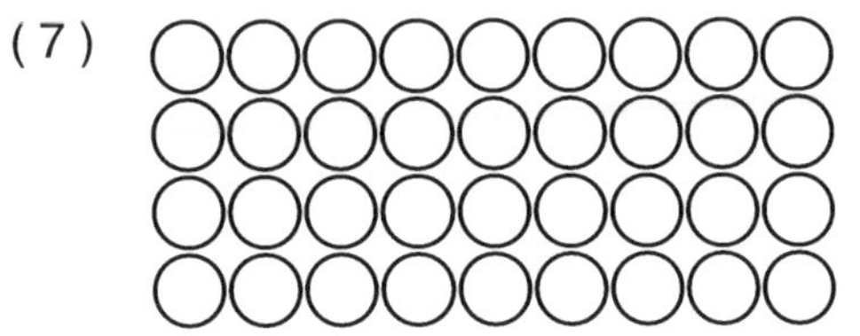

4 rows and 9 columns makes a total of 36.

(8) 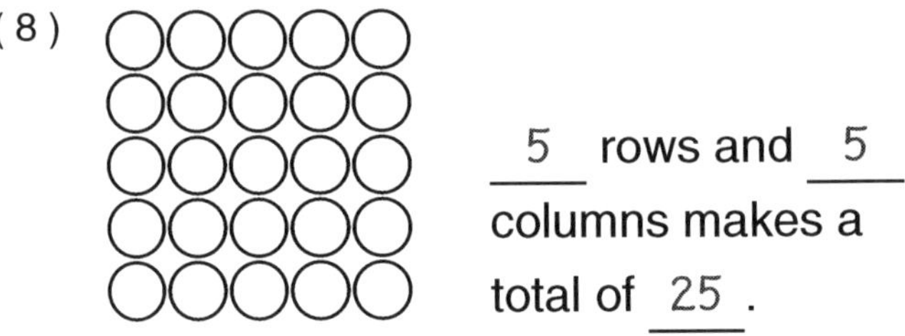

5 rows and 5 columns makes a total of 25.

(9) 1 rows and 10 columns makes a total of 10.

(10) 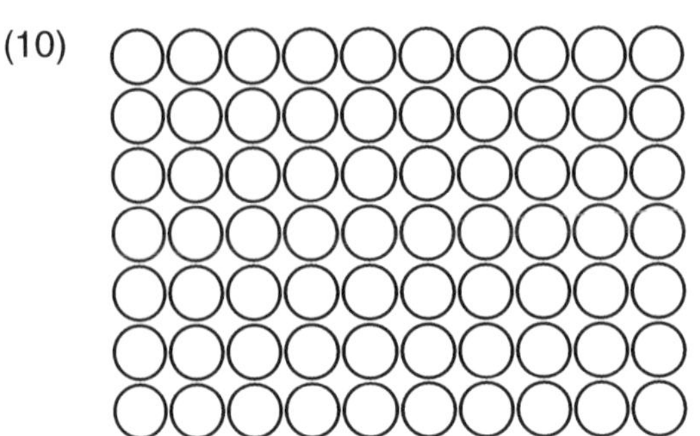

7 rows and 10 columns makes a total of 70.

Visual Multiplication
ANSWER KEY

 Use the dots to help you fill in the blanks to each of the multiplication problems.

(1) 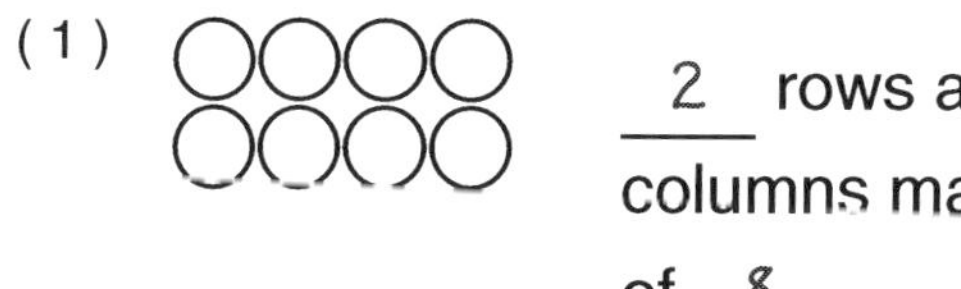

2 rows and 4 columns makes a total of 8.

(2) 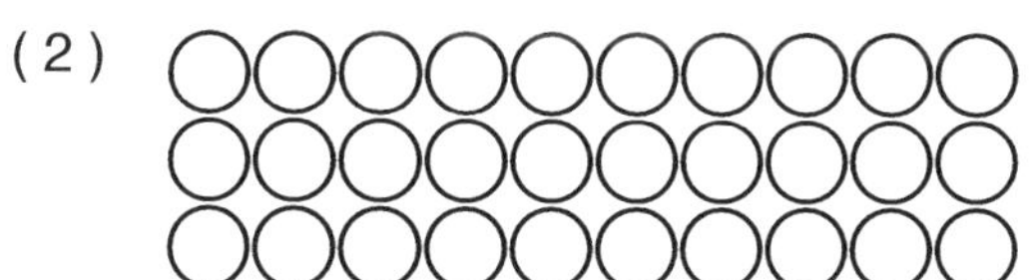

3 rows and 10 columns makes a total of 30.

(3) 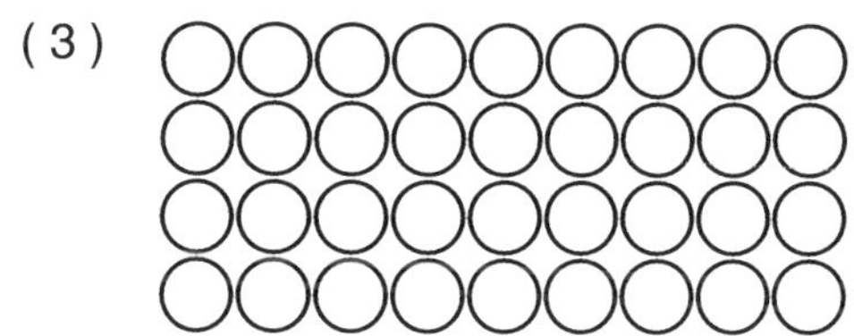

4 rows and 9 columns makes a total of 36.

(4) 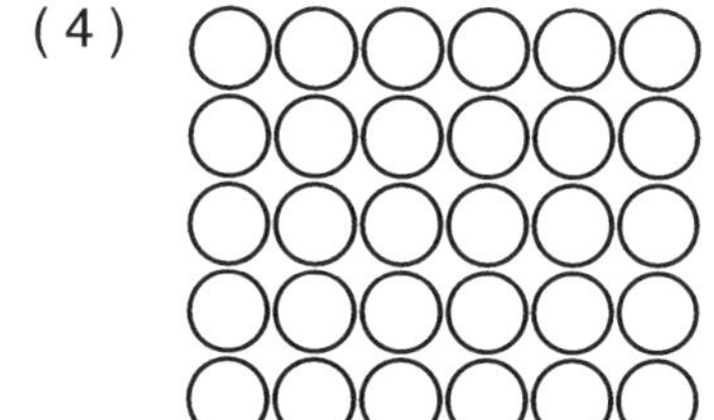

5 rows and 6 columns makes a total of 30.

(5) 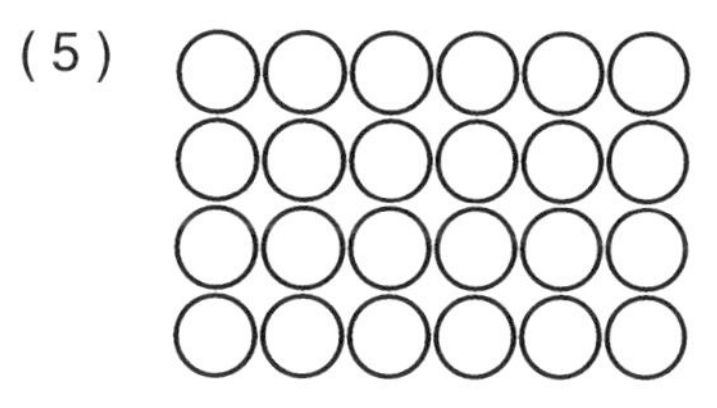

4 rows and 6 columns makes a total of 24.

(6)

5 rows and 1 columns makes a total of 5.

(7) 

2 rows and 9 columns makes a total of 18.

(8) 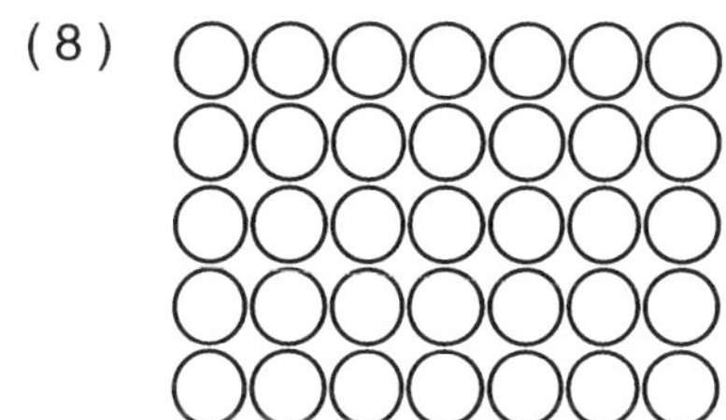

5 rows and 7 columns makes a total of 35.

(9) 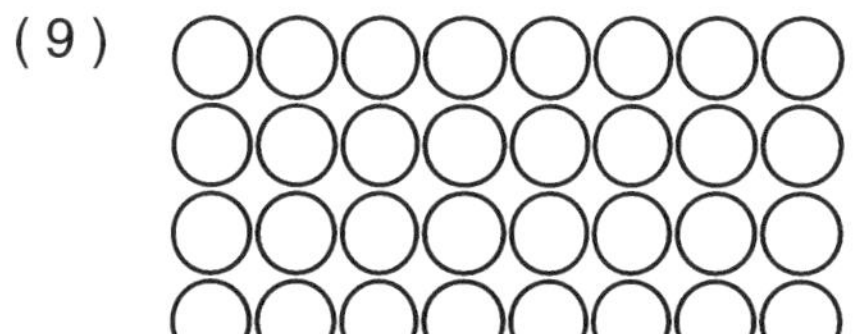

4 rows and 8 columns makes a total of 32.

(10) 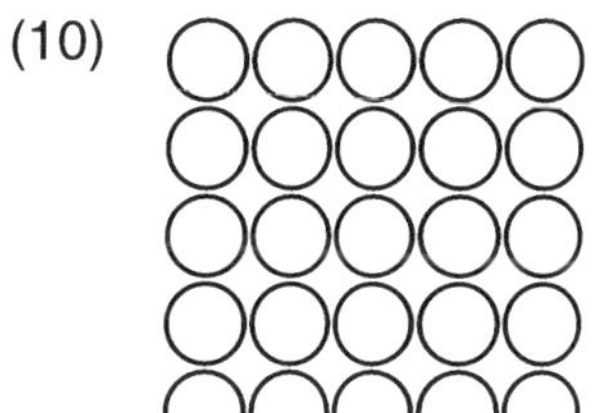

5 rows and 5 columns makes a total of 25.

Visual Multiplication
ANSWER KEY

 Use the dots to help you fill in the blanks to each of the multiplication problems.

(1) 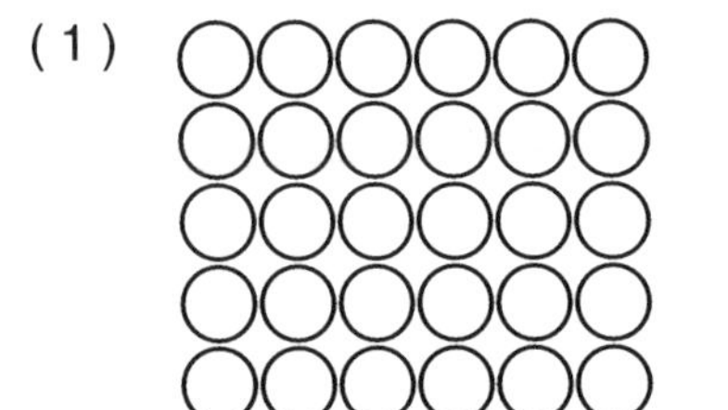

5 rows and 6 columns makes a total of 30.

(2) 

2 rows and 6 columns makes a total of 12.

(3) 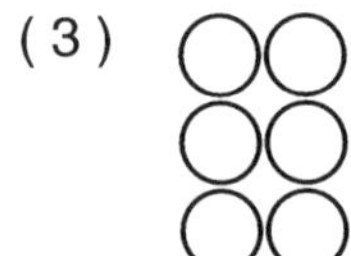

3 rows and 2 columns makes a total of 6.

(4) 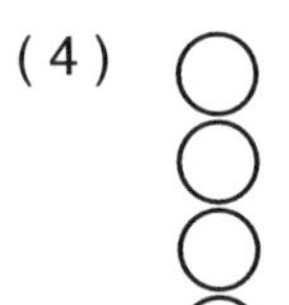

5 rows and 1 columns makes a total of 5.

(5) 

1 rows and 10 columns makes a total of 10.

(6) 

3 rows and 10 columns makes a total of 30.

(7)

4 rows and 2 columns makes a total of 8.

(8) 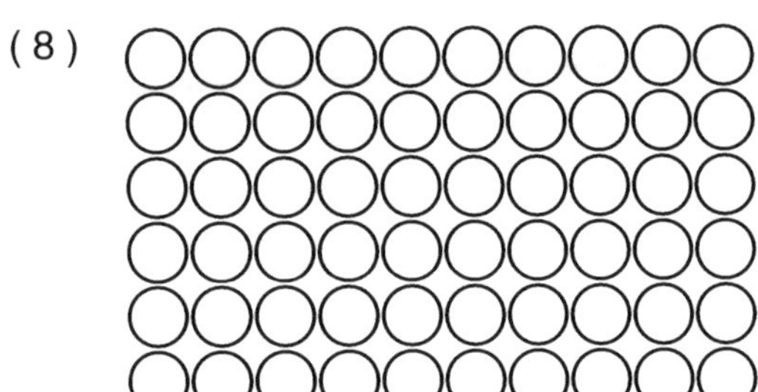

6 rows and 10 columns makes a total of 60.

(9) 

3 rows and 5 columns makes a total of 15.

(10) 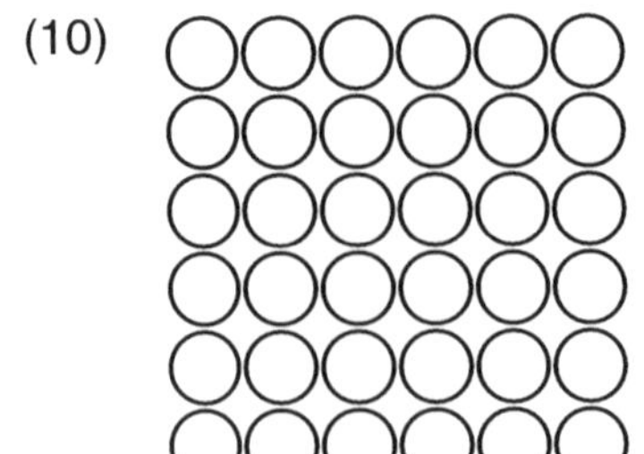

6 rows and 6 columns makes a total of 36.

(11)

1 rows and 9 columns makes a total of 9.

Visual Multiplication
ANSWER KEY

 Use the dots to help you fill in the blanks to each of the multiplication problems.

(1) 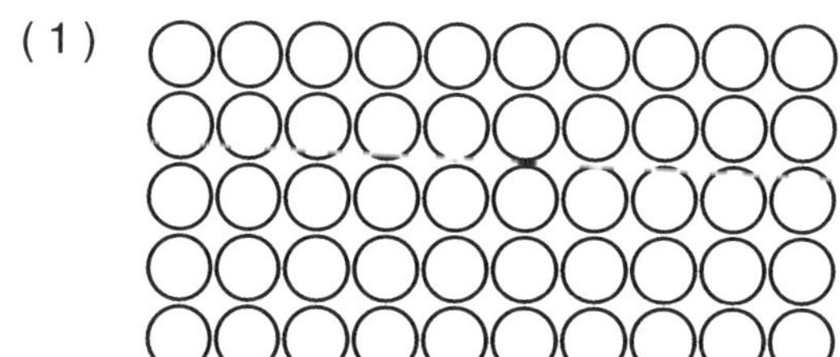

5 rows and 10 columns makes a total of 50.

(2) 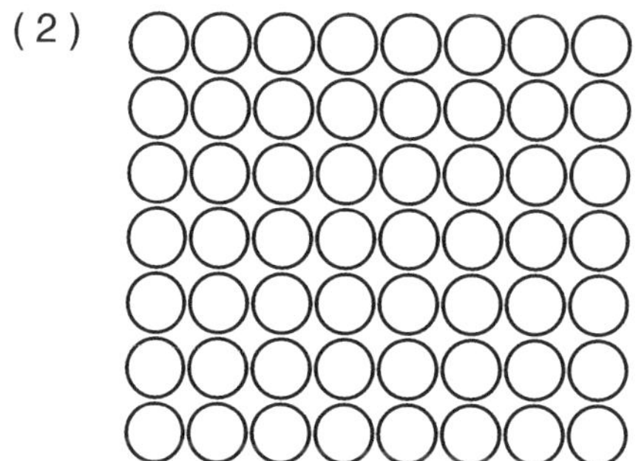

7 rows and 8 columns makes a total of 56.

(3) 

3 rows and 10 columns makes a total of 30.

(4) 

2 rows and 9 columns makes a total of 18.

(5) 2 rows and 1 columns makes a total of 2.

(6) 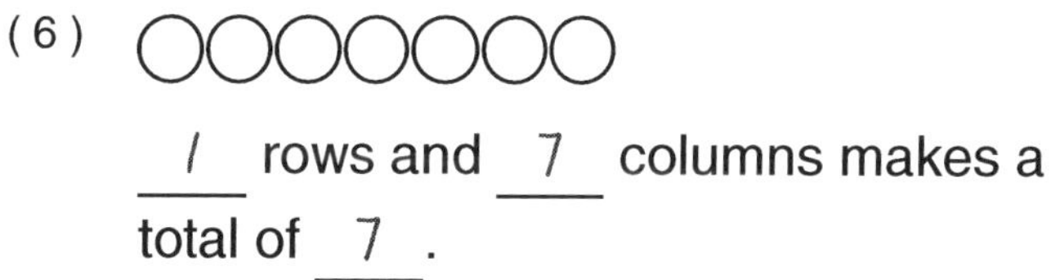

1 rows and 7 columns makes a total of 7.

(7) 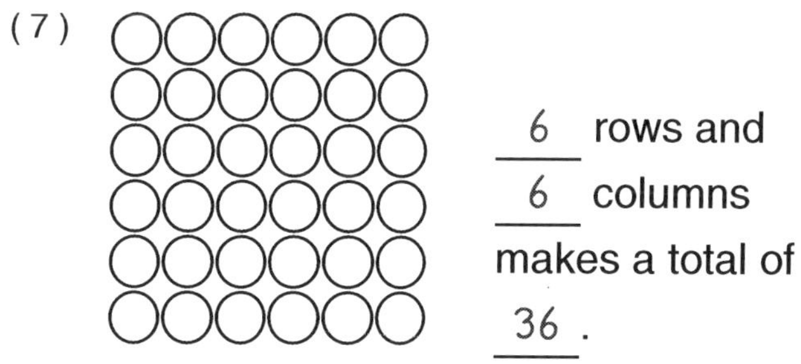

6 rows and 6 columns makes a total of 36.

(8) 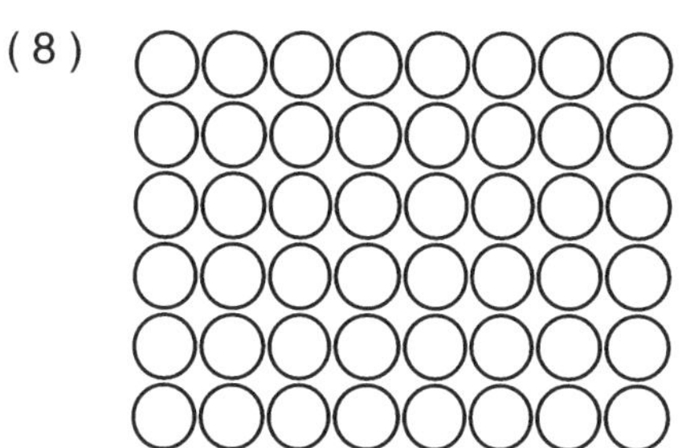

6 rows and 8 columns makes a total of 48.

(9) 

3 rows and 7 columns makes a total of 21.

Visual Multiplication
ANSWER KEY

Use the dots to help you fill in the blanks to each of the multiplication problems.

(1)

5 rows and 10 columns makes a total of 50.

(2)

2 rows and 7 columns makes a total of 14.

(3)

2 rows and 10 columns makes a total of 20.

(4)

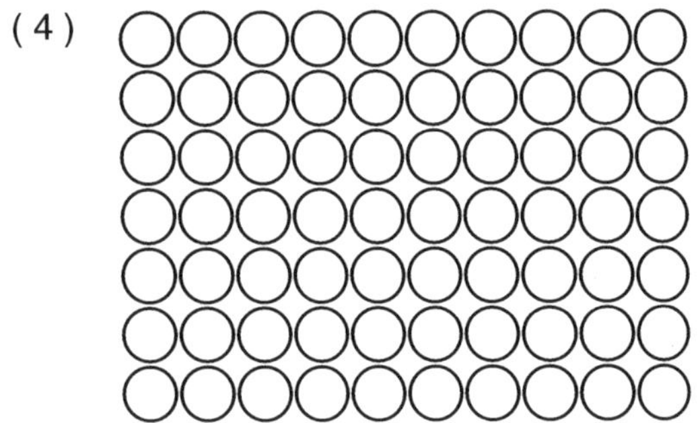

7 rows and 10 columns makes a total of 70.

(5)

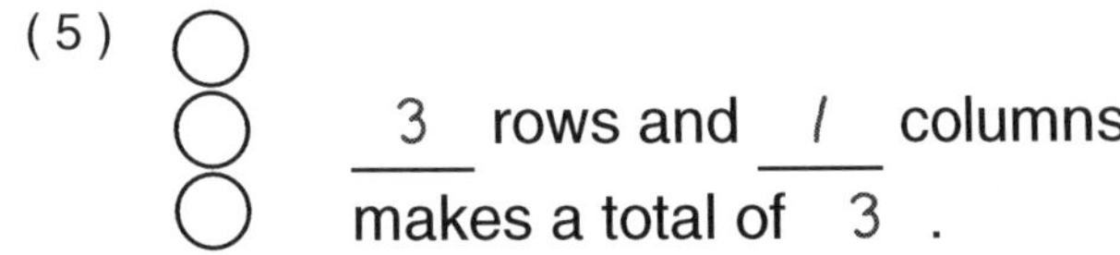

3 rows and 1 columns makes a total of 3.

(6)

1 rows and 6 columns makes a total of 6.

(7)

1 rows and 10 columns makes a total of 10.

(8)

5 rows and 1 columns makes a total of 5.

(9)

4 rows and 2 columns makes a total of 8.

(10)

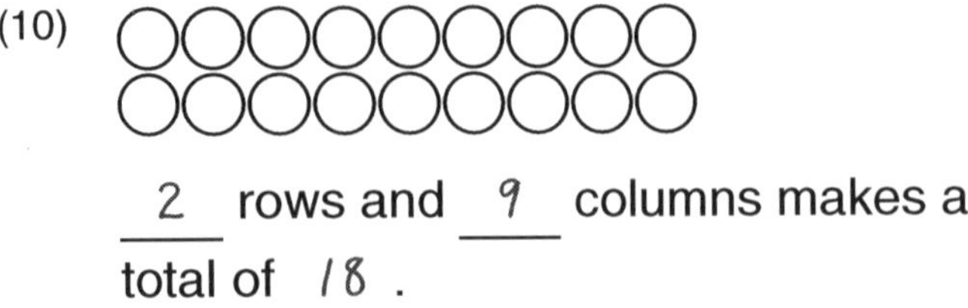

2 rows and 9 columns makes a total of 18.

(11)

5 rows and 2 columns makes a total of 10.

Visual Multiplication
ANSWER KEY

Use the dots to help you fill in the blanks to each of the multiplication problems.

(1)

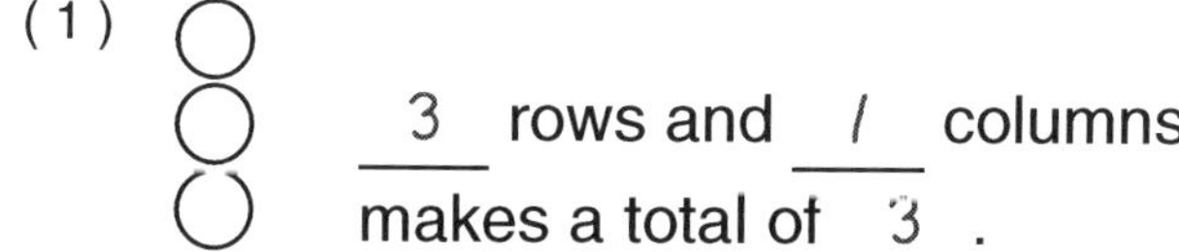

3 rows and 1 columns makes a total of 3.

(2)

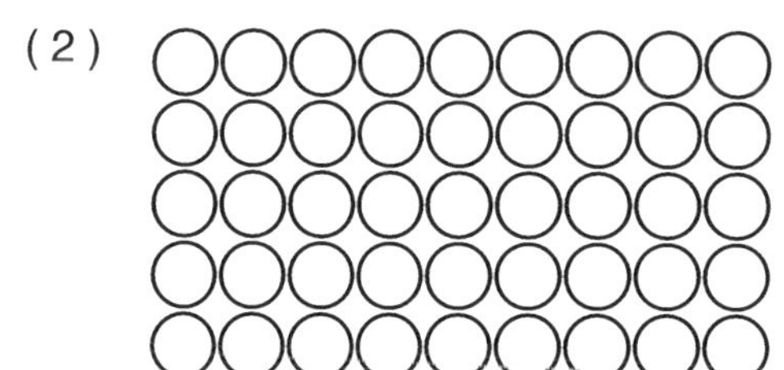

5 rows and 9 columns makes a total of 45.

(3)

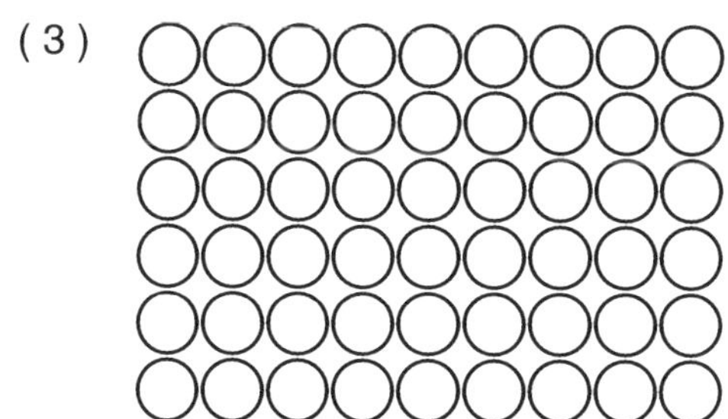

6 rows and 9 columns makes a total of 54.

(4)

2 rows and 2 columns makes a total of 4.

(5)

1 rows and 7 columns makes a total of 7.

(6)

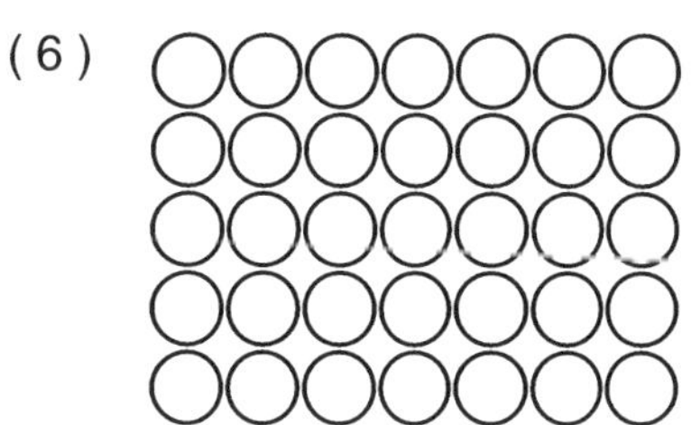

5 rows and 7 columns makes a total of 35.

(7)

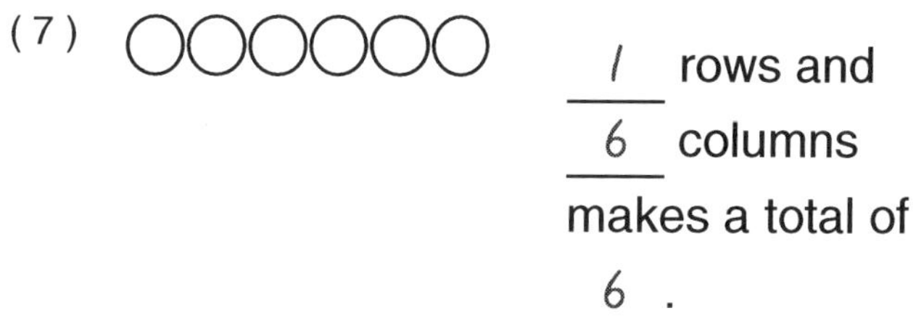

1 rows and 6 columns makes a total of 6.

(8)

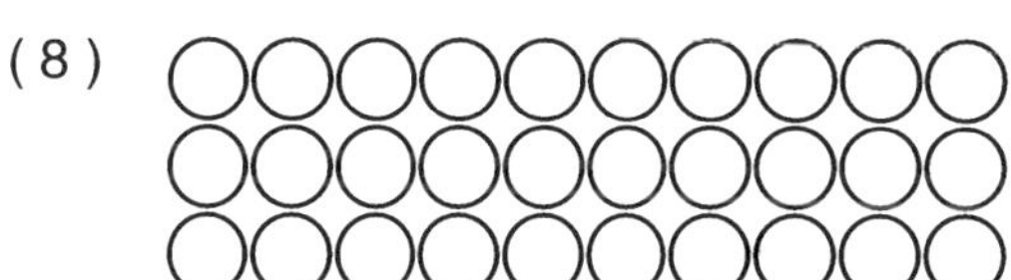

3 rows and 10 columns makes a total of 30.

(9)

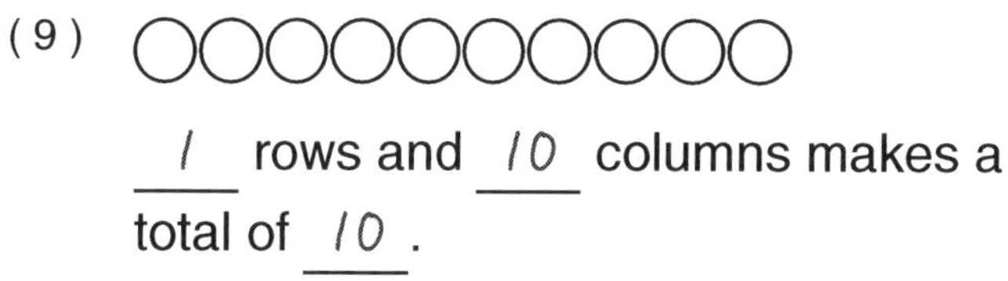

1 rows and 10 columns makes a total of 10.

(10)

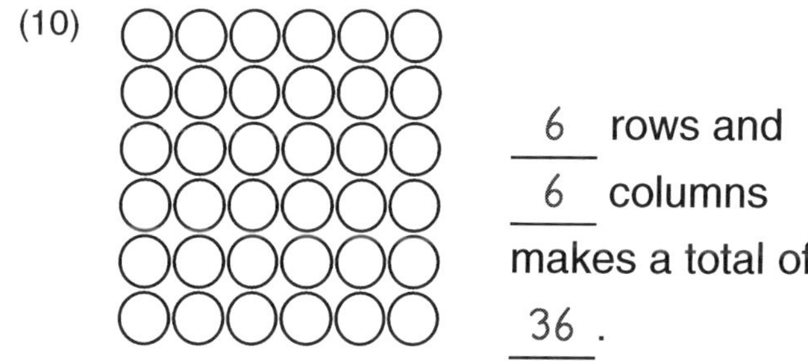

6 rows and 6 columns makes a total of 36.

Visual Multiplication
ANSWER KEY

 Use the dots to help you fill in the blanks to each of the multiplication problems.

(1) 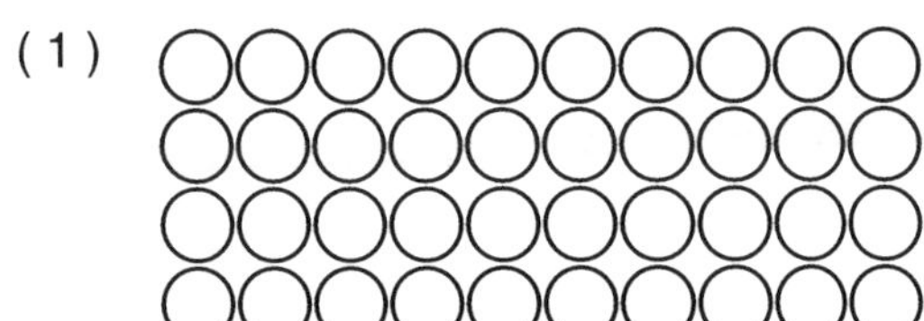

4 rows and 10 columns makes a total of 40.

(2) 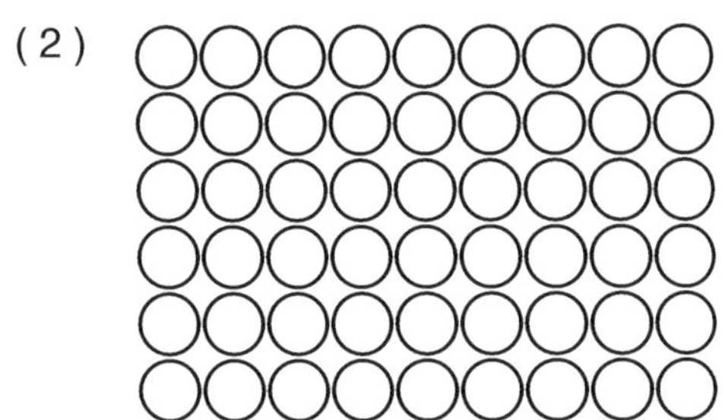

6 rows and 9 columns makes a total of 54.

(3) 3 rows and 2 columns makes a total of 6.

(4) 2 rows and 6 columns makes a total of 12.

(5) 1 rows and 8 columns makes a total of 8.

(6) 1 rows and 9 columns makes a total of 9.

(7) 1 rows and 5 columns makes a total of 5.

(8) 1 rows and 7 columns makes a total of 7.

(9) 4 rows and 7 columns makes a total of 28.

(10) 3 rows and 3 columns makes a total of 9.

(11) 3 rows and 8 columns makes a total of 24.

Visual Multiplication
ANSWER KEY

Use the dots to help you fill in the blanks to each of the multiplication problems.

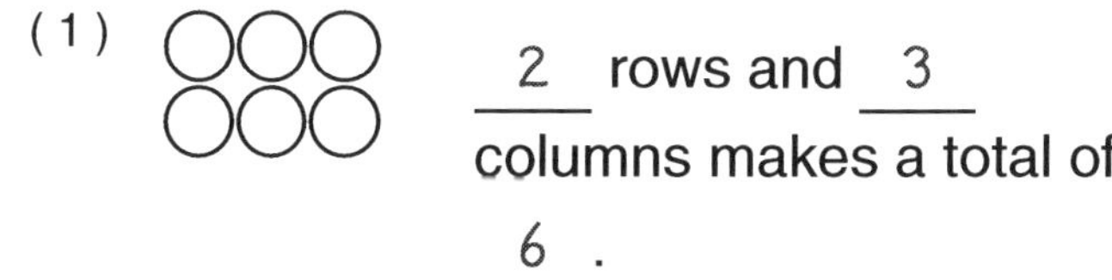

(1) 2 rows and 3 columns makes a total of 6.

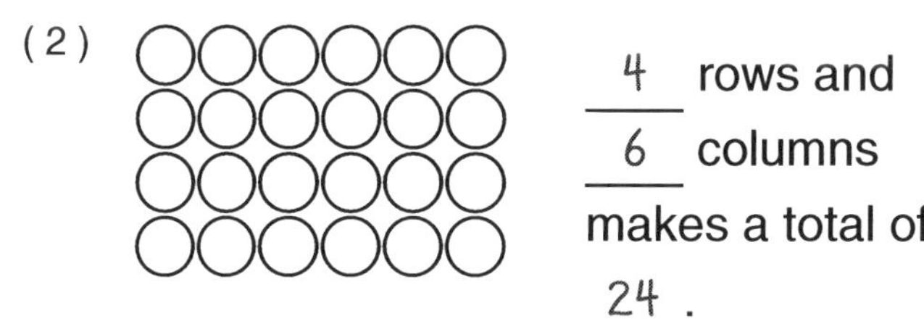

(2) 4 rows and 6 columns makes a total of 24.

(3) 1 rows and 2 columns makes a total of 2.

(4) 2 rows and 9 columns makes a total of 18.

(5) 3 rows and 1 columns makes a total of 3.

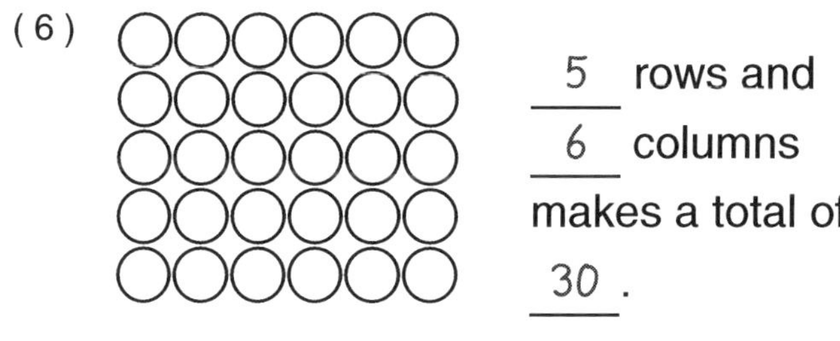

(6) 5 rows and 6 columns makes a total of 30.

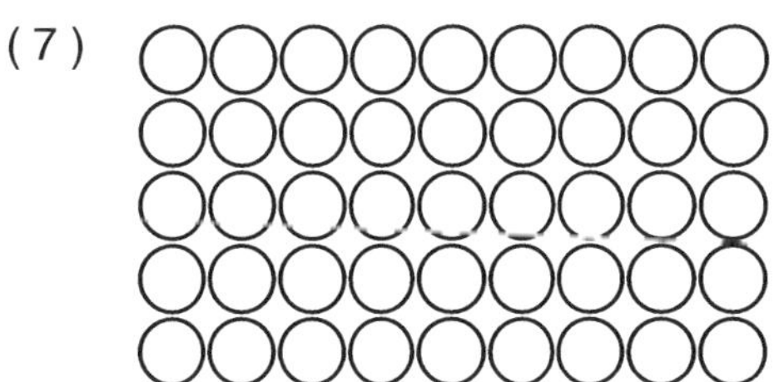

(7) 5 rows and 9 columns makes a total of 45.

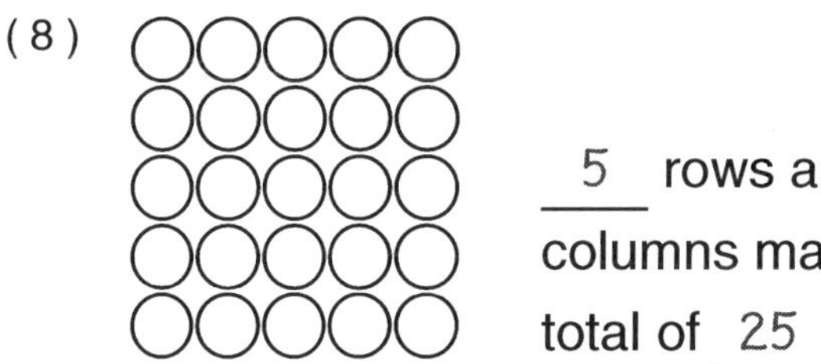

(8) 5 rows and 5 columns makes a total of 25.

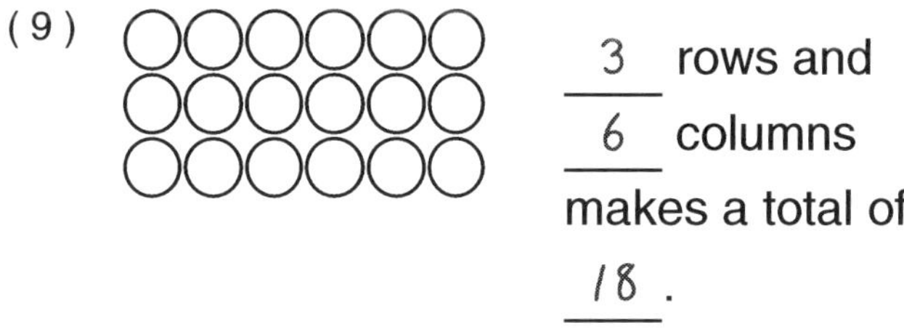

(9) 3 rows and 6 columns makes a total of 18.

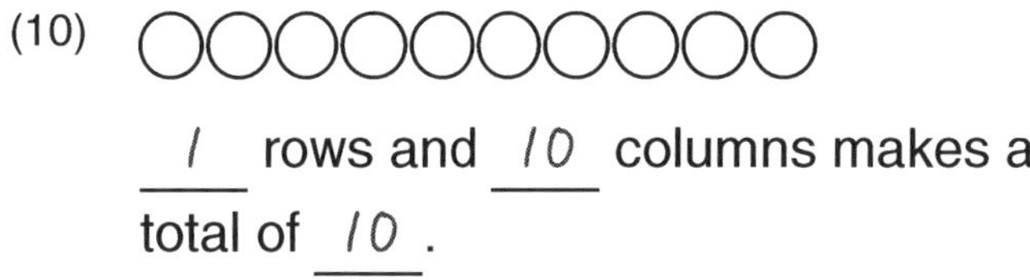

(10) 1 rows and 10 columns makes a total of 10.

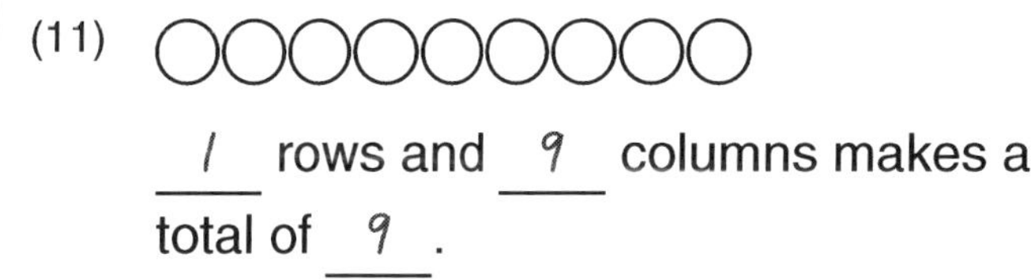

(11) 1 rows and 9 columns makes a total of 9.

Visual Multiplication
ANSWER KEY

Use the dots to help you fill in the blanks to each of the multiplication problems.

(1) 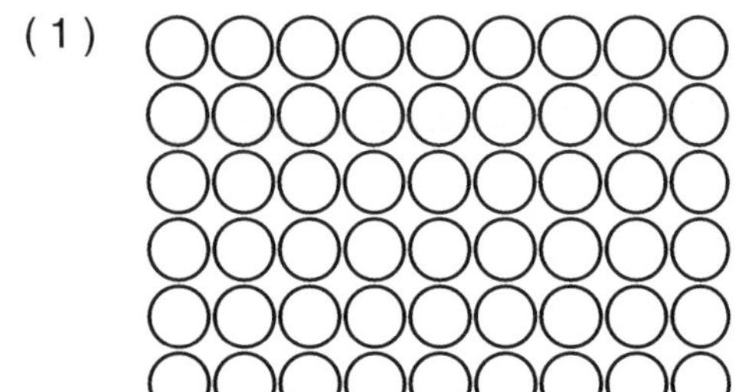

6 rows and 9 columns makes a total of 54.

(2) 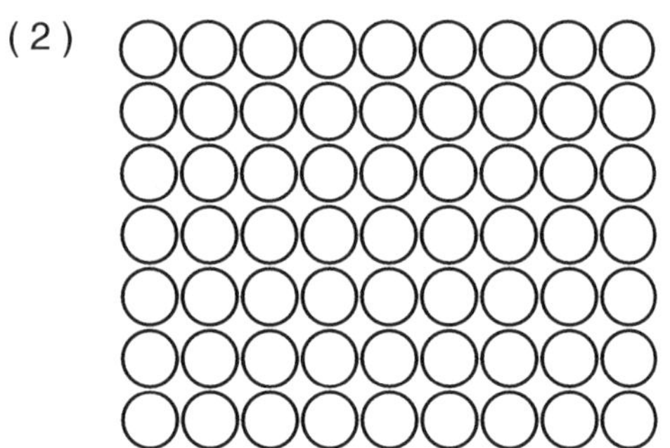

7 rows and 9 columns makes a total of 63.

(3) 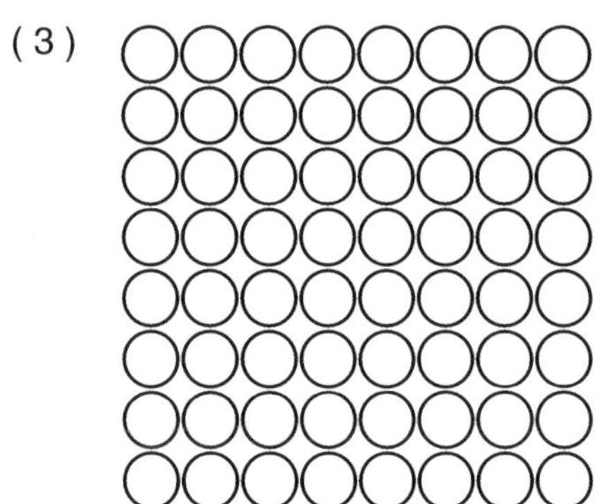

8 rows and 8 columns makes a total of 64.

(4) 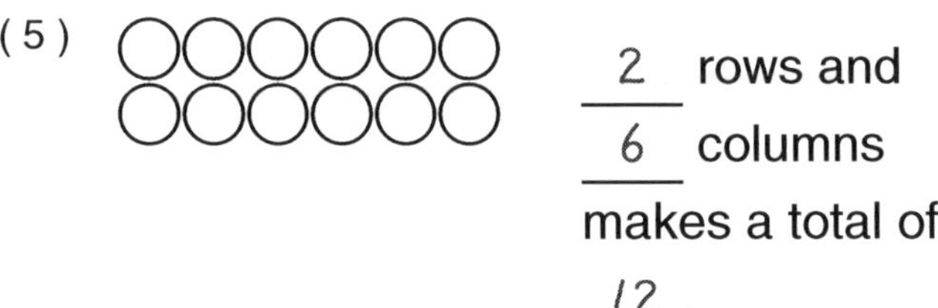

2 rows and 8 columns makes a total of 16.

(5) 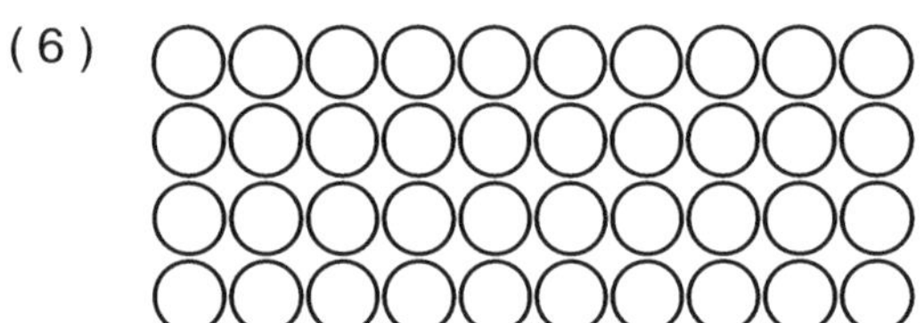

2 rows and 6 columns makes a total of 12.

(6) 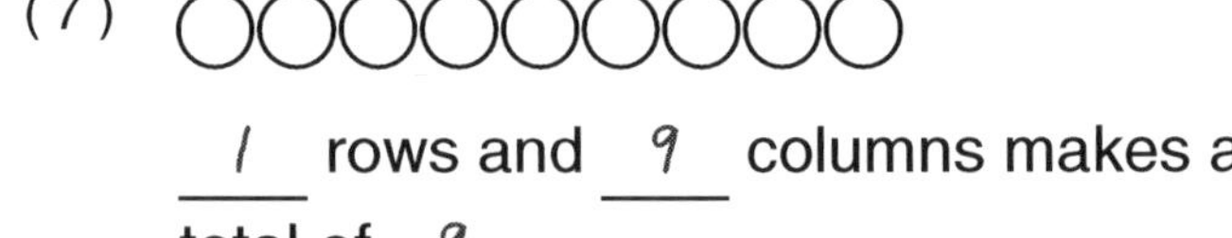

4 rows and 10 columns makes a total of 40.

(7)

1 rows and 9 columns makes a total of 9.

(8)

1 rows and 2 columns makes a total of 2.

(9) 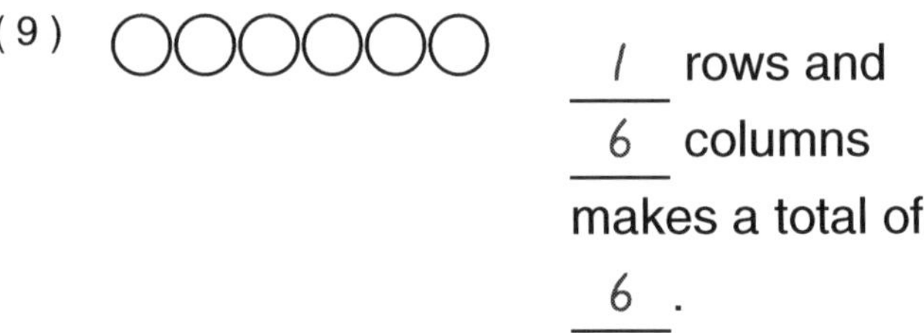

1 rows and 6 columns makes a total of 6.

Visual Multiplication
ANSWER KEY

Use the dots to help you fill in the blanks to each of the multiplication problems.

(1) 1 rows and 3 columns makes a total of 3.

(2) 4 rows and 3 columns makes a total of 12.

(3) 2 rows and 2 columns makes a total of 4.

(4) 5 rows and 10 columns makes a total of 50.

(5) 7 rows and 10 columns makes a total of 70.

(6) 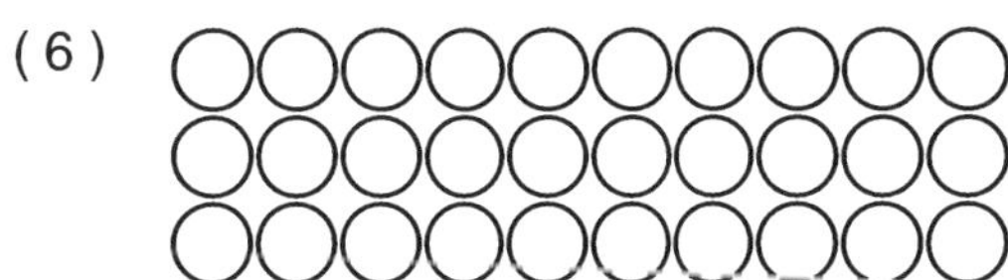

3 rows and 10 columns makes a total of 30.

(7) 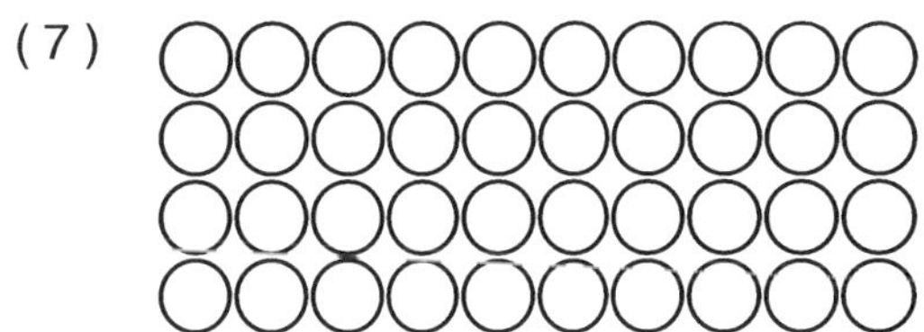

4 rows and 10 columns makes a total of 40.

(8) 

2 rows and 10 columns makes a total of 20.

(9) 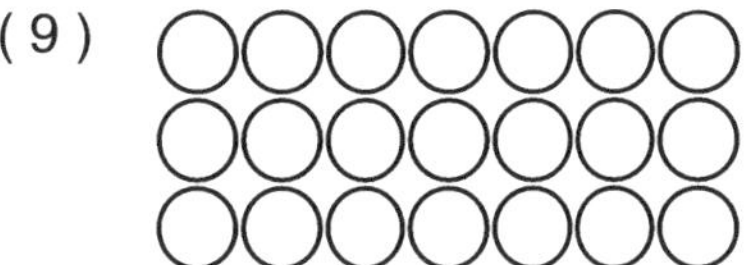

3 rows and 7 columns makes a total of 21.

(10) 

2 rows and 5 columns makes a total of 10.

Visual Multiplication
ANSWER KEY

Use the dots to help you fill in the blanks to each of the multiplication problems.

(1) 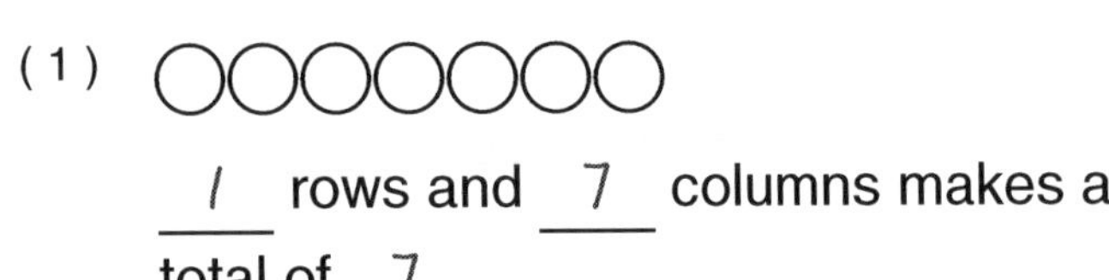

1 rows and 7 columns makes a total of 7 .

(2)

1 rows and 10 columns makes a total of 10 .

(3)

1 rows and 5 columns makes a total of 5 .

(4) 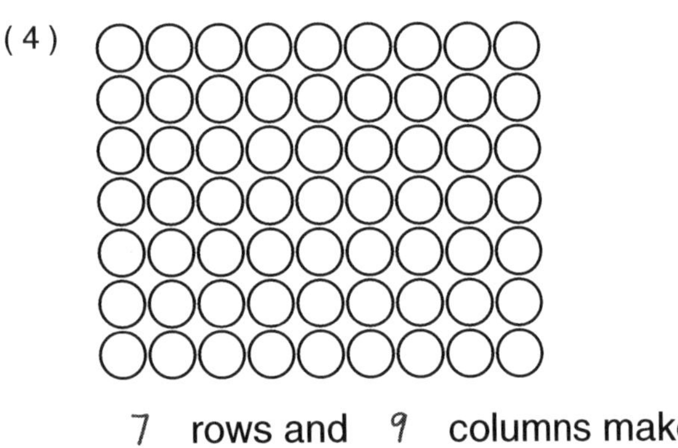

7 rows and 9 columns makes a total of 63 .

(5) 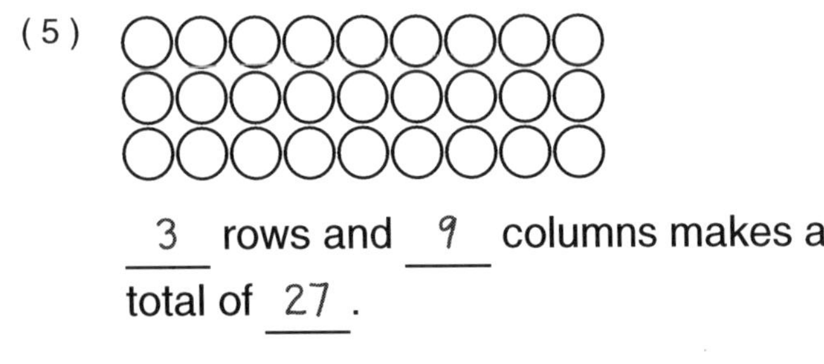

3 rows and 9 columns makes a total of 27 .

(6) 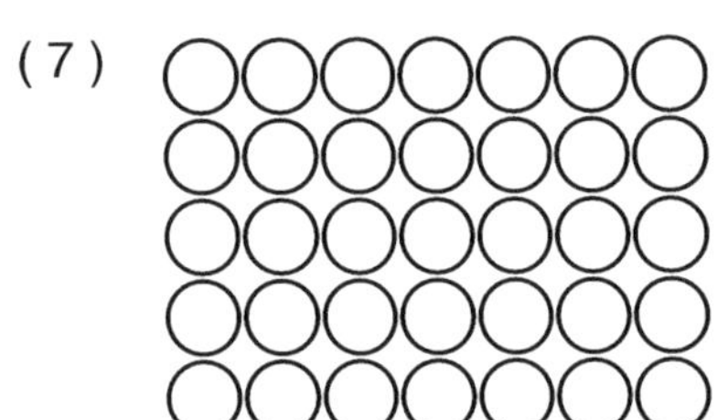

4 rows and 9 columns makes a total of 36 .

(7) 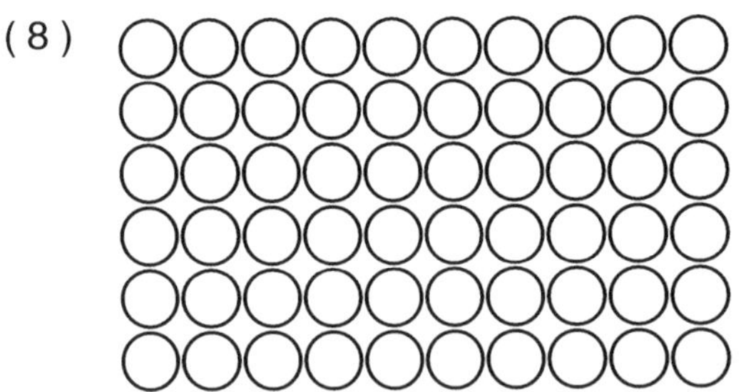

5 rows and 7 columns makes a total of 35 .

(8)

6 rows and 10 columns makes a total of 60 .

(9) 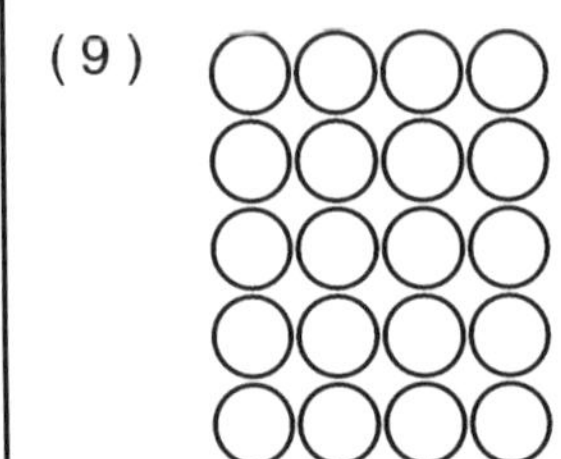

5 rows and 4 columns makes a total of 20 .

Visual Multiplication
ANSWER KEY

 Use the dots to help you fill in the blanks to each of the multiplication problems.

(1) 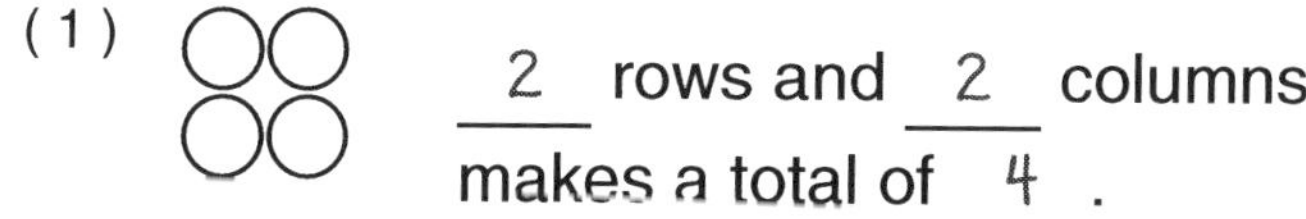

2 rows and 2 columns makes a total of 4.

(2) 

3 rows and 10 columns makes a total of 30.

(3) 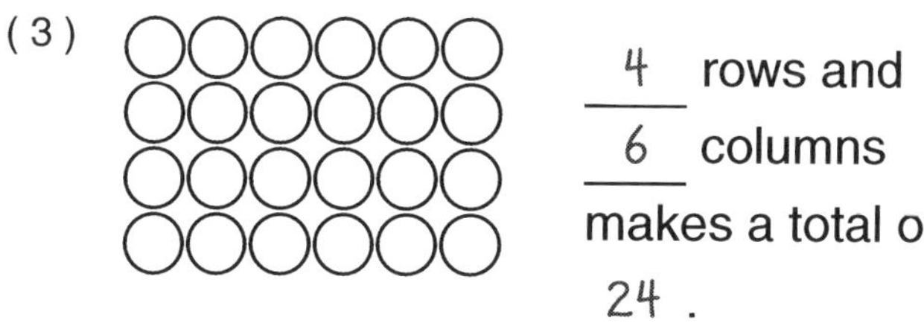

4 rows and 6 columns makes a total of 24.

(4) 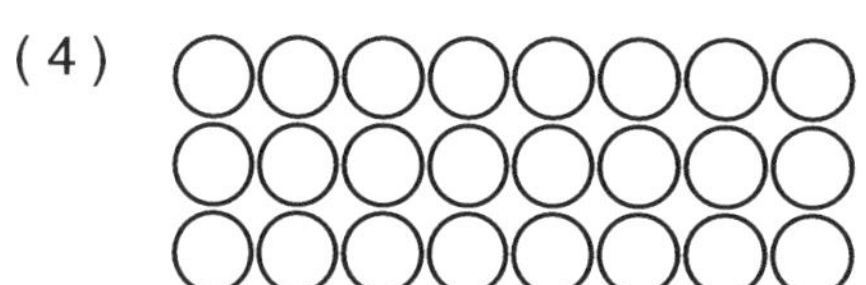

3 rows and 8 columns makes a total of 24.

(5) 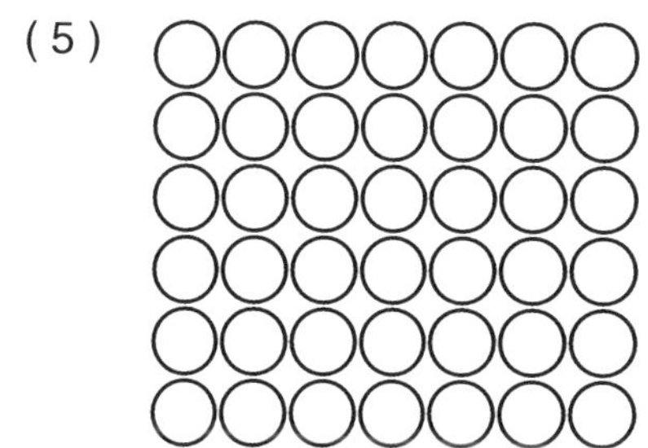

6 rows and 7 columns makes a total of 42.

(6) 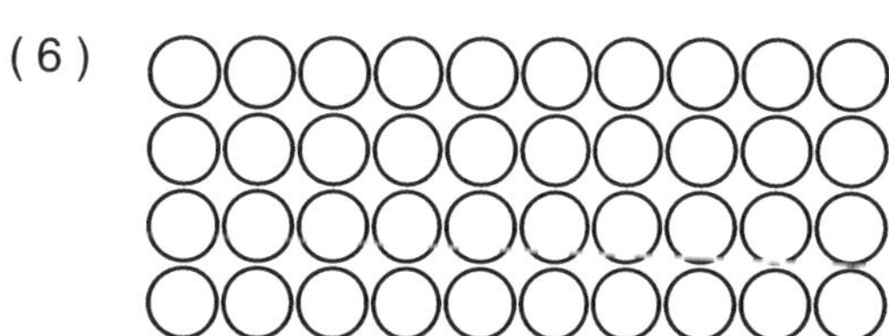

4 rows and 10 columns makes a total of 40.

(7) 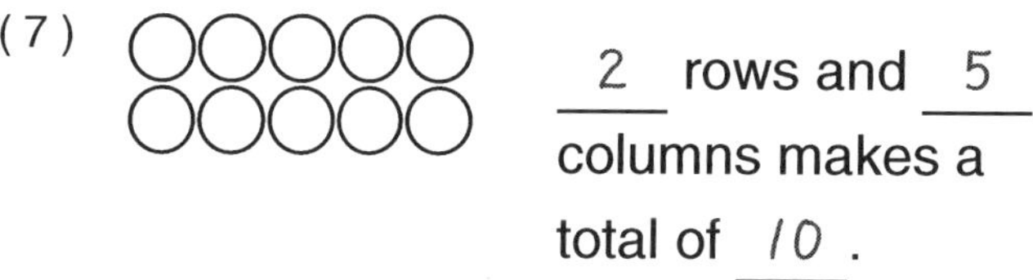

2 rows and 5 columns makes a total of 10.

(8) 9 rows and 9 columns makes a total of 9.

(9) 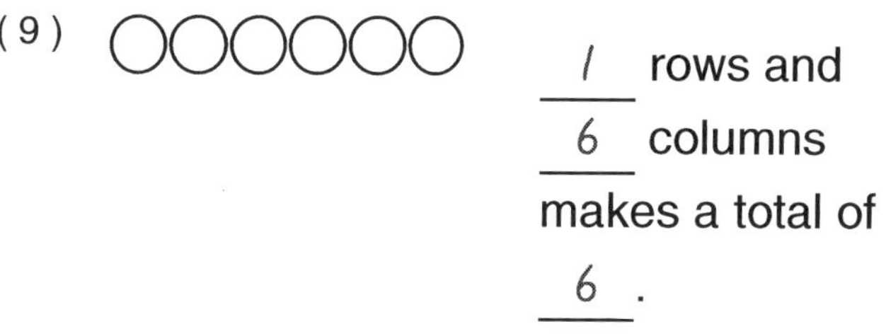

1 rows and 6 columns makes a total of 6.

(10) 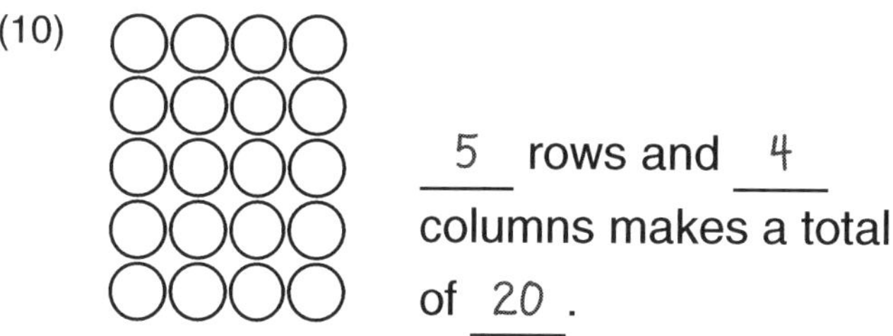

5 rows and 4 columns makes a total of 20.

(11) 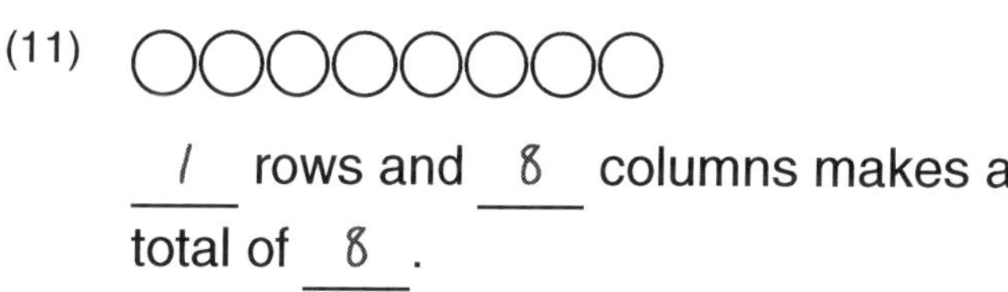

1 rows and 8 columns makes a total of 8.

Visual Multiplication
ANSWER KEY

 Use the dots to help you fill in the blanks to each of the multiplication problems.

(1) 

2 rows and 5 columns makes a total of 10.

(2) 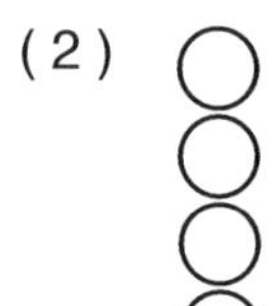

5 rows and 1 columns makes a total of 5.

(3) 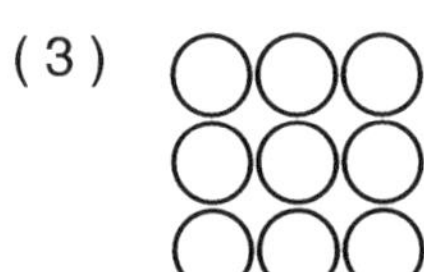

3 rows and 3 columns makes a total of 9.

(4) 

1 rows and 8 columns makes a total of 8.

(5) 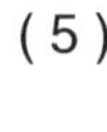 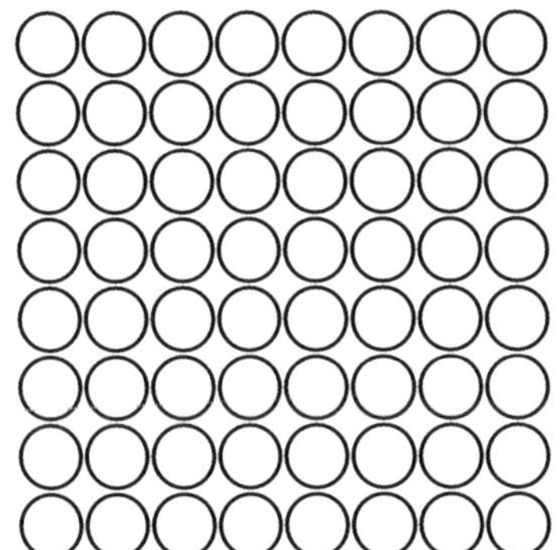

8 rows and 8 columns makes a total of 64.

(6) 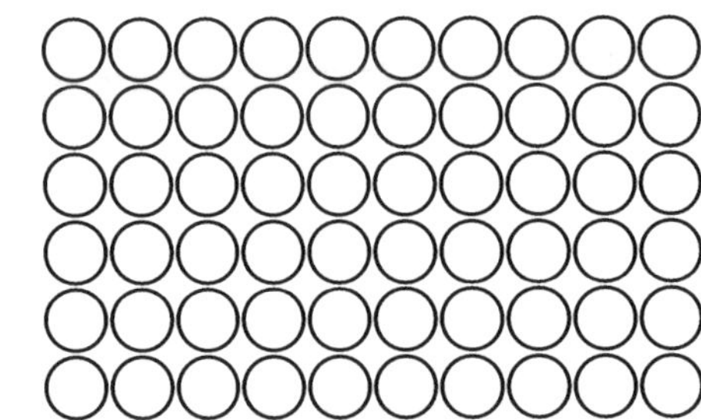

6 rows and 10 columns makes a total of 60.

(7) 

3 rows and 6 columns makes a total of 18.

(8) 

1 rows and 10 columns makes a total of 10.

(9) 

3 rows and 9 columns makes a total of 27.

(10) 

2 rows and 2 columns makes a total of 4.

(11)

1 rows and 2 columns makes a total of 2.

Visual Multiplication
ANSWER KEY

 Use the dots to help you fill in the blanks to each of the multiplication problems.

(1) 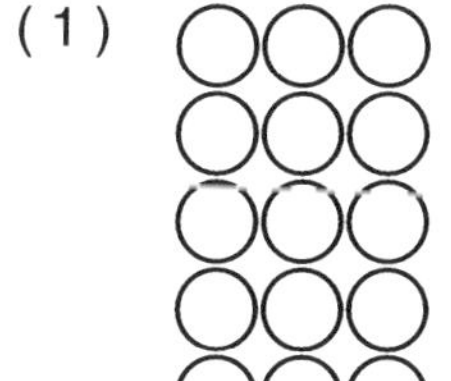

5 rows and 3 columns makes a total of 15.

(2) 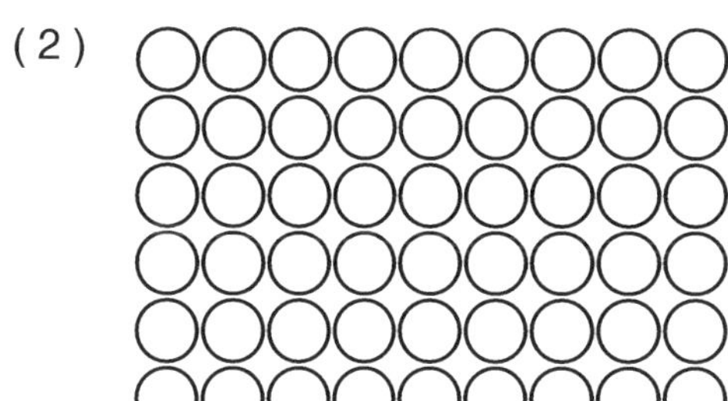

6 rows and 9 columns makes a total of 54.

(3) 

3 rows and 10 columns makes a total of 30.

(4) 

2 rows and 9 columns makes a total of 18.

(5) 

1 rows and 9 columns makes a total of 9.

(6) 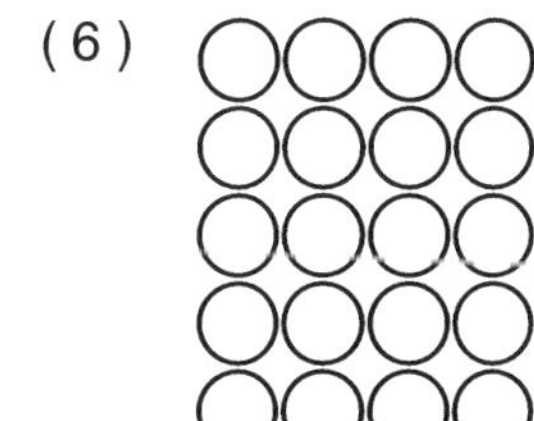

5 rows and 4 columns makes a total of 20.

(7) 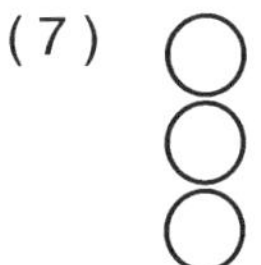

5 rows and 1 columns makes a total of 5.

(8) 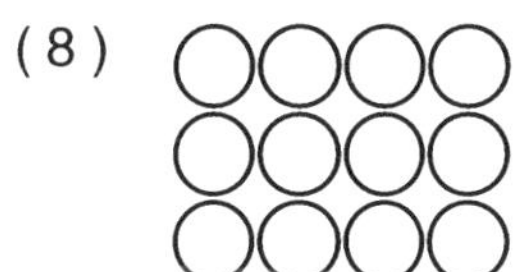

3 rows and 4 columns makes a total of 12.

(9) 

2 rows and 7 columns makes a total of 14.

(10) 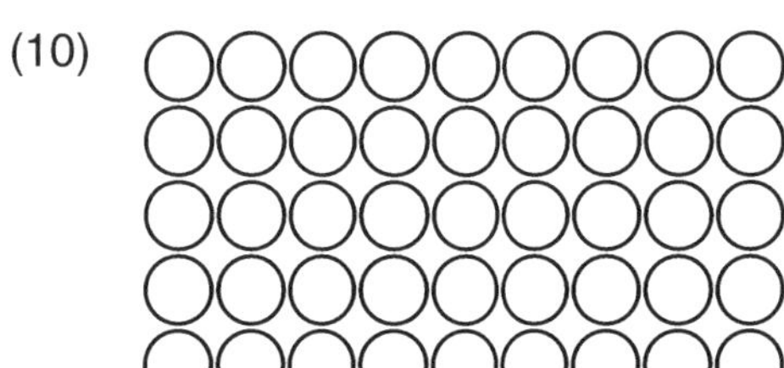

5 rows and 9 columns makes a total of 45.

Visual Multiplication
ANSWER KEY

Use the dots to help you fill in the blanks to each of the multiplication problems.

(1)

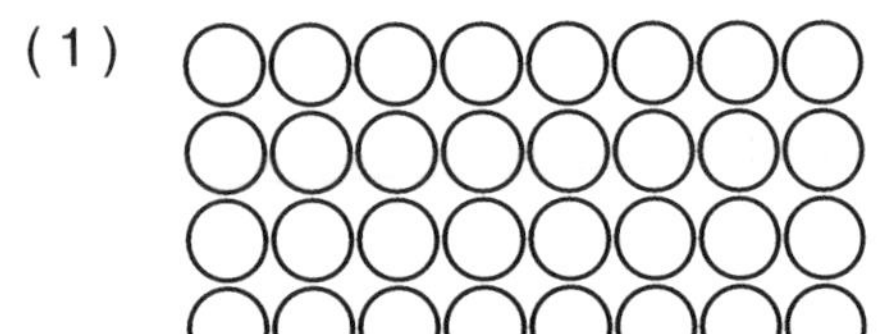

4 rows and 8 columns makes a total of 32.

(2)

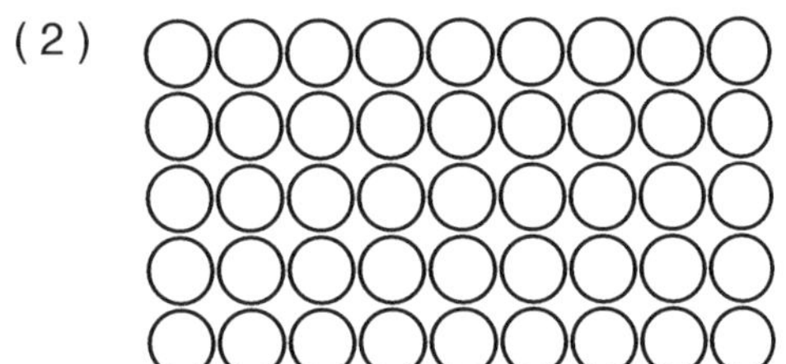

5 rows and 9 columns makes a total of 45.

(3)

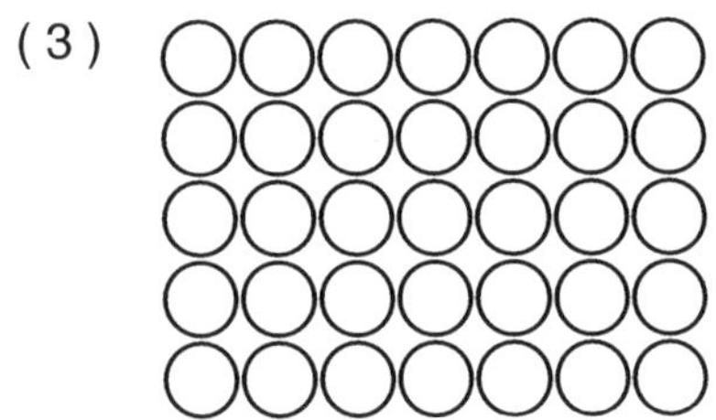

5 rows and 7 columns makes a total of 35.

(4)

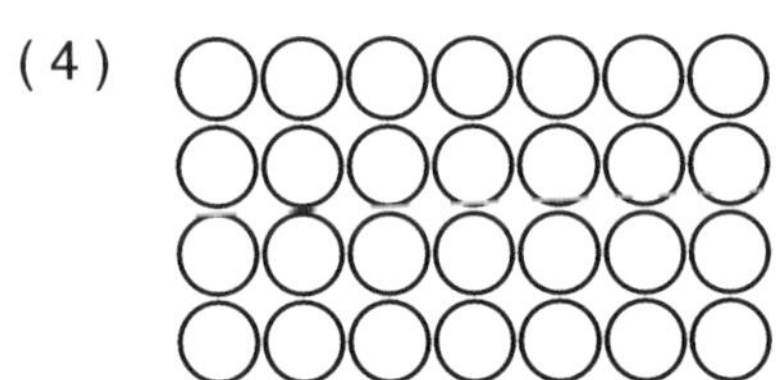

4 rows and 7 columns makes a total of 28.

(5)

1 rows and 7 columns makes a total of 7.

(6)

2 rows and 6 columns makes a total of 12.

(7)

2 rows and 9 columns makes a total of 18.

(8)

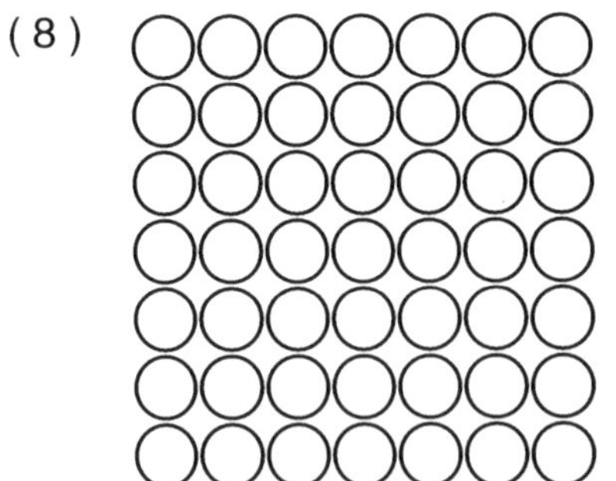

7 rows and 7 columns makes a total of 49.

(9)

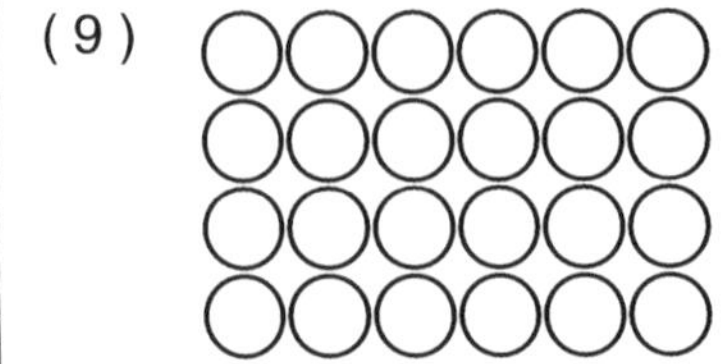

4 rows and 6 columns makes a total of 24.

Visual Multiplication
ANSWER KEY

Use the dots to help you fill in the blanks to each of the multiplication problems.

(1)

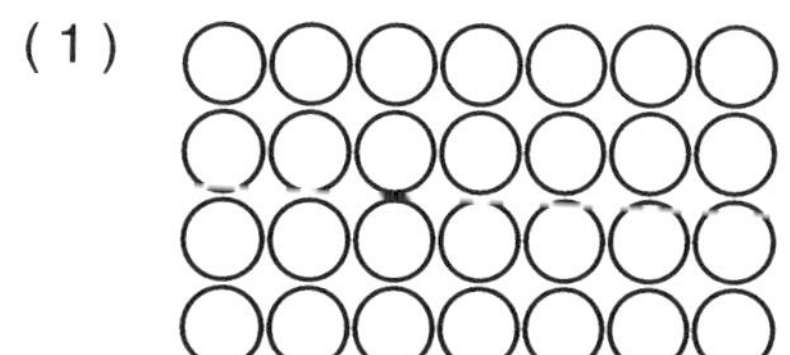

4 rows and 7 columns makes a total of 28.

(2)

3 rows and 3 columns makes a total of 9.

(3)

7 rows and 7 columns makes a total of 49.

(4)

4 rows and 1 columns makes a total of 4.

(5)

4 rows and 6 columns makes a total of 24.

(6)

3 rows and 10 columns makes a total of 30.

(7)

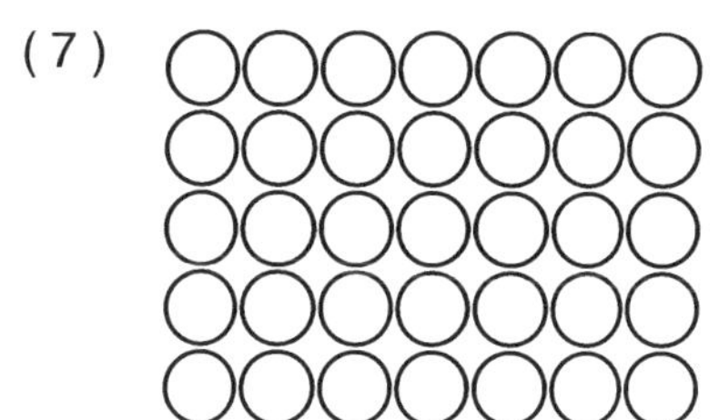

5 rows and 7 columns makes a total of 35.

(8)

4 rows and 3 columns makes a total of 12.

(9)

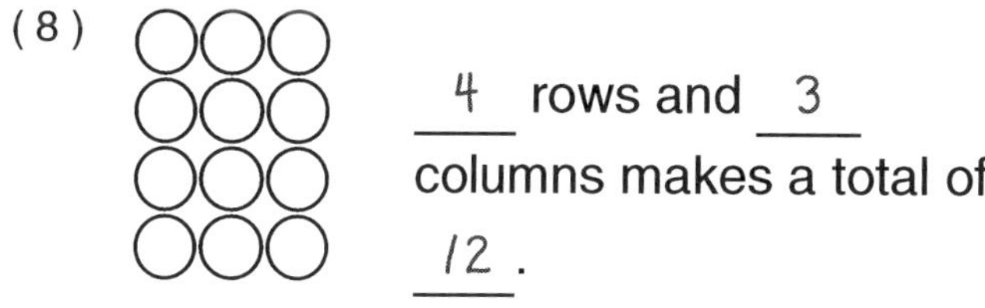

3 rows and 8 columns makes a total of 24.

(10)

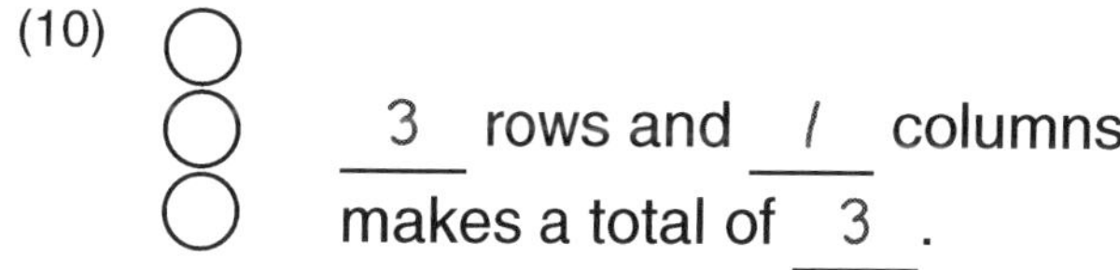

3 rows and 1 columns makes a total of 3.

Visual Multiplication
ANSWER KEY

 Use the dots to help you fill in the blanks to each of the multiplication problems.

(1) 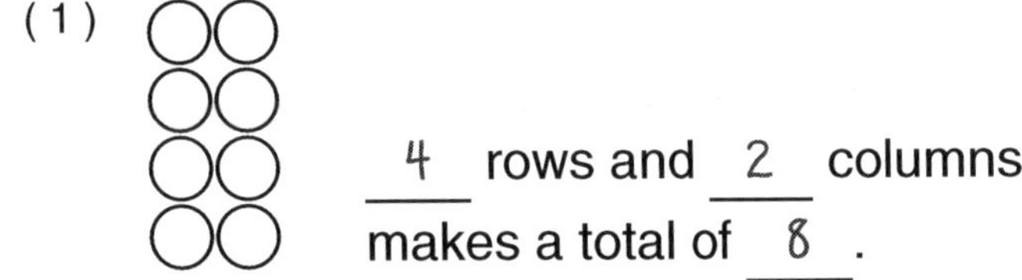

4 rows and 2 columns makes a total of 8 .

(2) 1 rows and 10 columns makes a total of 10 .

(3) 3 rows and 2 columns makes a total of 6 .

(4) 4 rows and 6 columns makes a total of 24 .

(5) 2 rows and 2 columns makes a total of 4 .

(6) 4 rows and 8 columns makes a total of 32 .

(7) 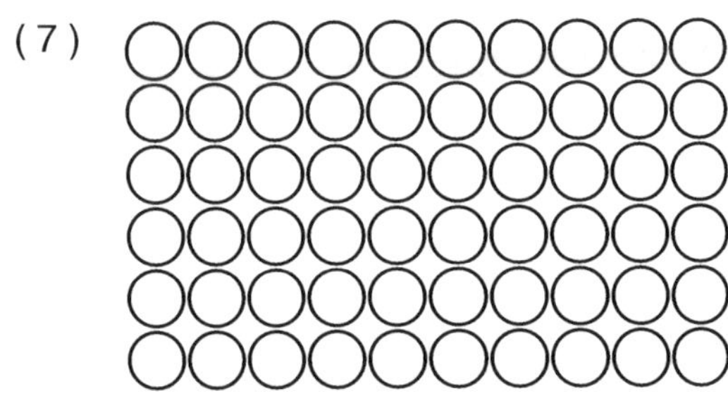

6 rows and 10 columns makes a total of 60 .

(8) 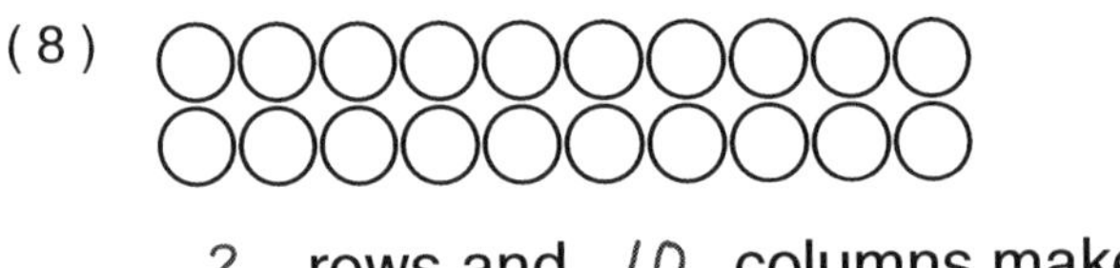

2 rows and 10 columns makes a total of 20 .

(9) 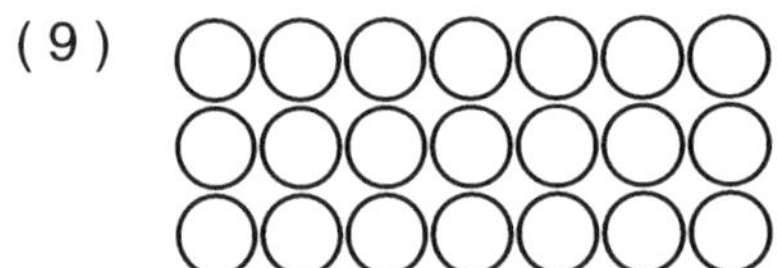

3 rows and 7 columns makes a total of 21 .

(10) 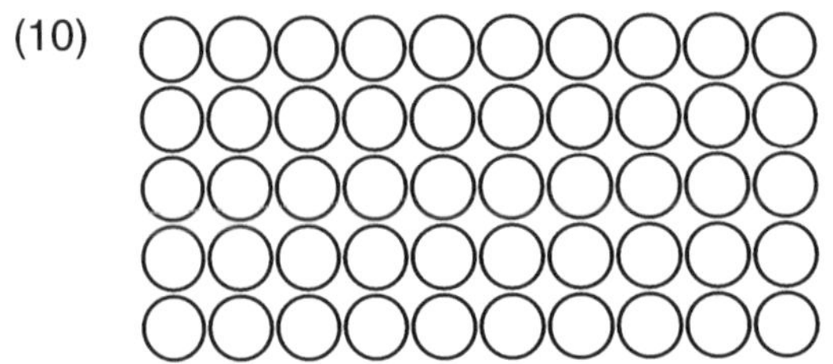

5 rows and 10 columns makes a total of 50 .

Visual Multiplication
ANSWER KEY

 Use the dots to help you fill in the blanks to each of the multiplication problems.

(1) 

3 rows and 7 columns makes a total of 21.

(2) 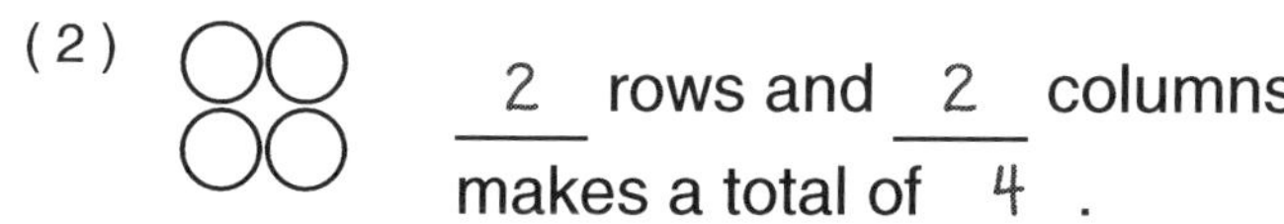

2 rows and 2 columns makes a total of 4.

(3) 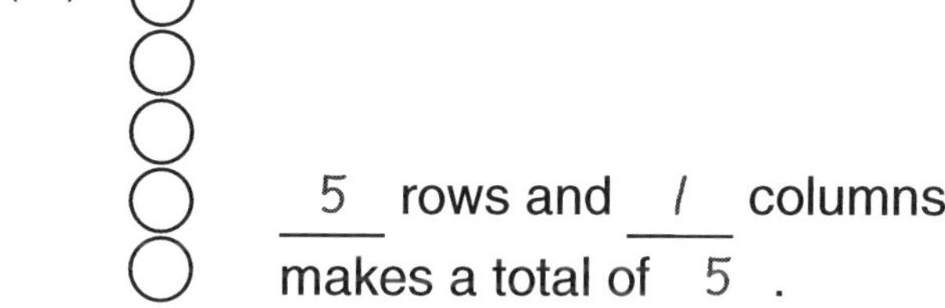

5 rows and 1 columns makes a total of 5.

(4) 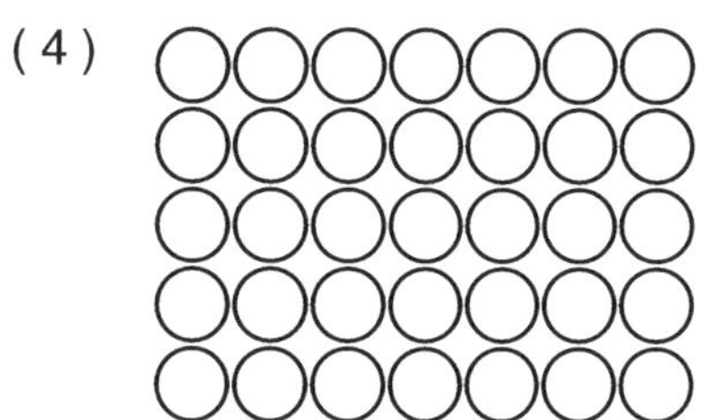

5 rows and 7 columns makes a total of 35.

(5) 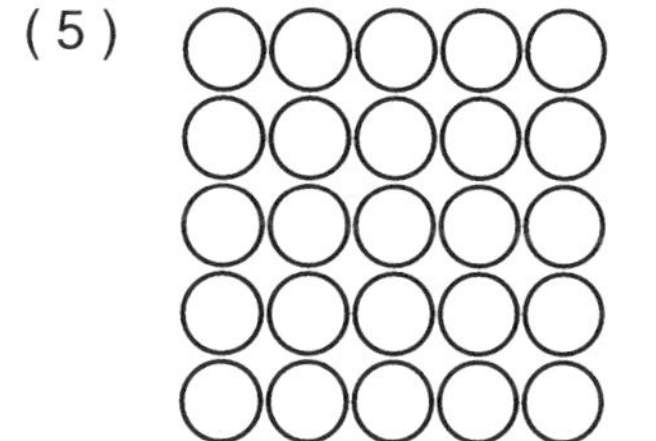

5 rows and 5 columns makes a total of 25.

(6) 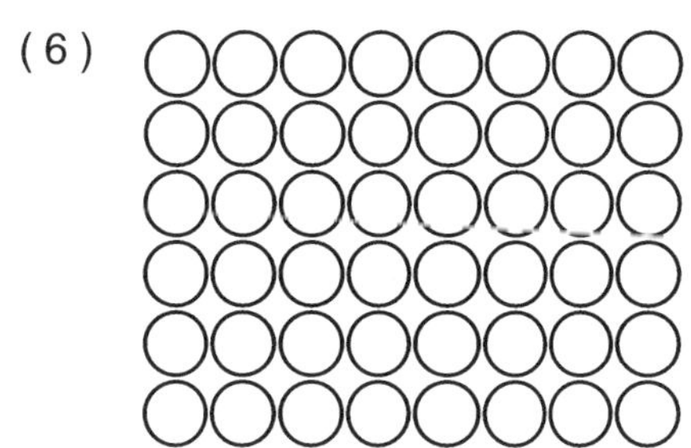

6 rows and 8 columns makes a total of 48.

(7) 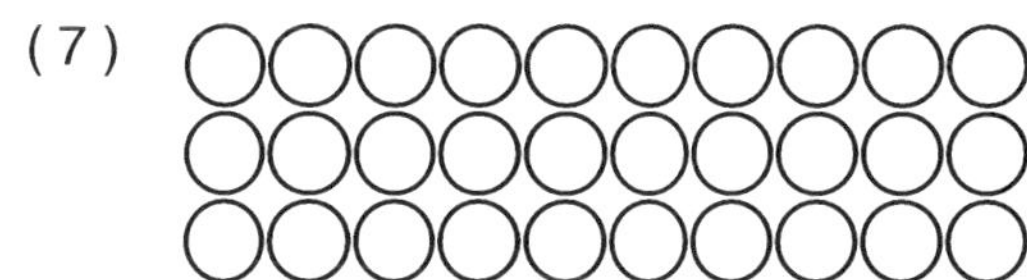

3 rows and 10 columns makes a total of 30.

(8) 

2 rows and 8 columns makes a total of 16.

(9) ○○○○○○○○

1 rows and 8 columns makes a total of 8.

(10) 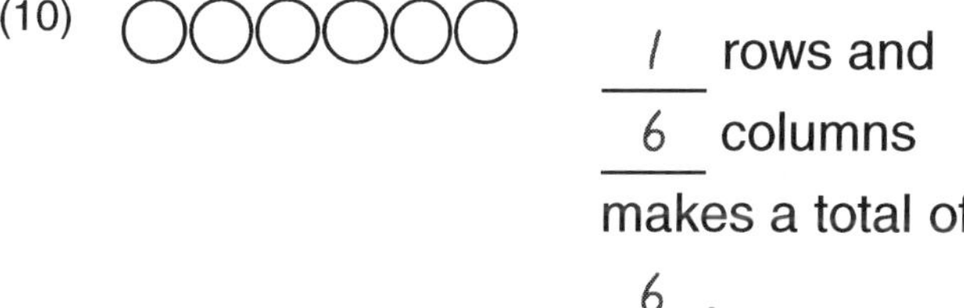

1 rows and 6 columns makes a total of 6.

Visual Multiplication
ANSWER KEY

Use the dots to help you fill in the blanks to each of the multiplication problems.

(1) 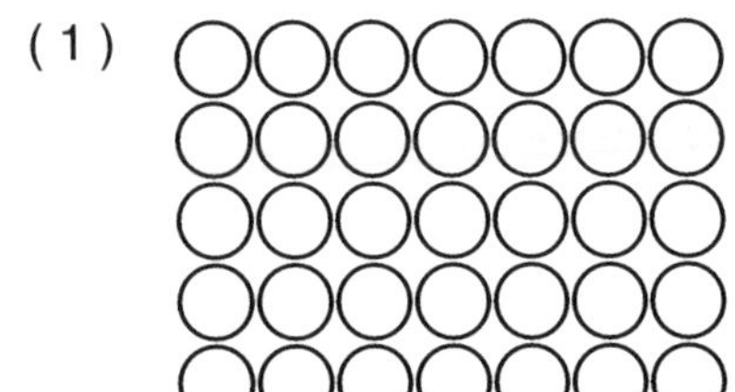

5 rows and 7 columns makes a total of 35.

(2) 

1 rows and 10 columns makes a total of 10.

(3) 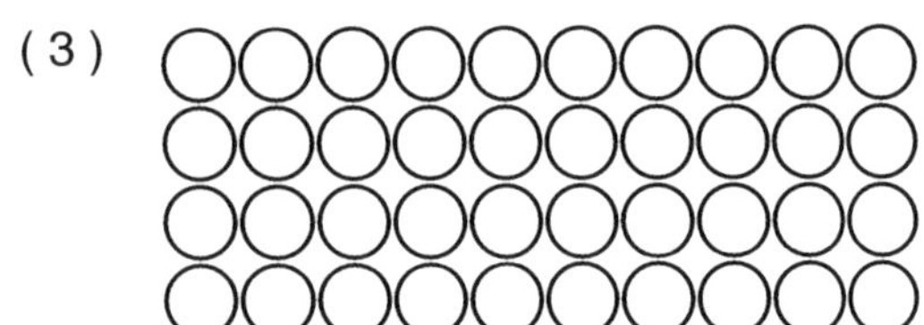

4 rows and 10 columns makes a total of 40.

(4) 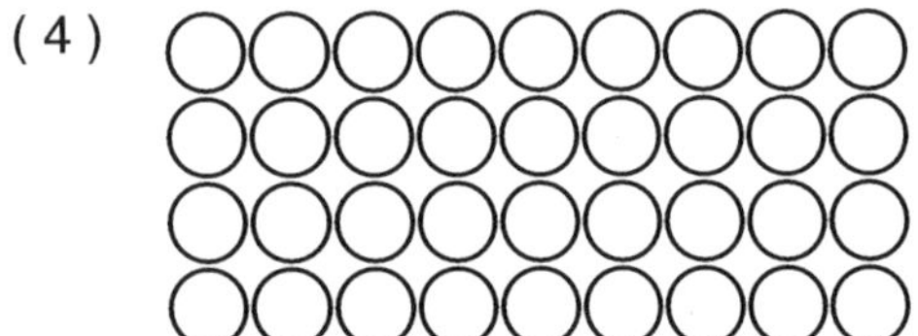

4 rows and 9 columns makes a total of 36.

(5) 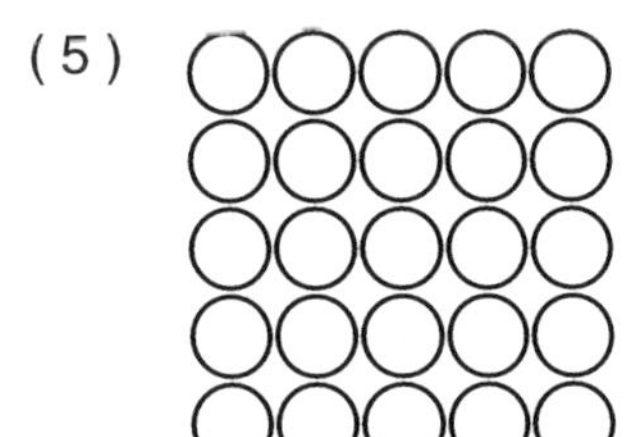

5 rows and 5 columns makes a total of 25.

(6) 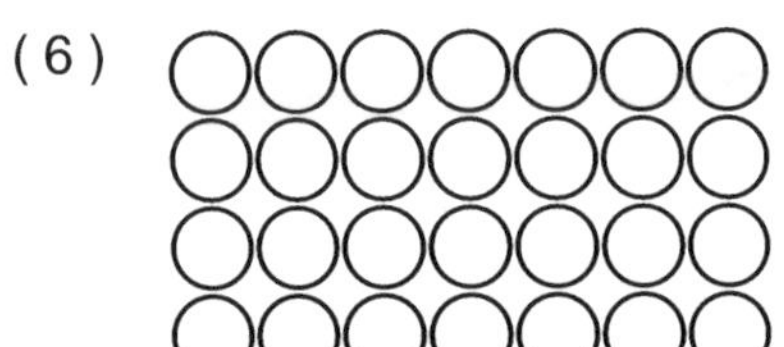

4 rows and 7 columns makes a total of 28.

(7) 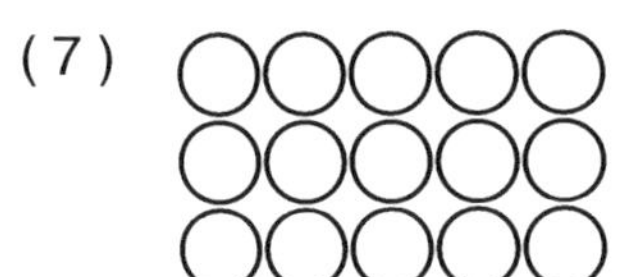

3 rows and 5 columns makes a total of 15.

(8)

1 rows and 7 columns makes a total of 7.

(9) 

3 rows and 10 columns makes a total of 30.

(10)

1 rows and 6 columns makes a total of 6.

(11)

2 rows and 1 columns makes a total of 2.

Visual Multiplication
ANSWER KEY

Use the dots to help you fill in the blanks to each of the multiplication problems.

(1)

1 rows and 7 columns makes a total of 7.

(2)

5 rows and 2 columns makes a total of 10.

(3)

2 rows and 6 columns makes a total of 12.

(4)

1 rows and 5 columns makes a total of 5.

(5)

5 rows and 9 columns makes a total of 45.

(6)

7 rows and 10 columns makes a total of 70.

(7)

1 rows and 4 columns makes a total of 4.

(8)

3 rows and 7 columns makes a total of 21.

(9)

4 rows and 10 columns makes a total of 40.

(10)

2 rows and 2 columns makes a total of 4.

Visual Multiplication
ANSWER KEY

 Use the dots to help you fill in the blanks to each of the multiplication problems.

(1)

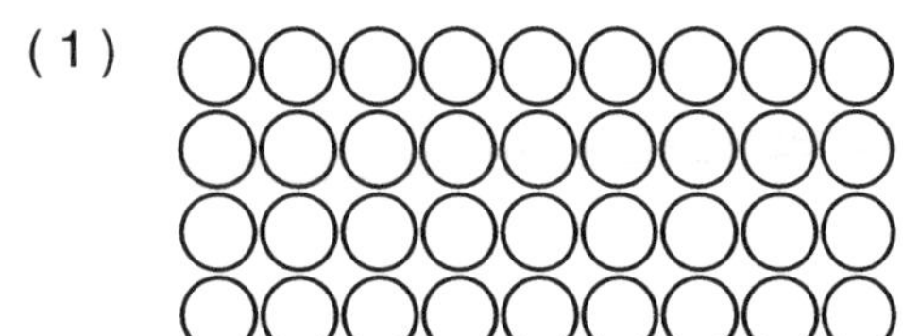

4 rows and 9 columns makes a total of 36.

(2)

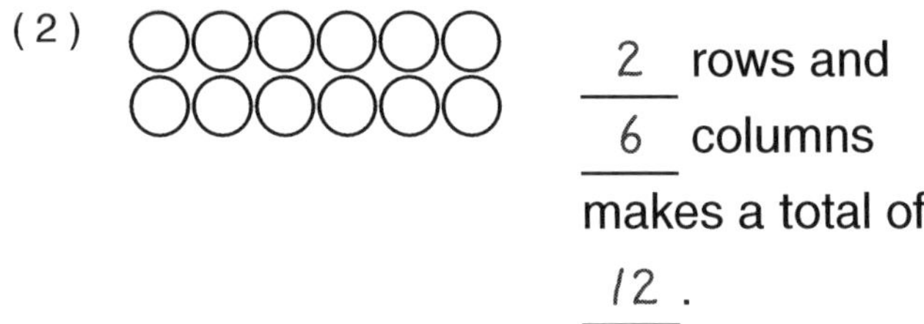

2 rows and 6 columns makes a total of 12.

(3)

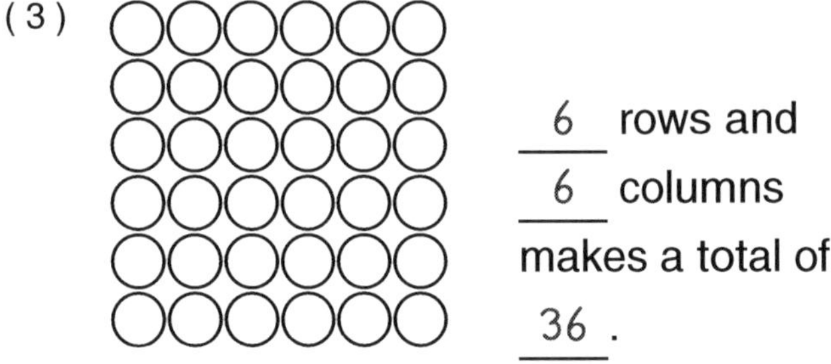

6 rows and 6 columns makes a total of 36.

(4)

1 rows and 10 columns makes a total of 10.

(5)

1 rows and 3 columns makes a total of 3.

(6)

1 rows and 2 columns makes a total of 2.

(7)

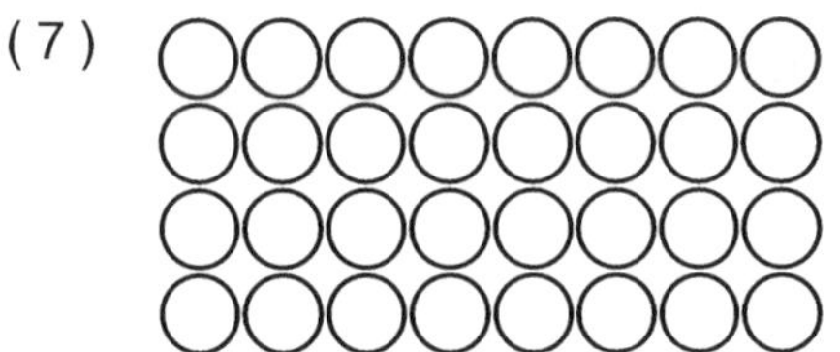

4 rows and 8 columns makes a total of 32.

(8)

5 rows and 2 columns makes a total of 10.

(9)

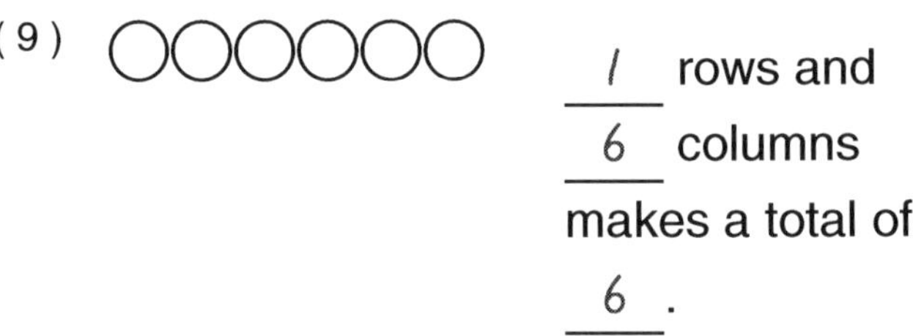

1 rows and 6 columns makes a total of 6.

(10)

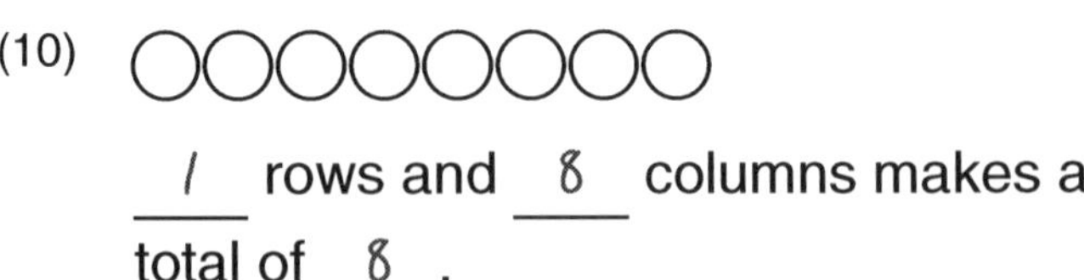

1 rows and 8 columns makes a total of 8.

(11)

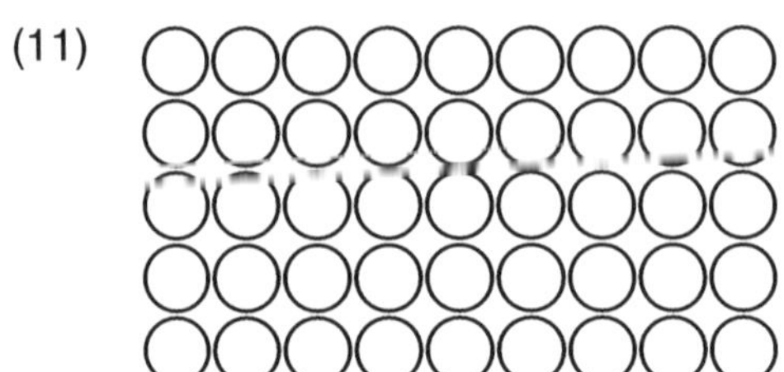

5 rows and 9 columns makes a total of 45.

Visual Multiplication
ANSWER KEY

 Use the dots to help you fill in the blanks to each of the multiplication problems.

(1) 

3 rows and 5 columns makes a total of 15.

(2) 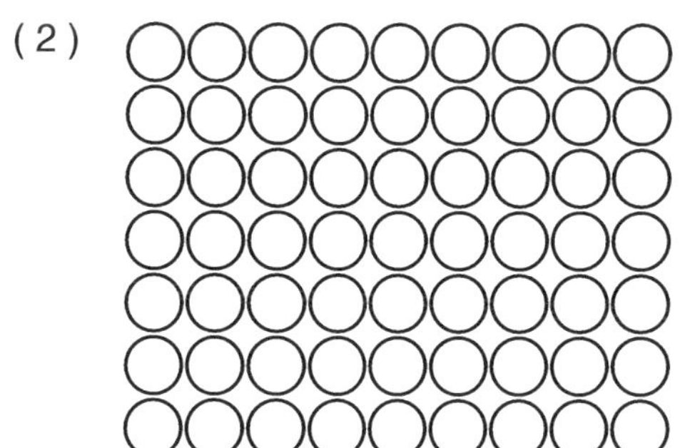

7 rows and 9 columns makes a total of 63.

(3) 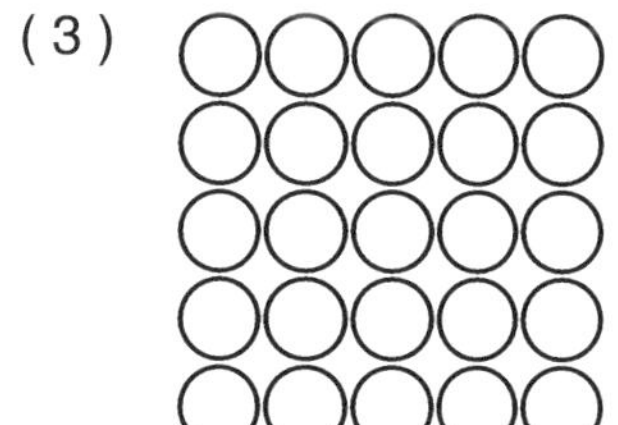

5 rows and 5 columns makes a total of 25.

(4) 1 rows and 4 columns makes a total of 4.

(5) 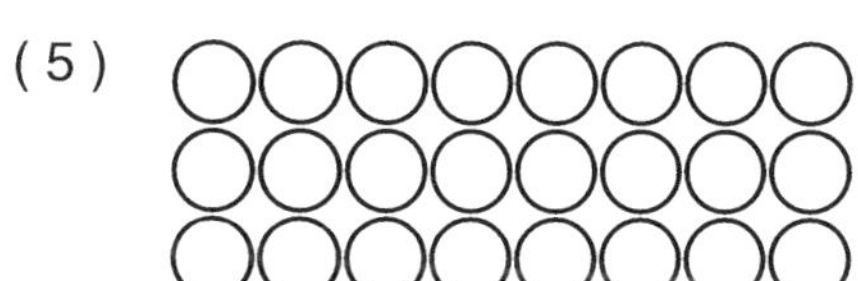

3 rows and 8 columns makes a total of 24.

(6) 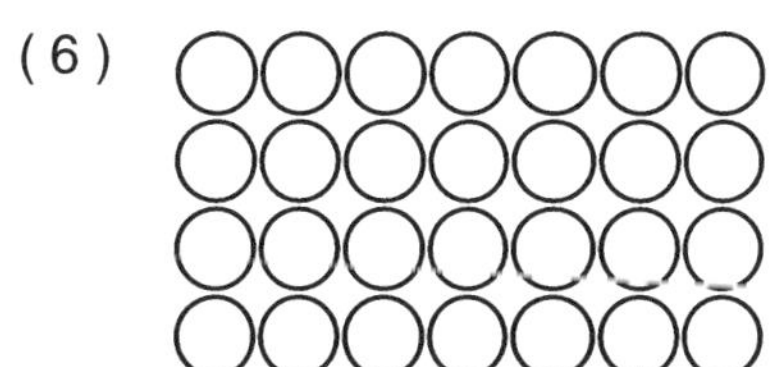

4 rows and 7 columns makes a total of 28.

(7) 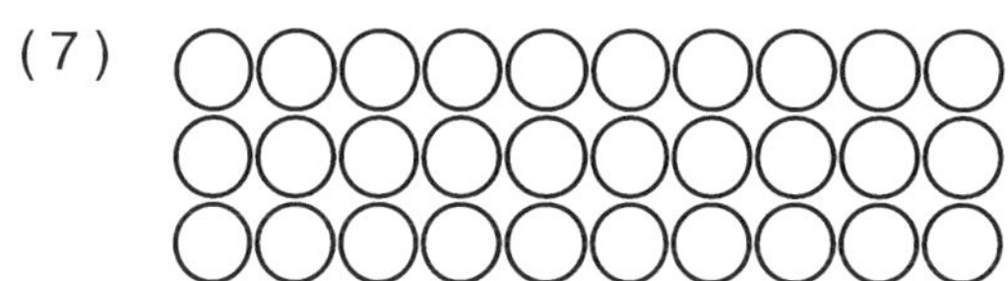

3 rows and 10 columns makes a total of 30.

(8) 

3 rows and 7 columns makes a total of 21.

(9) 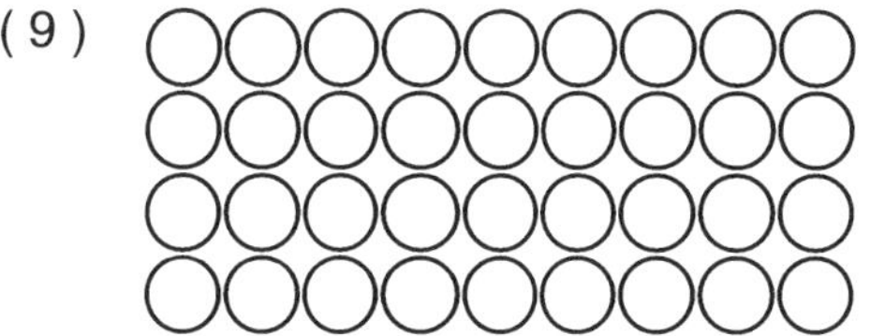

4 rows and 9 columns makes a total of 36.

(10) 

1 rows and 9 columns makes a total of 9.

Visual Multiplication
ANSWER KEY

 Use the dots to help you fill in the blanks to each of the multiplication problems.

(1) 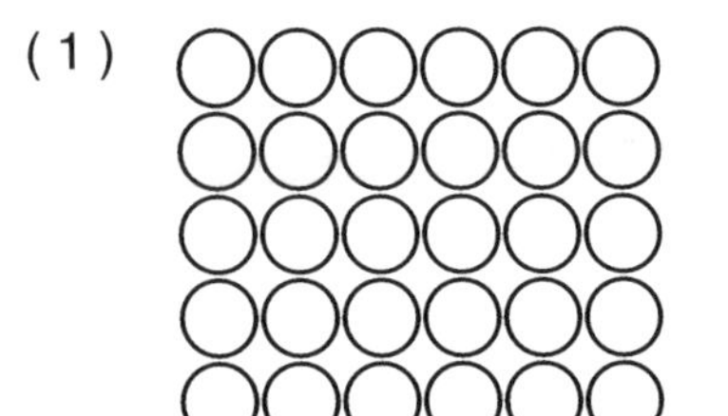

5 rows and 6 columns makes a total of 30.

(2) 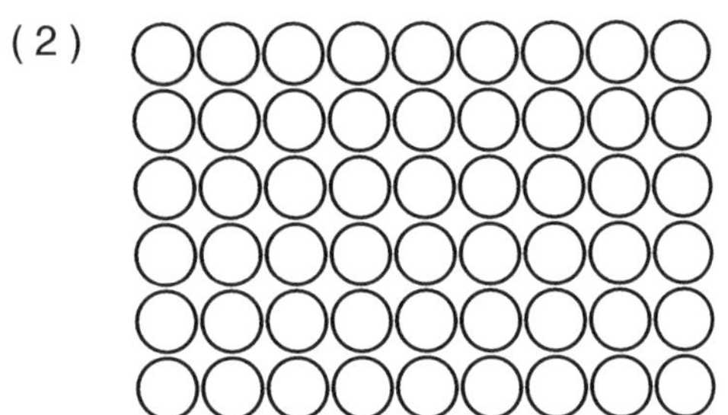

6 rows and 9 columns makes a total of 54.

(3) 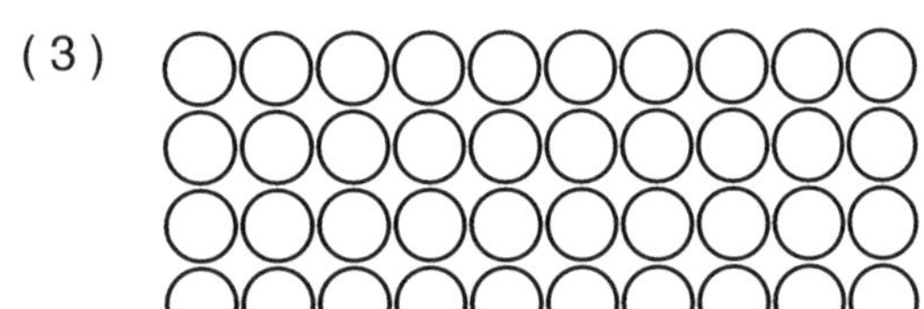

4 rows and 10 columns makes a total of 40.

(4) 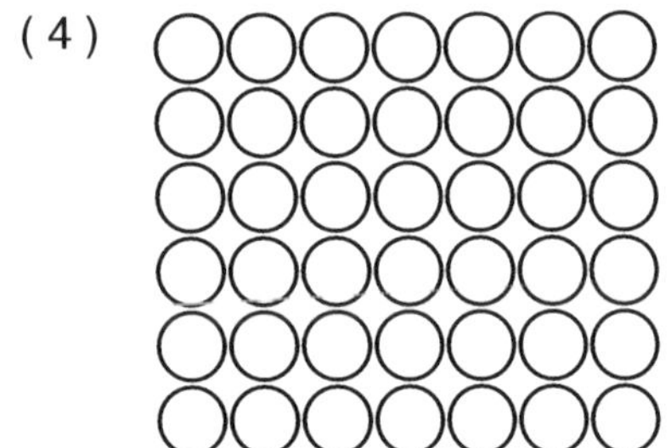

6 rows and 7 columns makes a total of 42.

(5) 2 rows and 1 columns makes a total of 2.

(6) 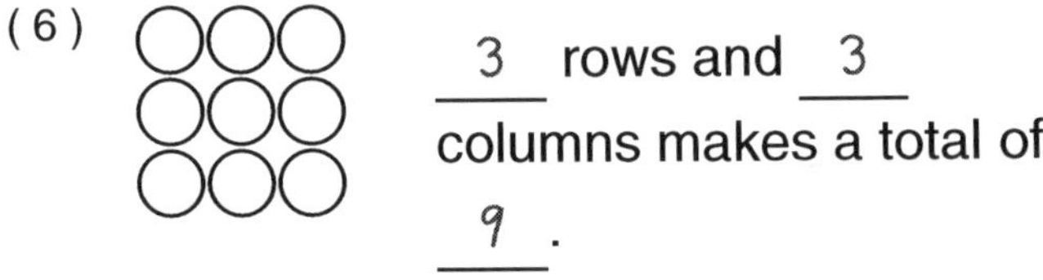

3 rows and 3 columns makes a total of 9.

(7) 

3 rows and 8 columns makes a total of 24.

(8) 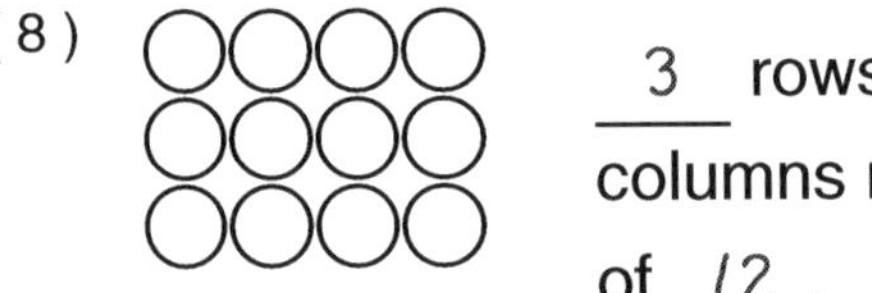

3 rows and 4 columns makes a total of 12.

(9) 

2 rows and 4 columns makes a total of 8.

(10) 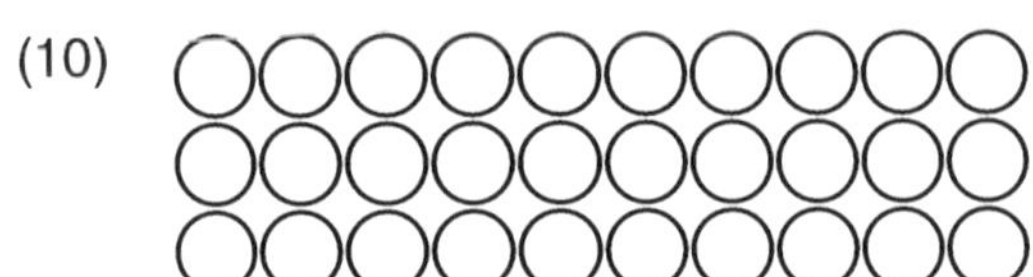

3 rows and 10 columns makes a total of 30.

Visual Multiplication
ANSWER KEY

 Use the dots to help you fill in the blanks to each of the multiplication problems.

(1) 

3 rows and 10 columns makes a total of 30.

(2) 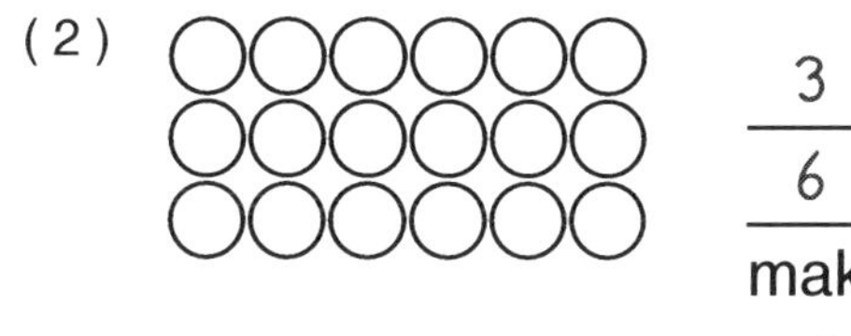

3 rows and 6 columns makes a total of 18.

(3) 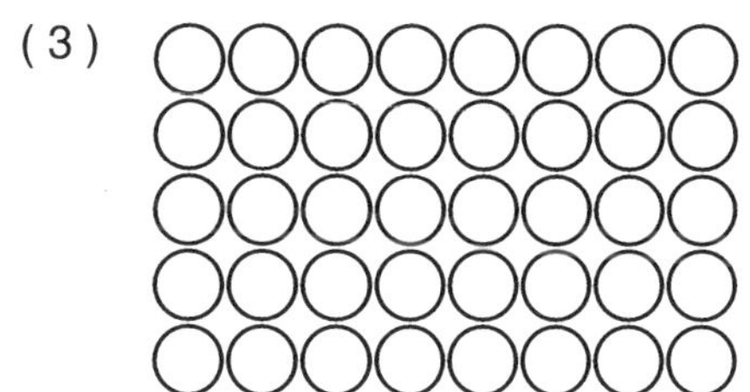

5 rows and 8 columns makes a total of 40.

(4) 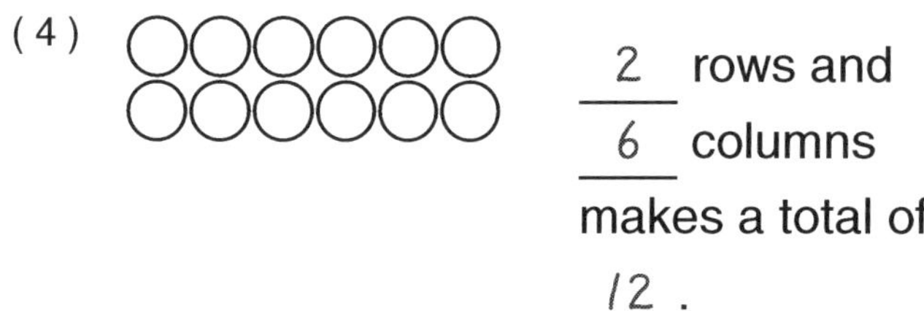

2 rows and 6 columns makes a total of 12.

(5) 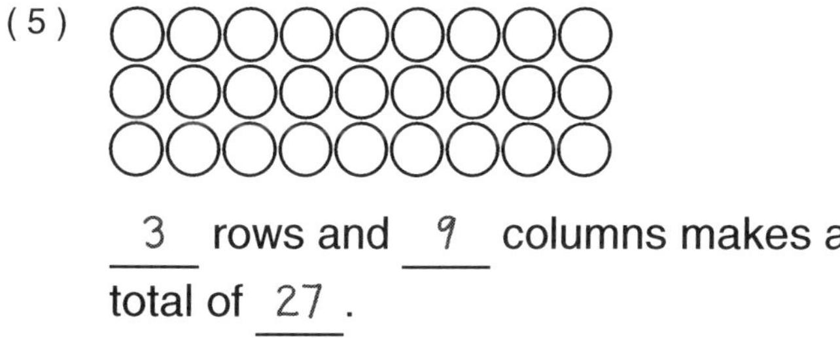

3 rows and 9 columns makes a total of 27.

(6) 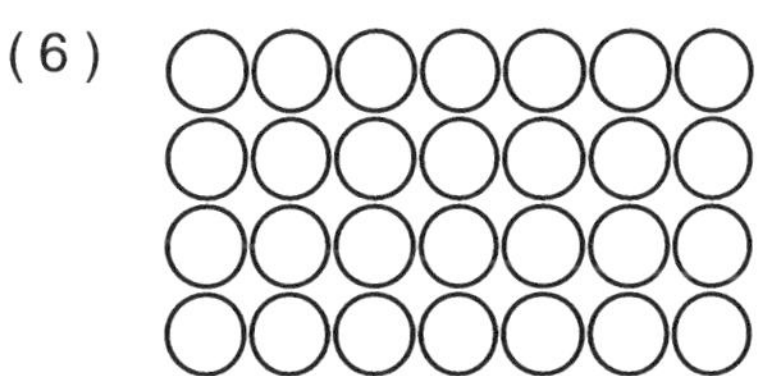

4 rows and 7 columns makes a total of 28.

(7) 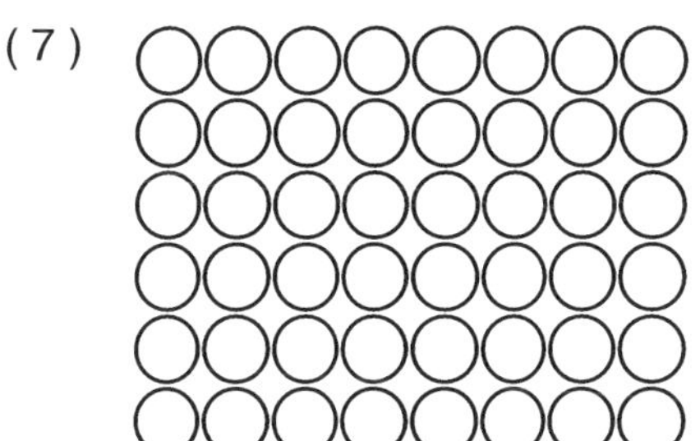

6 rows and 8 columns makes a total of 48.

(8) 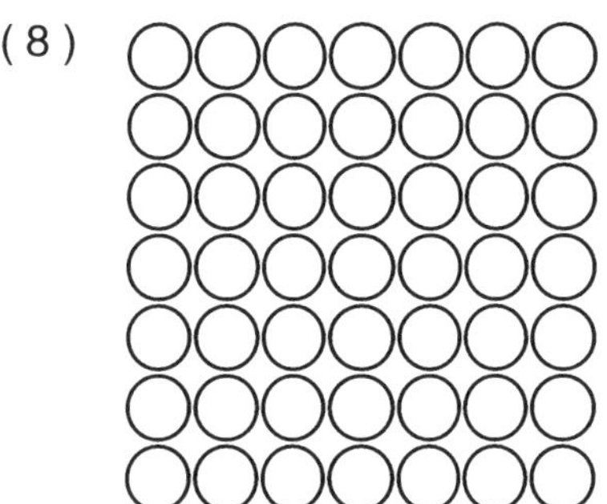

7 rows and 7 columns makes a total of 49.

(9) 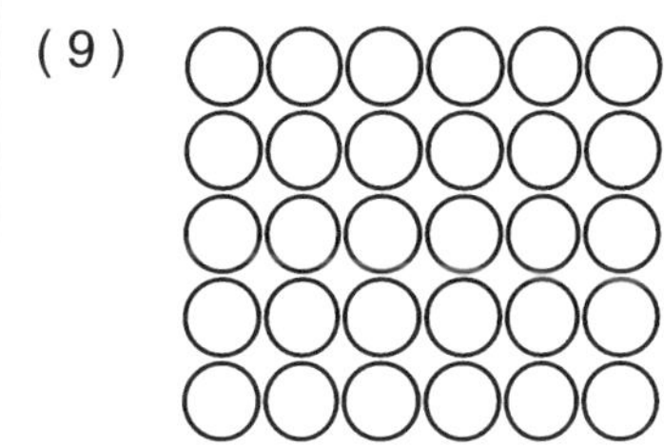

5 rows and 6 columns makes a total of 30.

Visual Multiplication
ANSWER KEY

 Use the dots to help you fill in the blanks to each of the multiplication problems.

(1) 1 rows and 3 columns makes a total of 3.

(2) 5 rows and 6 columns makes a total of 30.

(3) 8 rows and 8 columns makes a total of 64.

(4)

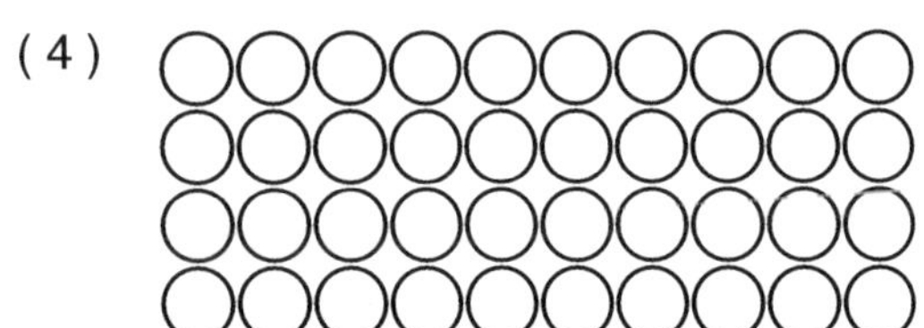

4 rows and 10 columns makes a total of 40.

(5) 1 rows and 7 columns makes a total of 7.

(6) 1 rows and 4 columns makes a total of 4.

(7)

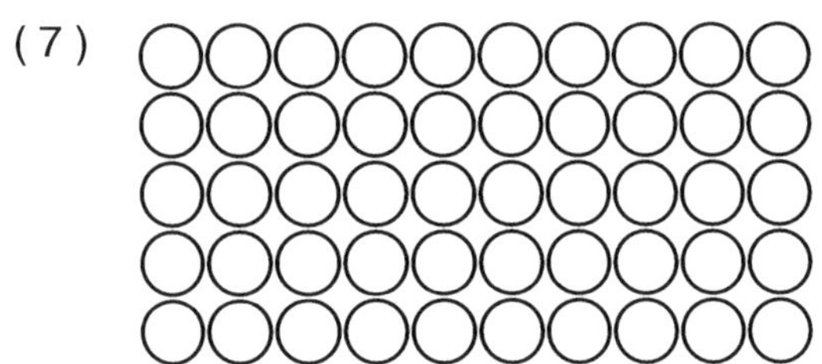

5 rows and 10 columns makes a total of 50.

(8)

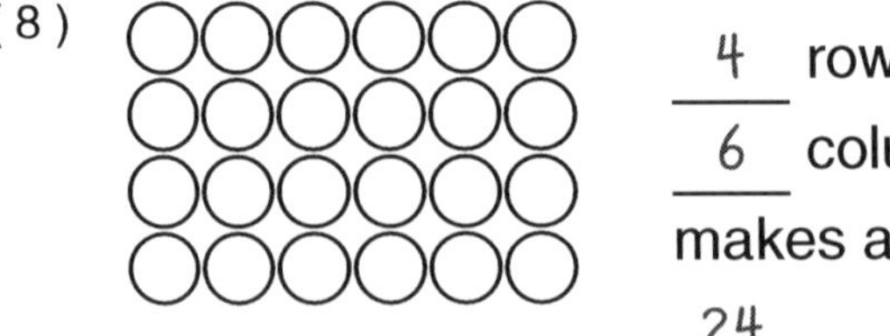

4 rows and 6 columns makes a total of 24.

(9)

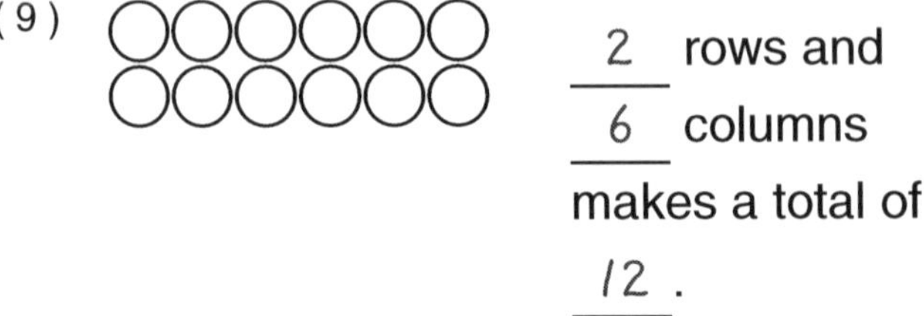

2 rows and 6 columns makes a total of 12.

Visual Multiplication
ANSWER KEY

 Use the dots to help you fill in the blanks to each of the multiplication problems.

(1) 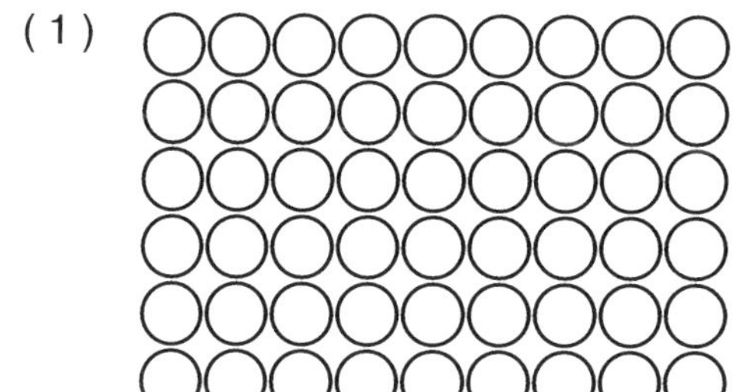

6 rows and 9 columns makes a total of 54.

(2) 

2 rows and 7 columns makes a total of 14.

(3) 2 rows and 2 columns makes a total of 4.

(4) 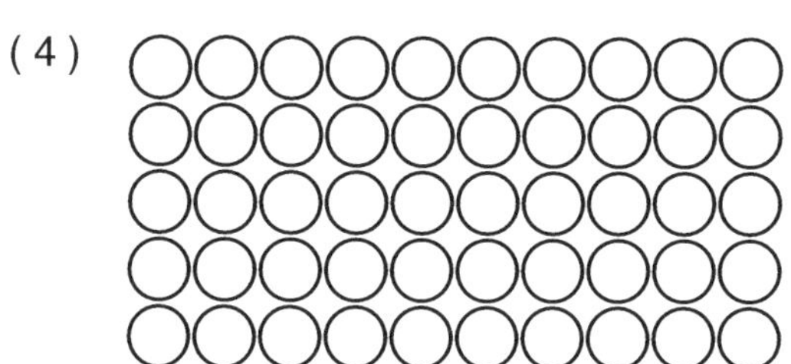

5 rows and 10 columns makes a total of 50.

(5) 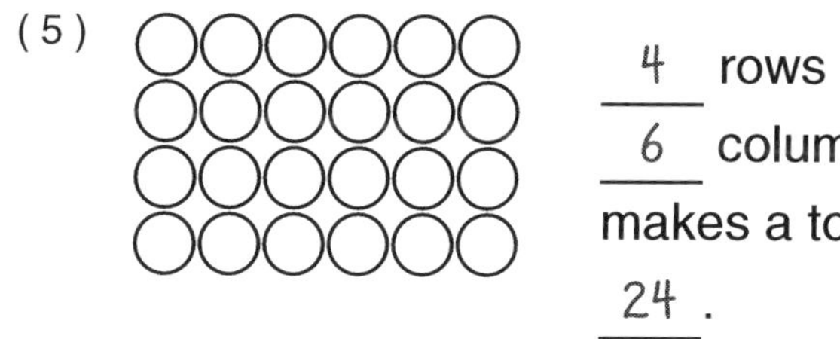

4 rows and 6 columns makes a total of 24.

(6) 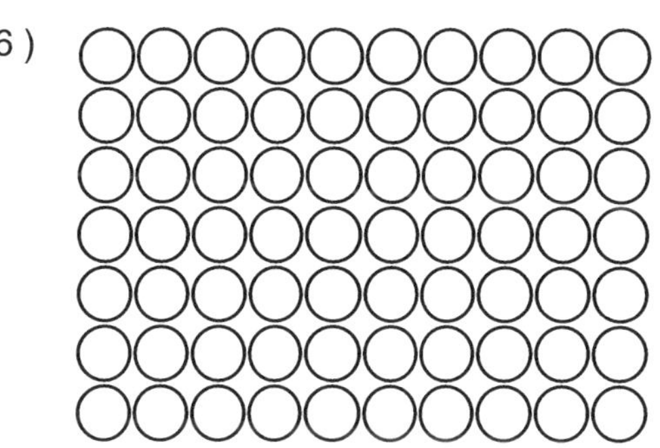

7 rows and 10 columns makes a total of 70.

(7) 

1 rows and 4 columns makes a total of 4.

(8) 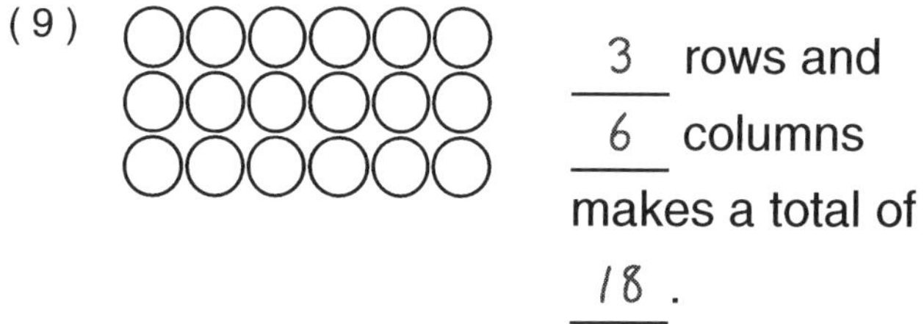

2 rows and 9 columns makes a total of 18.

(9) 3 rows and 6 columns makes a total of 18.

(10) 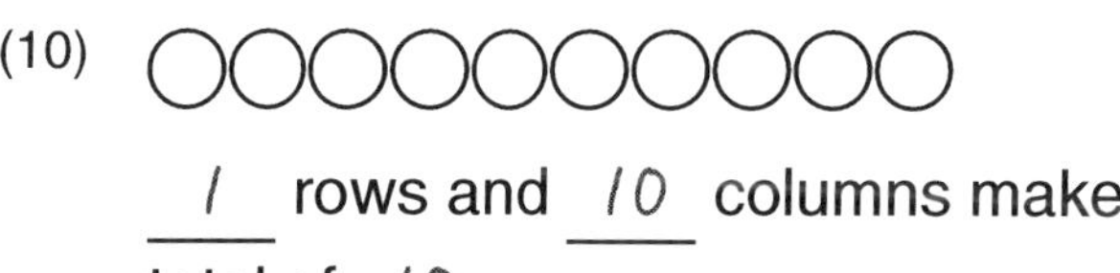

1 rows and 10 columns makes a total of 10.

Visual Multiplication
ANSWER KEY

 Use the dots to help you fill in the blanks to each of the multiplication problems.

(1) 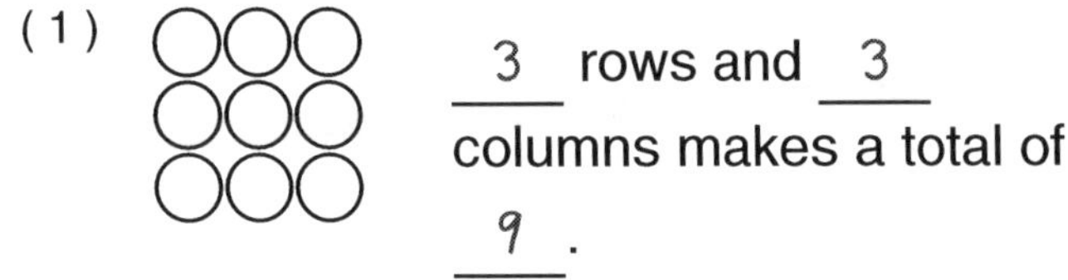

3 rows and 3 columns makes a total of 9.

(2) 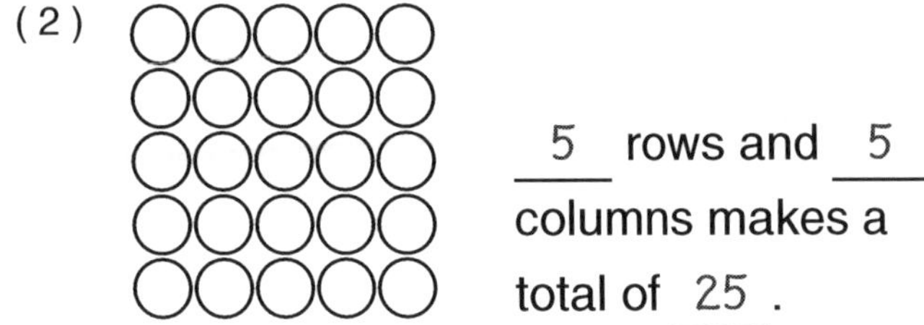

5 rows and 5 columns makes a total of 25.

(3) 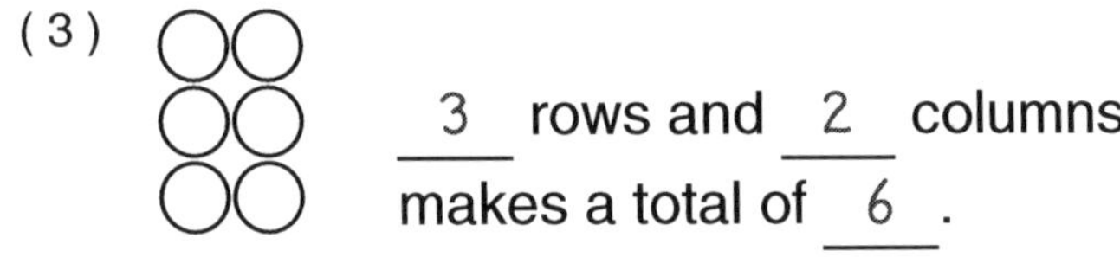

3 rows and 2 columns makes a total of 6.

(4) 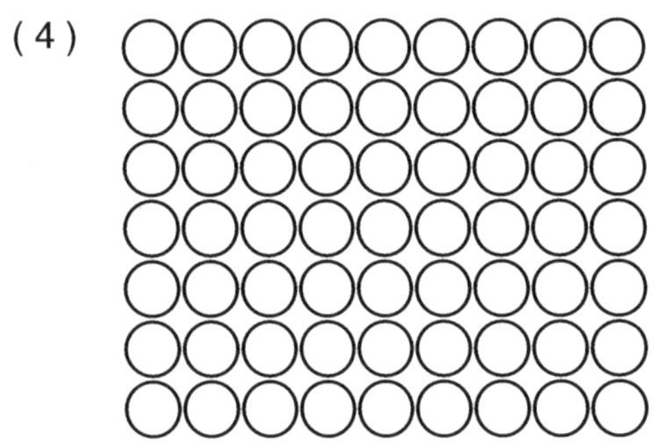

7 rows and 9 columns makes a total of 63.

(5) 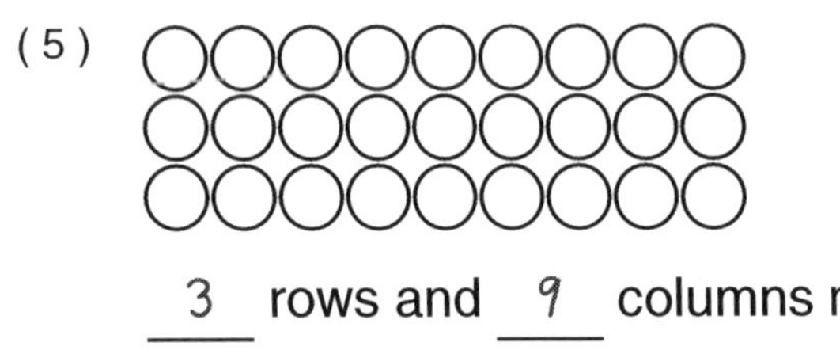

3 rows and 9 columns makes a total of 27.

(6) 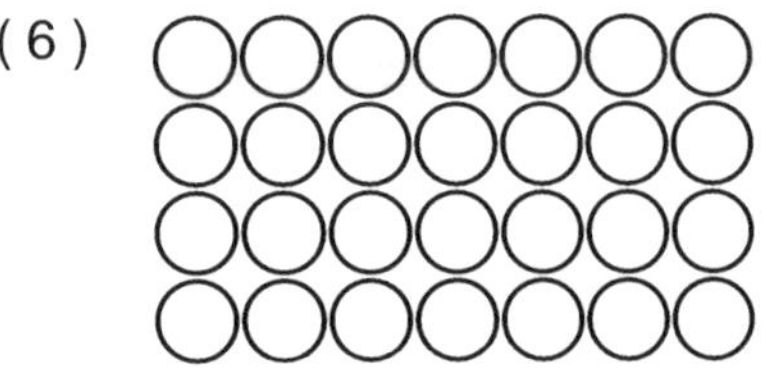

4 rows and 7 columns makes a total of 28.

(7) 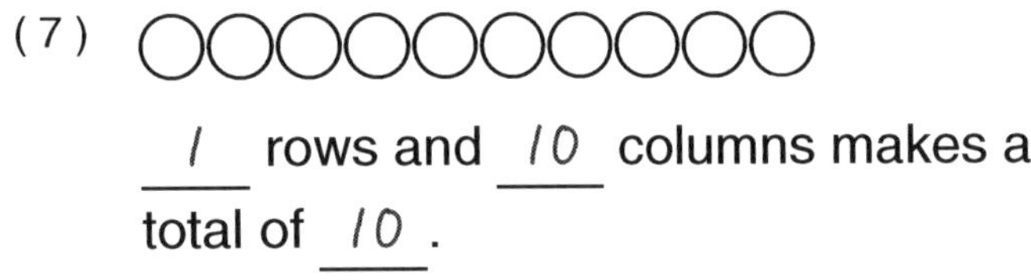

1 rows and 10 columns makes a total of 10.

(8) 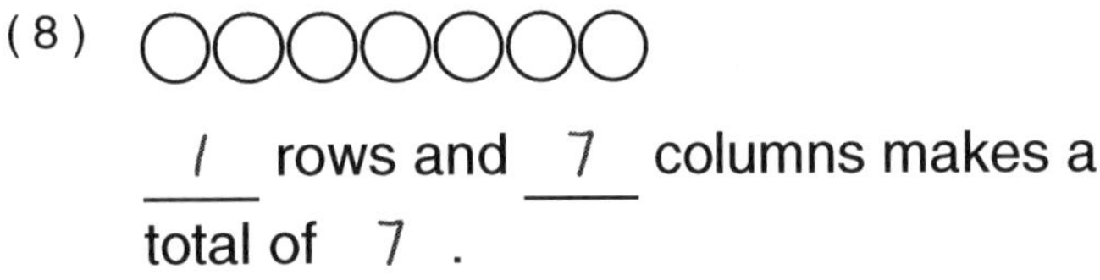

1 rows and 7 columns makes a total of 7.

(9) 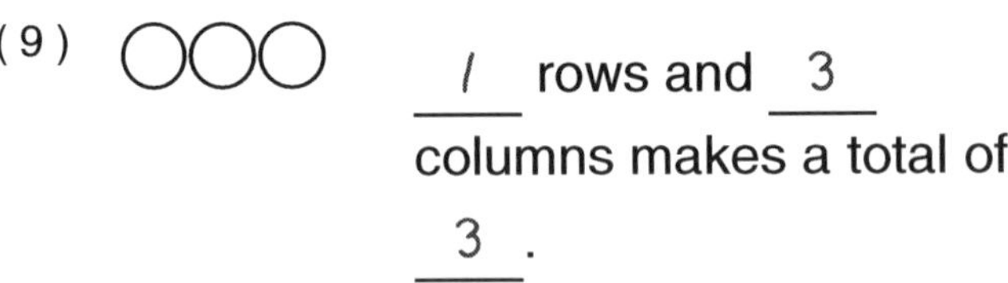

1 rows and 3 columns makes a total of 3.

(10) 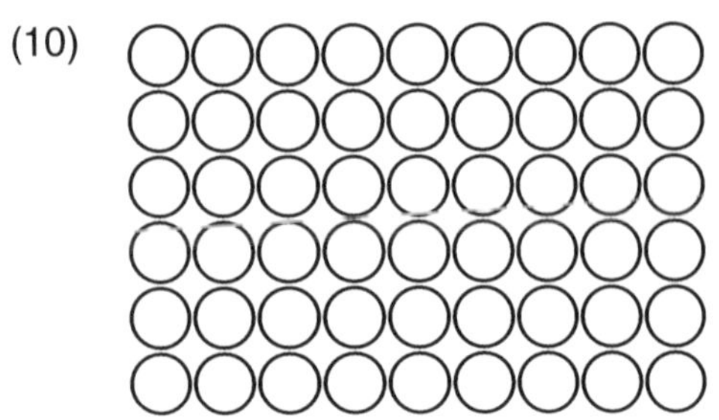

6 rows and 9 columns makes a total of 54.

Visual Multiplication
ANSWER KEY

 Use the dots to help you fill in the blanks to each of the multiplication problems.

(1)

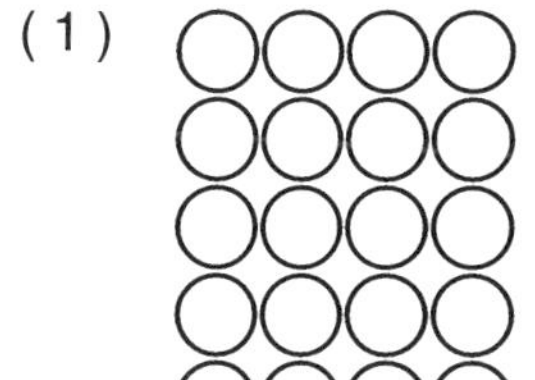

5 rows and 4 columns makes a total of 20.

(2) 3 rows and 1 columns makes a total of 3.

(3) 2 rows and 4 columns makes a total of 8.

(4) 4 rows and 6 columns makes a total of 24.

(5) 3 rows and 7 columns makes a total of 21.

(6)

2 rows and 9 columns makes a total of 18.

(7)

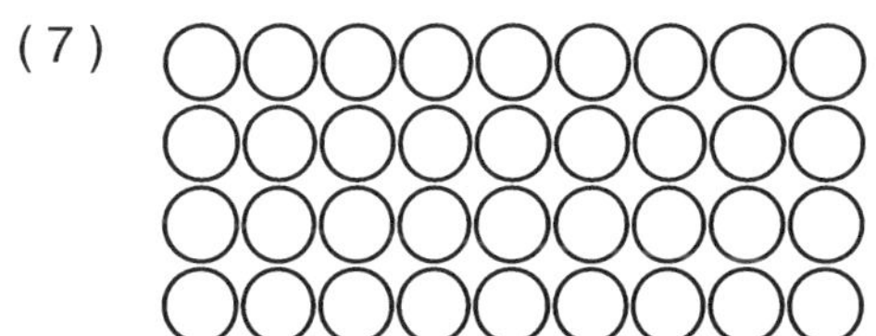

4 rows and 9 columns makes a total of 36.

(8)

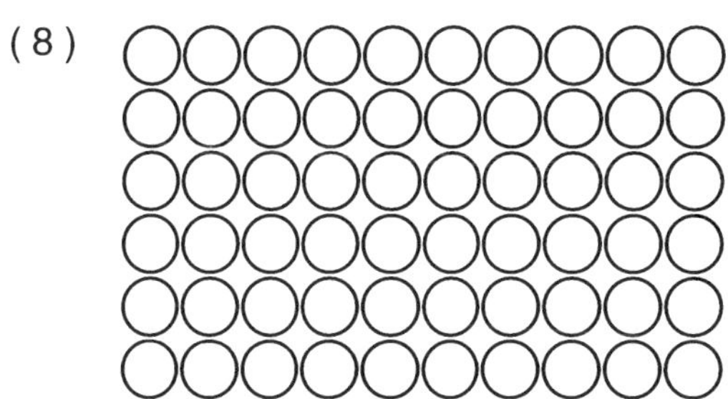

6 rows and 10 columns makes a total of 60.

(9)

1 rows and 8 columns makes a total of 8.

(10) 3 rows and 2 columns makes a total of 6.

(11)

2 rows and 10 columns makes a total of 20.

Visual Multiplication
ANSWER KEY

Use the dots to help you fill in the blanks to each of the multiplication problems.

(1) 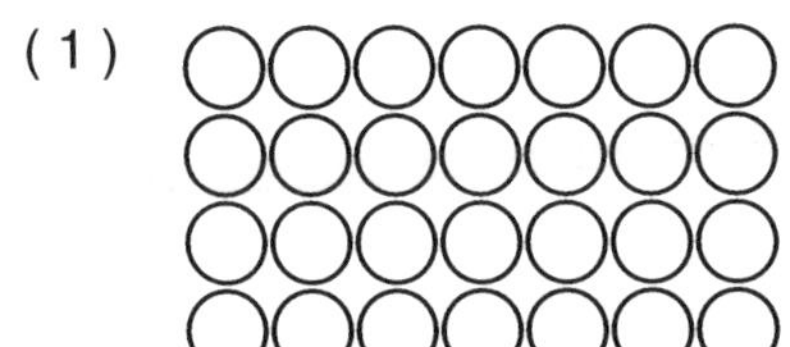

4 rows and 7 columns makes a total of 28.

(2) 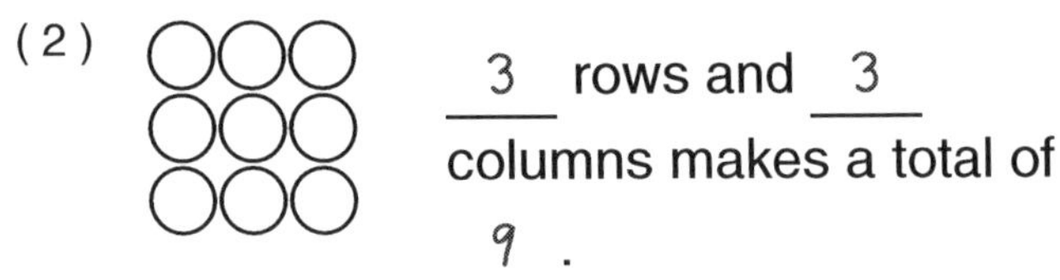

3 rows and 3 columns makes a total of 9.

(3) 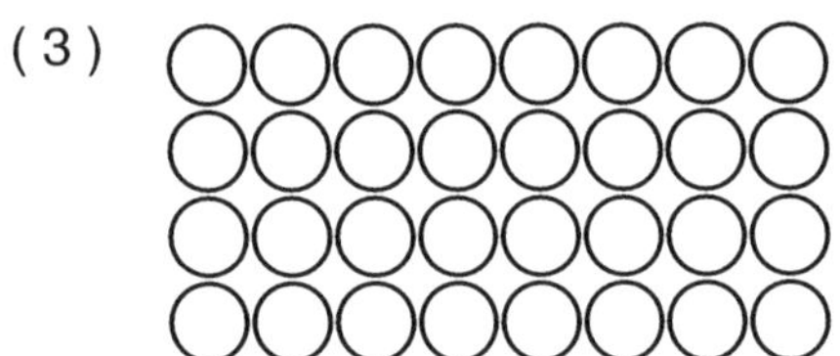

4 rows and 8 columns makes a total of 32.

(4) 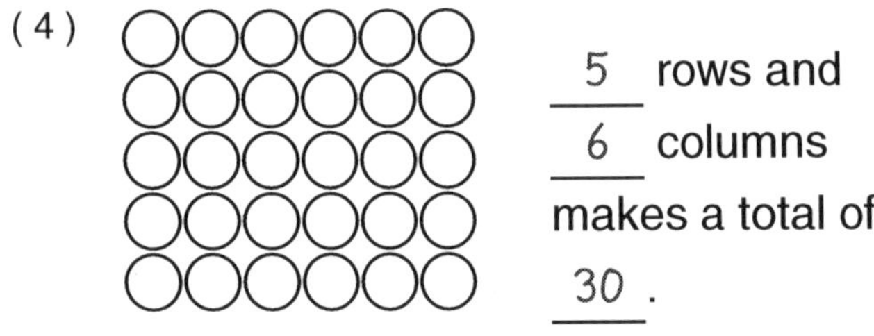

5 rows and 6 columns makes a total of 30.

(5) 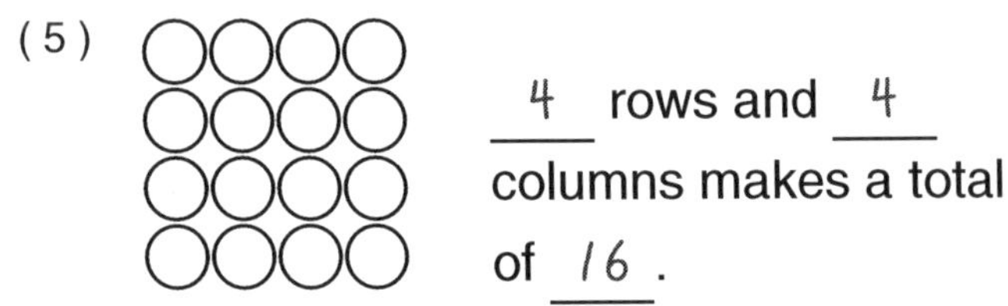

4 rows and 4 columns makes a total of 16.

(6)

2 rows and 4 columns makes a total of 8.

(7) 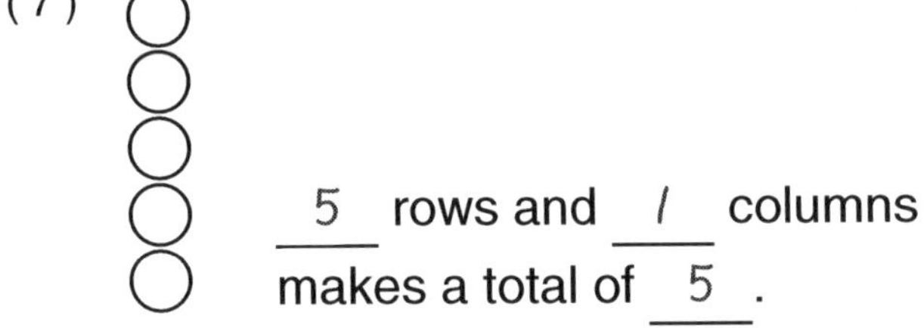

5 rows and 1 columns makes a total of 5.

(8) 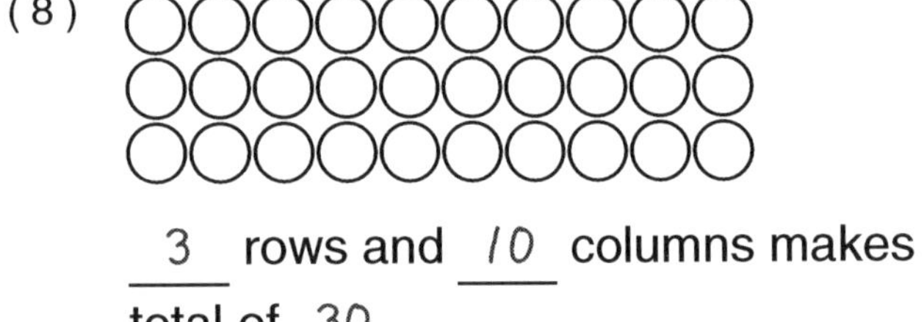

3 rows and 10 columns makes a total of 30.

(9) 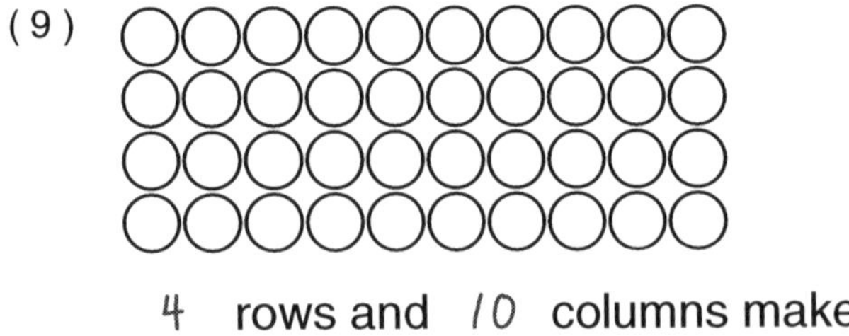

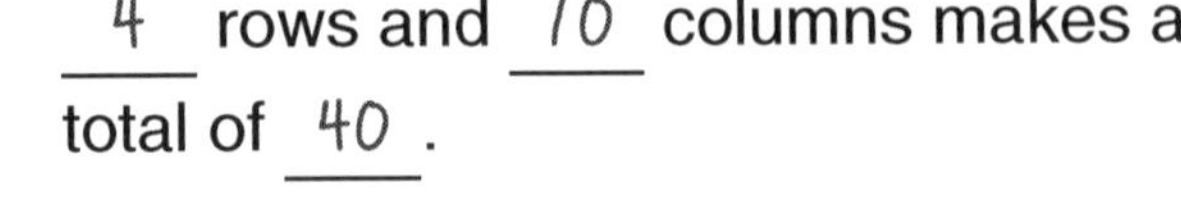

4 rows and 10 columns makes a total of 40.

(10) 

2 rows and 9 columns makes a total of 18.

Visual Multiplication
ANSWER KEY

 Use the dots to help you fill in the blanks to each of the multiplication problems.

(1) 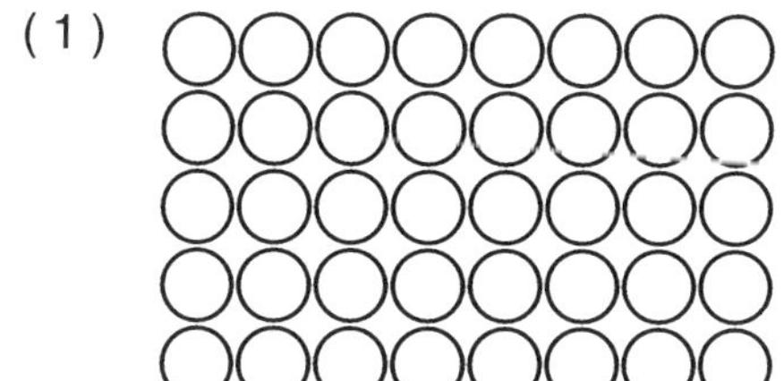

5 rows and 8 columns makes a total of 40 .

(2) 

3 rows and 9 columns makes a total of 27 .

(3) 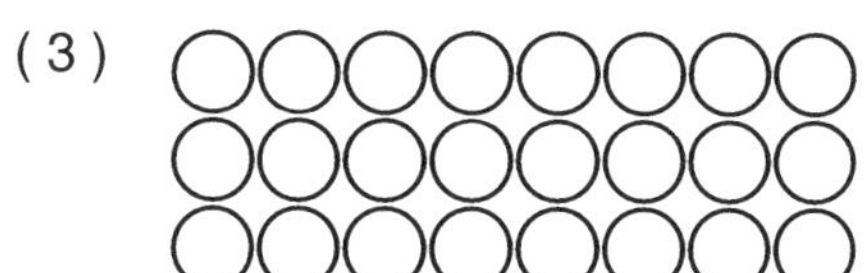

3 rows and 8 columns makes a total of 24 .

(4) 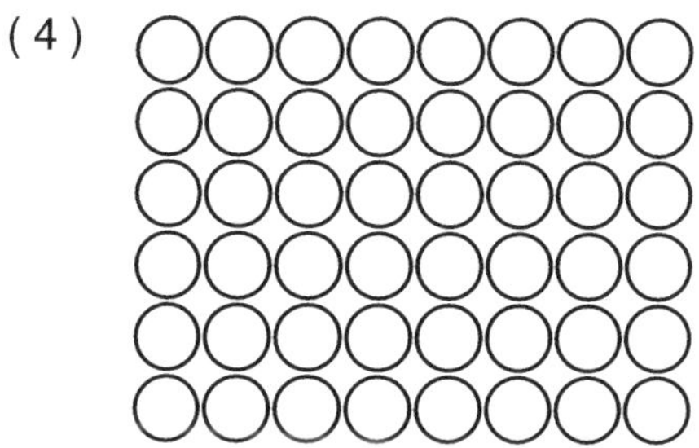

6 rows and 8 columns makes a total of 48 .

(5) 3 rows and 3 columns makes a total of 9 .

(6) 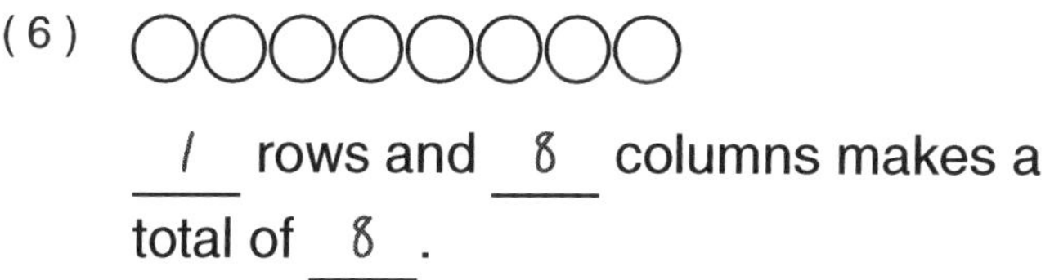

1 rows and 8 columns makes a total of 8 .

(7) 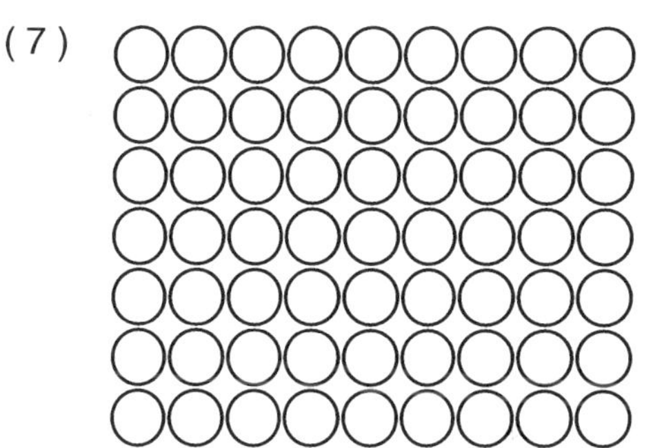

7 rows and 9 columns makes a total of 63 .

(8) 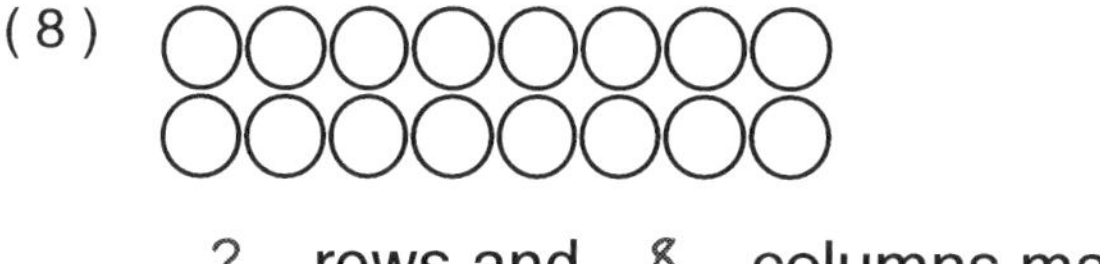

2 rows and 8 columns makes a total of 16 .

(9) 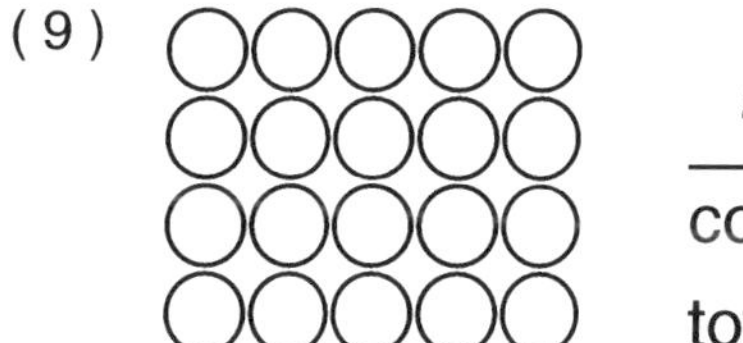

4 rows and 5 columns makes a total of 20 .

Visual Multiplication
ANSWER KEY

Use the dots to help you fill in the blanks to each of the multiplication problems.

(1)

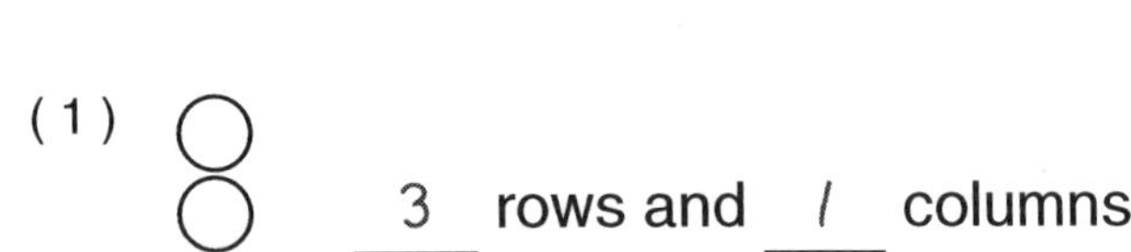

3 rows and 1 columns makes a total of 3.

(2) 2 rows and 3 columns makes a total of 6.

(3) 4 rows and 5 columns makes a total of 20.

(4) 2 rows and 7 columns makes a total of 14.

(5) 4 rows and 2 columns makes a total of 8.

(6) 1 rows and 6 columns makes a total of 6.

(7) 4 rows and 1 columns makes a total of 4.

(8)

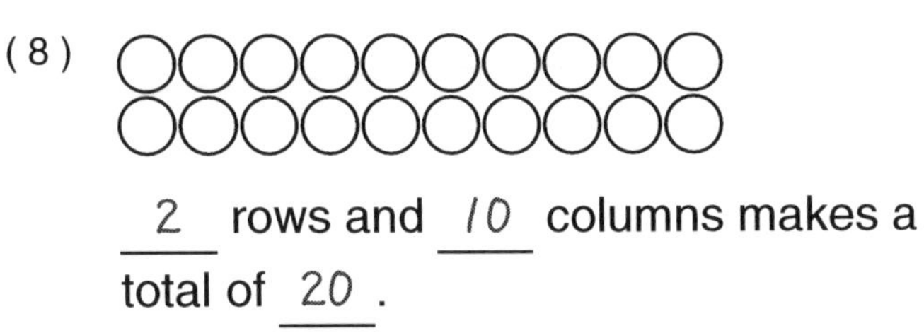

2 rows and 10 columns makes a total of 20.

(9)

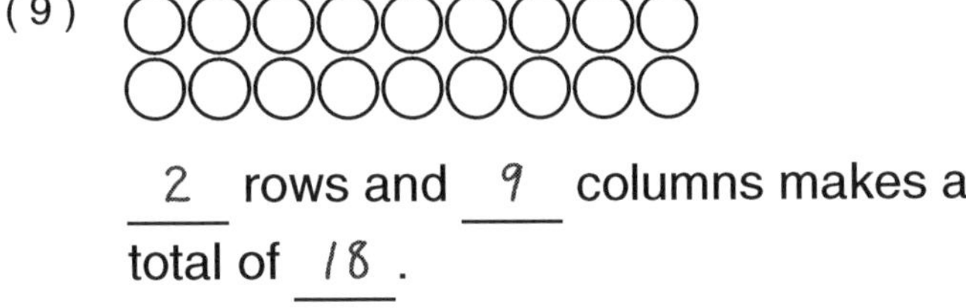

2 rows and 9 columns makes a total of 18.

(10)

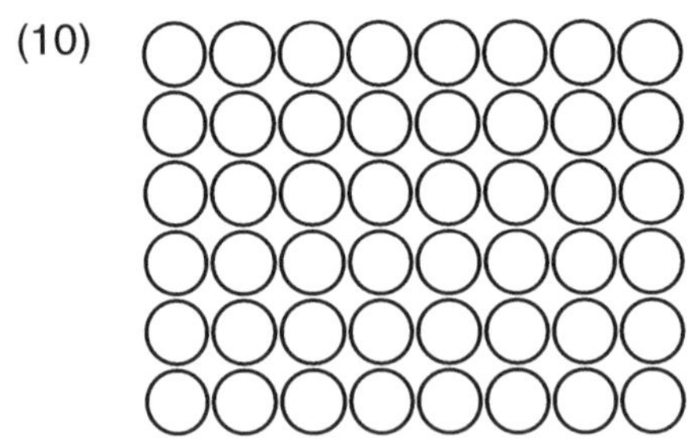

6 rows and 8 columns makes a total of 48.

(11)

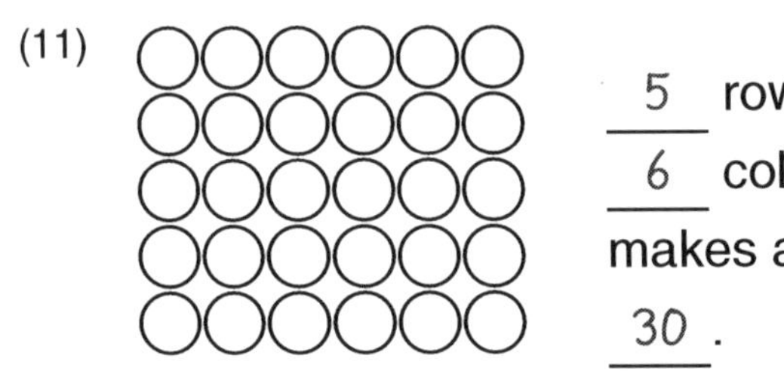

5 rows and 6 columns makes a total of 30.

Visual Multiplication
ANSWER KEY

Use the dots to help you fill in the blanks to each of the multiplication problems.

(1) 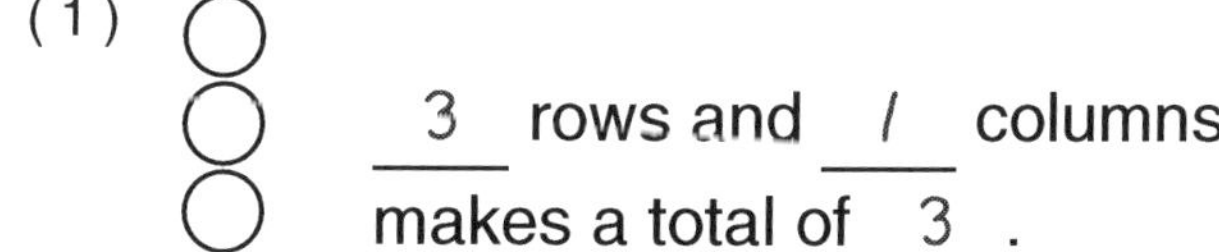

3 rows and 1 columns makes a total of 3.

(2) 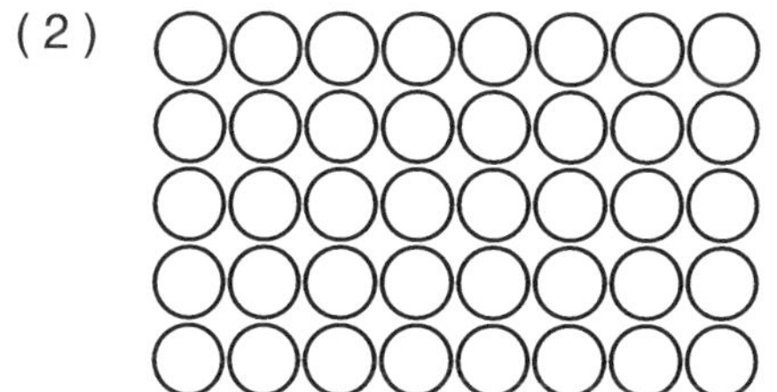

5 rows and 8 columns makes a total of 40.

(3) 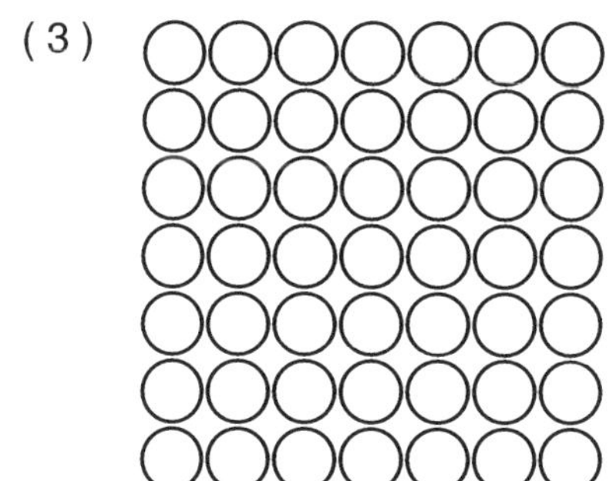

7 rows and 7 columns makes a total of 49.

(4) 2 rows and 6 columns makes a total of 12.

(5) 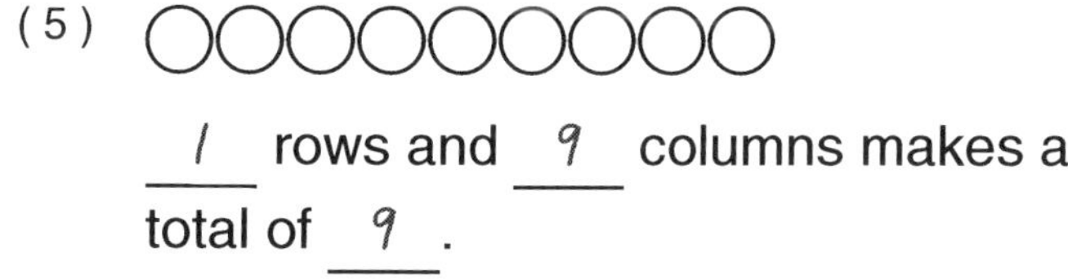

1 rows and 9 columns makes a total of 9.

(6) 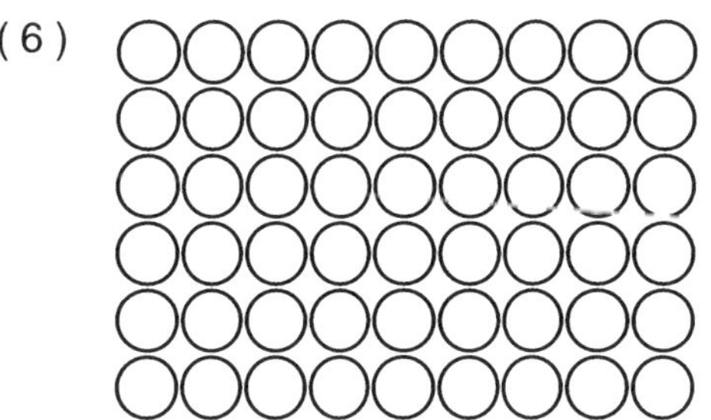

6 rows and 9 columns makes a total of 54.

(7) 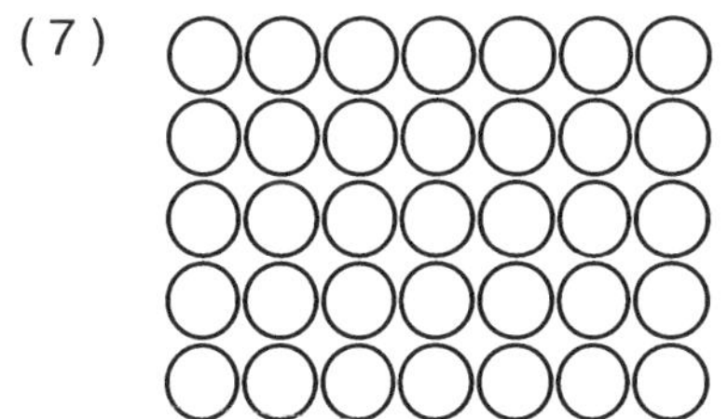

5 rows and 7 columns makes a total of 35.

(8) 

3 rows and 10 columns makes a total of 30.

(9) 

3 rows and 9 columns makes a total of 27.

Visual Multiplication
ANSWER KEY

 Use the dots to help you fill in the blanks to each of the multiplication problems.

(1) 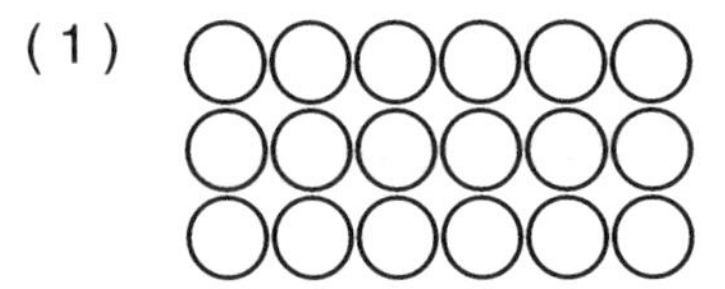

3 rows and 6 columns makes a total of 18.

(2) 

1 rows and 5 columns makes a total of 5.

(3) 

3 rows and 7 columns makes a total of 21.

(4) 

2 rows and 9 columns makes a total of 18.

(5) 

3 rows and 10 columns makes a total of 30.

(6) 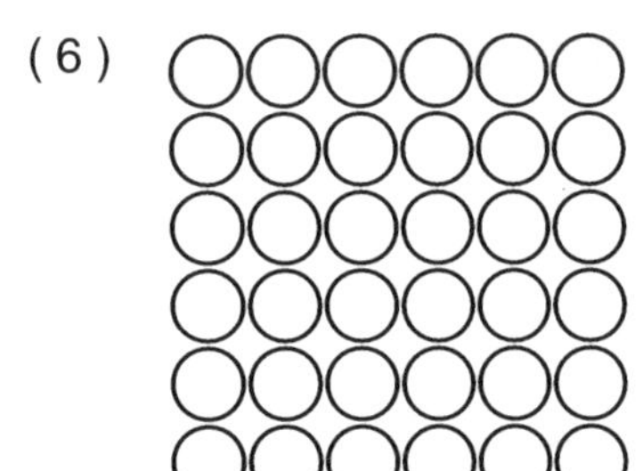

6 rows and 6 columns makes a total of 36.

(7) 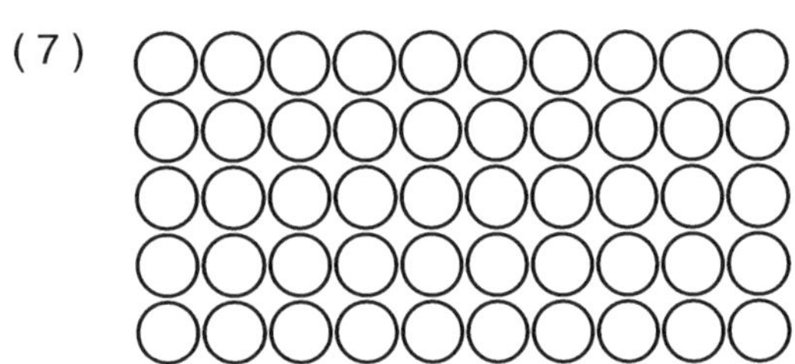

5 rows and 10 columns makes a total of 50.

(8) 

2 rows and 8 columns makes a total of 16.

(9)

3 rows and 1 columns makes a total of 3.

(10) 

1 rows and 6 columns makes a total of 6.

Visual Multiplication
ANSWER KEY

 Use the dots to help you fill in the blanks to each of the multiplication problems.

(1)

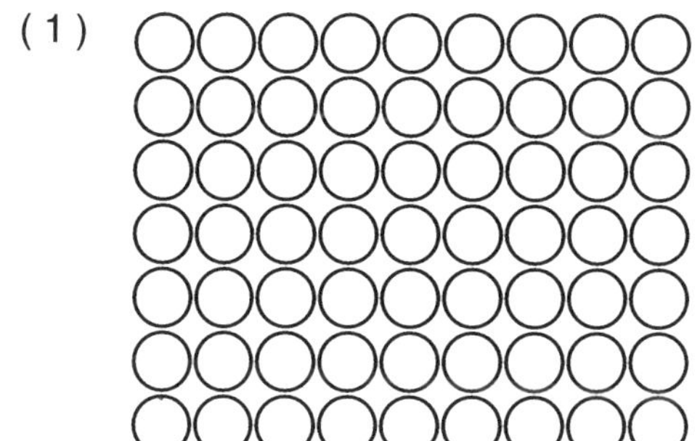

7 rows and 9 columns makes a total of 63.

(2) 2 rows and 4 columns makes a total of 8.

(3) 5 rows and 7 columns makes a total of 35.

(4)

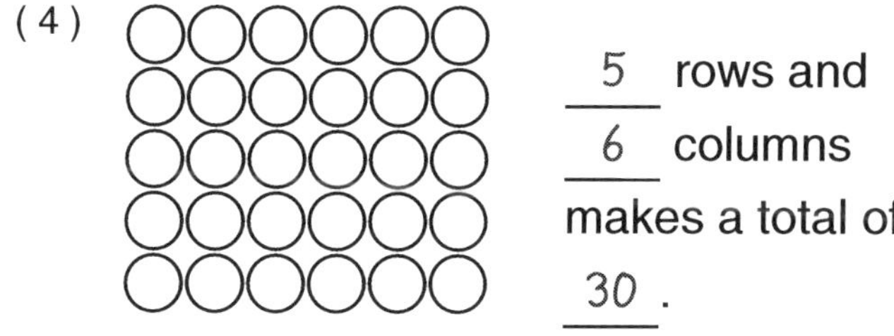

5 rows and 6 columns makes a total of 30.

(5) 2 rows and 1 columns makes a total of 2.

(6)

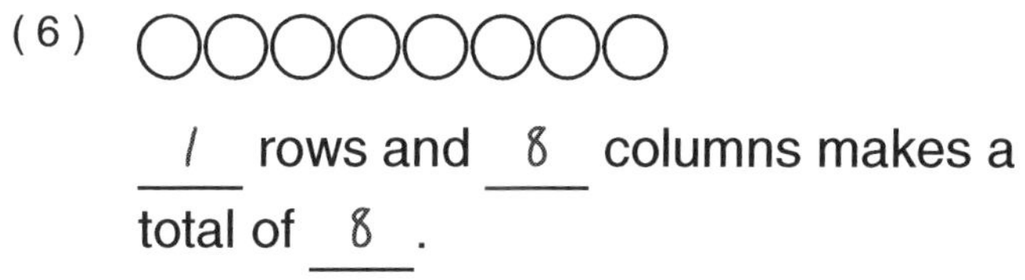

1 rows and 8 columns makes a total of 8.

(7)

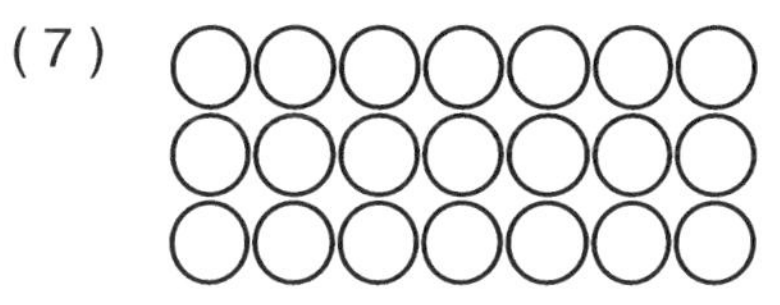

3 rows and 7 columns makes a total of 21.

(8)

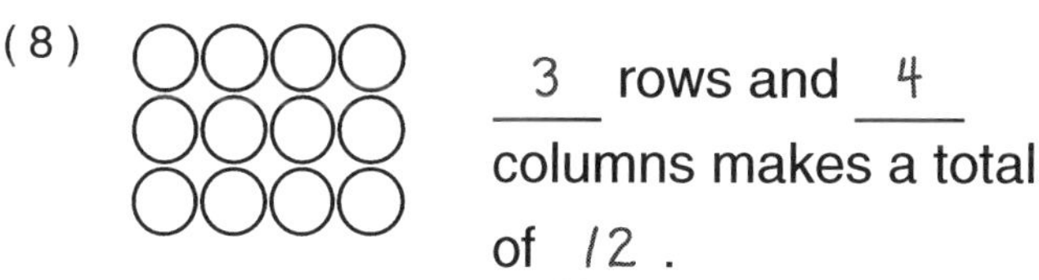

3 rows and 4 columns makes a total of 12.

(9)

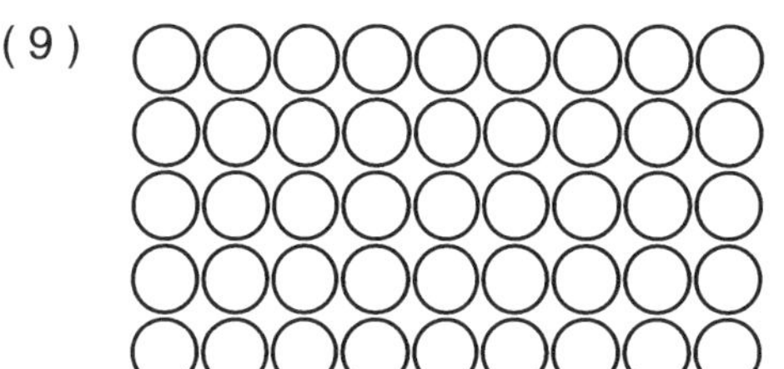

5 rows and 9 columns makes a total of 45.

(10) 4 rows and 1 columns makes a total of 4.

Visual Multiplication
ANSWER KEY

 Use the dots to help you fill in the blanks to each of the multiplication problems.

(1) 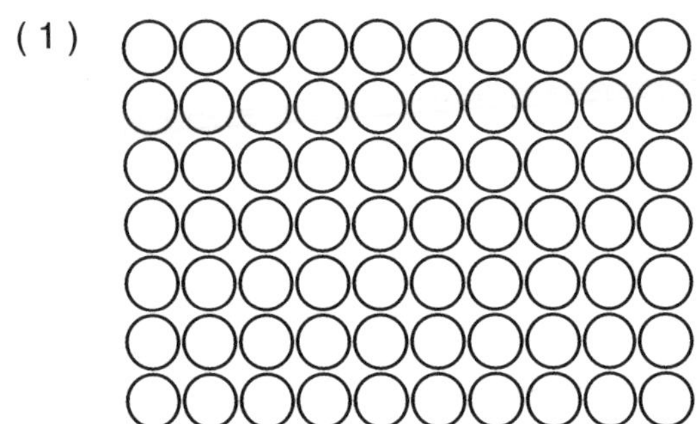

7 rows and 10 columns makes a total of 70.

(2) 

2 rows and 9 columns makes a total of 18.

(3) 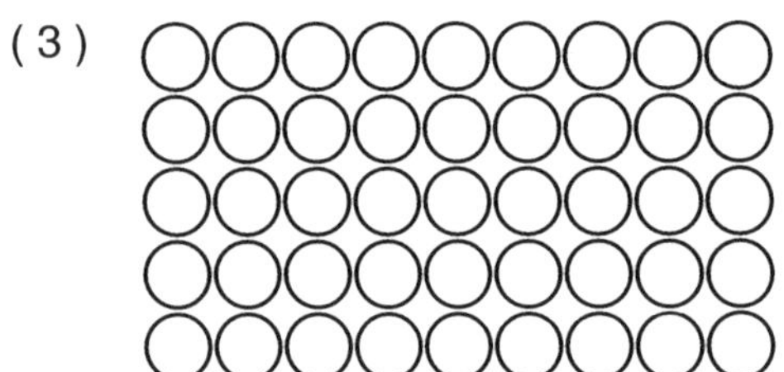

5 rows and 9 columns makes a total of 45.

(4) 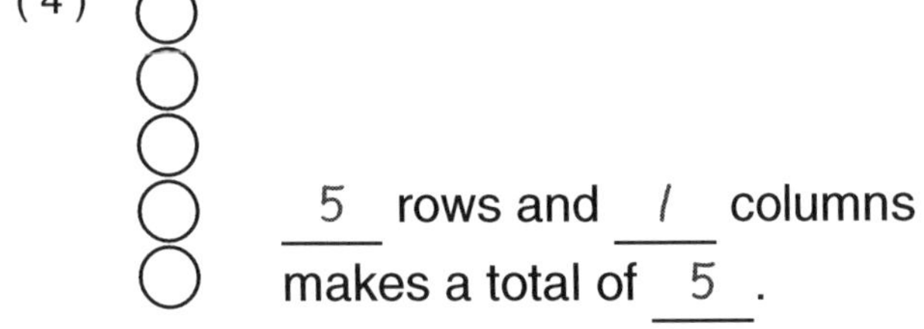

5 rows and 1 columns makes a total of 5.

(5) 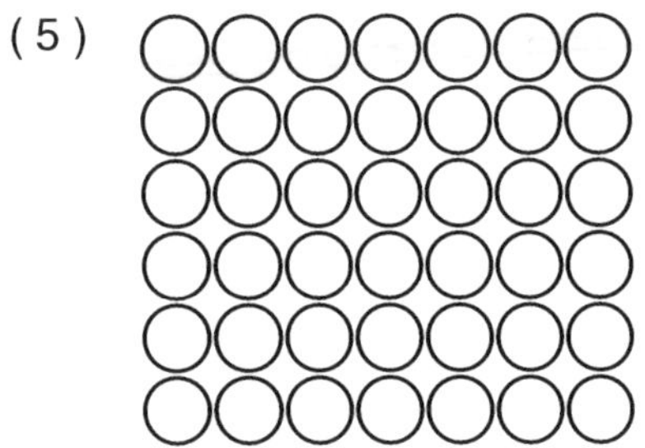

6 rows and 7 columns makes a total of 42.

(6) 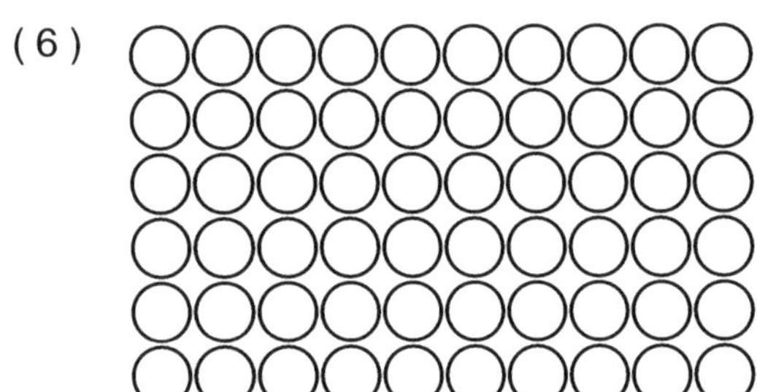

6 rows and 10 columns makes a total of 60.

(7) 

2 rows and 7 columns makes a total of 14.

(8) 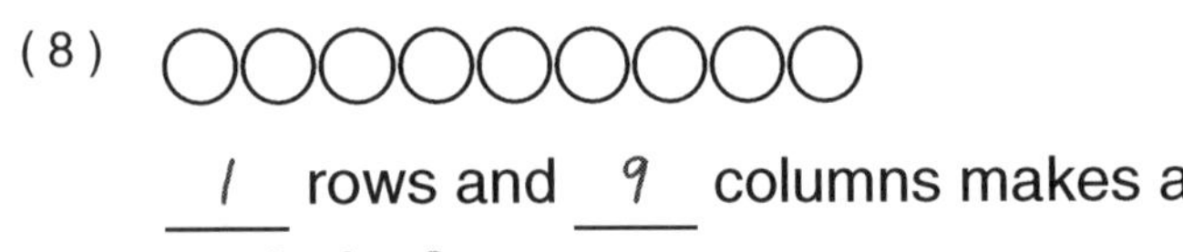

1 rows and 9 columns makes a total of 9.

Visual Multiplication
ANSWER KEY

 Use the dots to help you fill in the blanks to each of the multiplication problems.

(1) 

3 rows and 7 columns makes a total of 21.

(2) 1 rows and 6 columns makes a total of 6.

(3) 1 rows and 10 columns makes a total of 10.

(4) 2 rows and 6 columns makes a total of 12.

(5) 4 rows and 3 columns makes a total of 12.

(6) 3 rows and 4 columns makes a total of 12.

(7) 3 rows and 6 columns makes a total of 18.

(8) 5 rows and 1 columns makes a total of 5.

(9) 7 rows and 9 columns makes a total of 63.

(10) 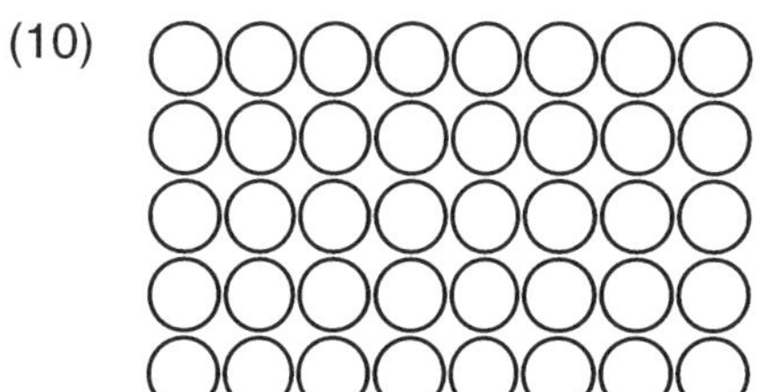

5 rows and 8 columns makes a total of 40.

Visual Multiplication
ANSWER KEY

Use the dots to help you fill in the blanks to each of the multiplication problems.

(1) 

1 rows and 4 columns makes a total of 4.

(2) 

1 rows and 7 columns makes a total of 7.

(3) 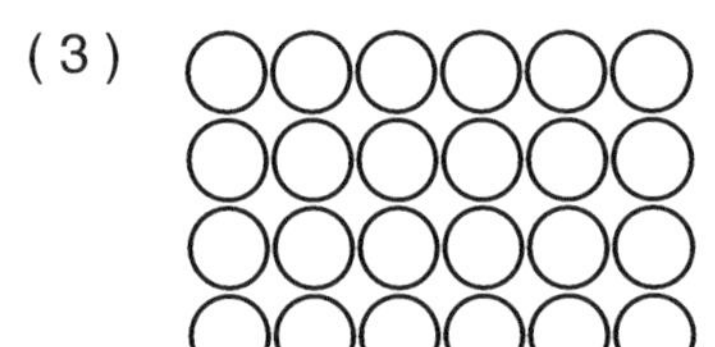

4 rows and 6 columns makes a total of 24.

(4)

1 rows and 10 columns makes a total of 10.

(5) 

3 rows and 6 columns makes a total of 18.

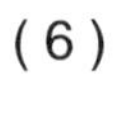

(6) 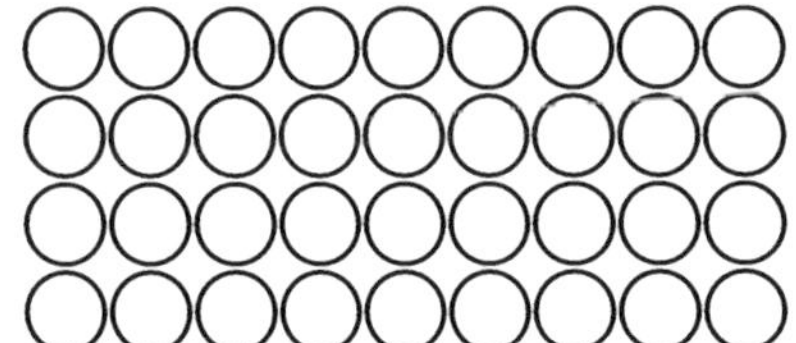

4 rows and 9 columns makes a total of 36.

(7) 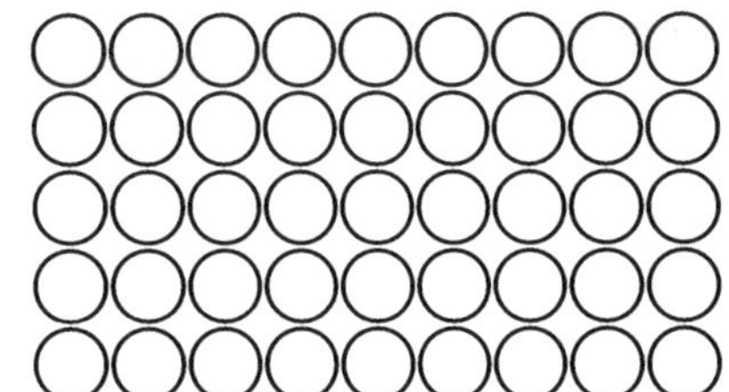

5 rows and 9 columns makes a total of 45.

(8) 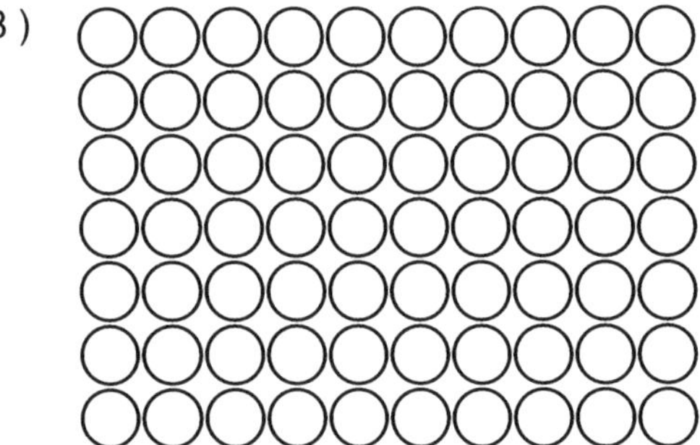

7 rows and 10 columns makes a total of 70.

(9) 

3 rows and 3 columns makes a total of 9.

(10) 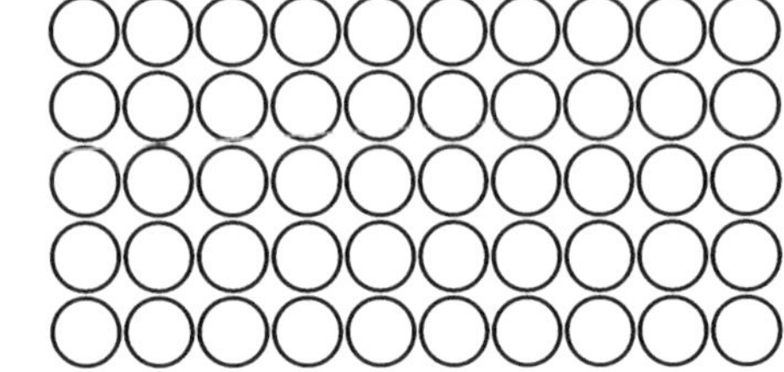

5 rows and 10 columns makes a total of 50.

Visual Multiplication
ANSWER KEY

Use the dots to help you fill in the blanks to each of the multiplication problems.

(1) 

2 rows and 5 columns makes a total of 10.

(2) 

2 rows and 6 columns makes a total of 12.

(3) 

1 rows and 4 columns makes a total of 4.

(4) 

1 rows and 3 columns makes a total of 3.

(5) 

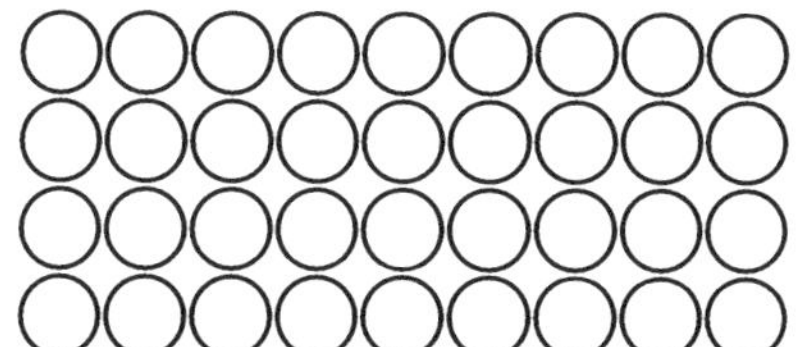

4 rows and 9 columns makes a total of 36.

(6)

1 rows and 6 columns makes a total of 6.

(7) 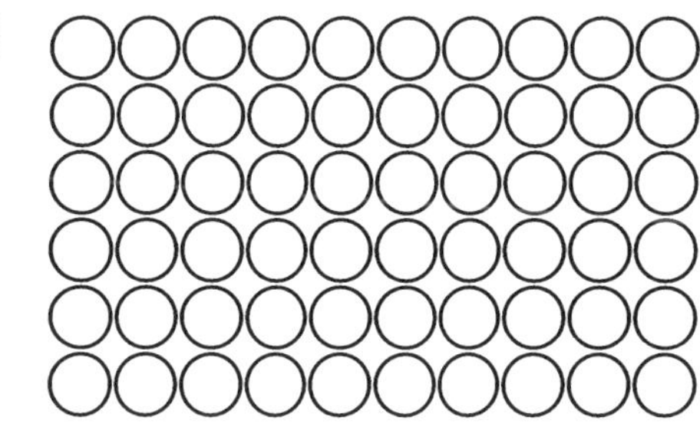

6 rows and 10 columns makes a total of 60.

(8) 

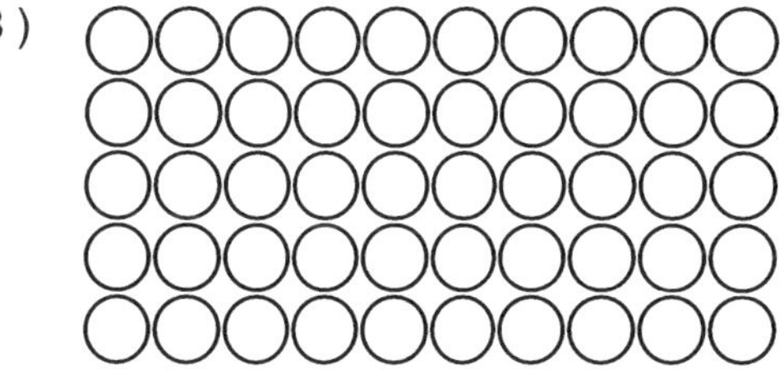

5 rows and 10 columns makes a total of 50.

(9)

5 rows and 1 columns makes a total of 5.

(10) 

3 rows and 5 columns makes a total of 15

(11) 

1 rows and 9 columns makes a total of 9.

Visual Multiplication
ANSWER KEY

 Use the dots to help you fill in the blanks to each of the multiplication problems.

(1) 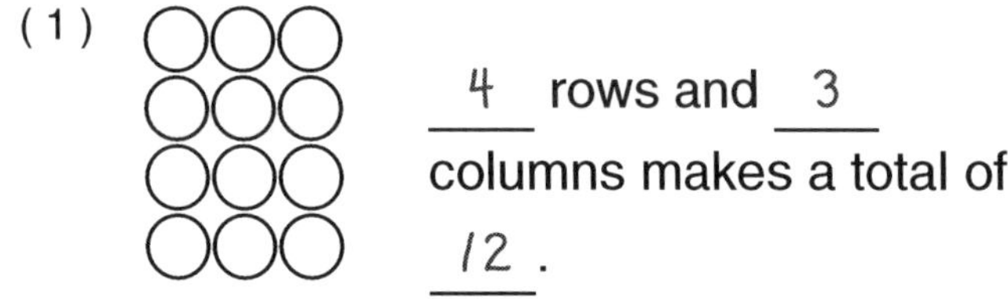
4 rows and 3 columns makes a total of 12.

(2) 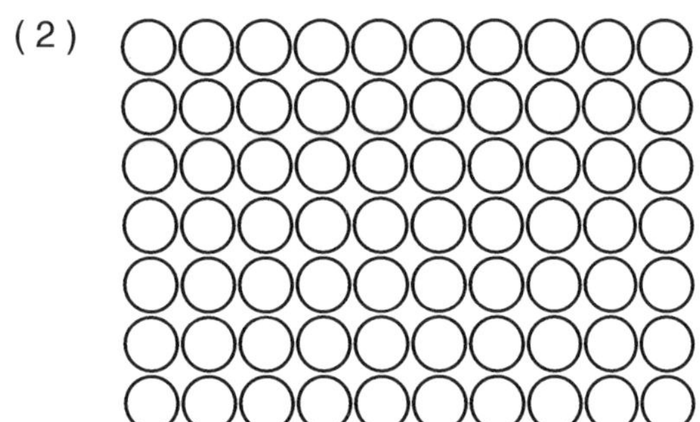
7 rows and 10 columns makes a total of 70.

(3) 1 rows and 5 columns makes a total of 5.

(4) 1 rows and 6 columns makes a total of 6.

(5) 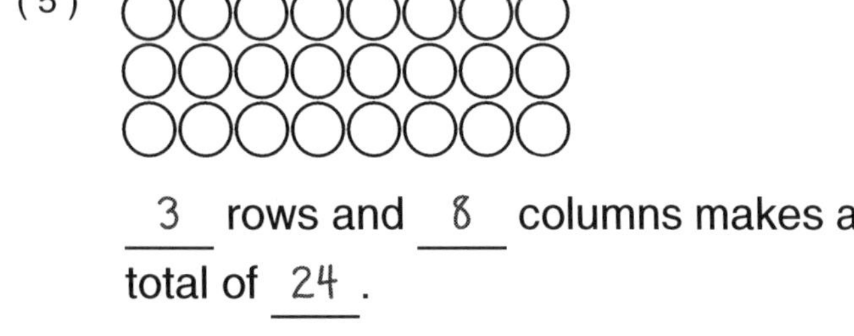
3 rows and 8 columns makes a total of 24.

(6) 4 rows and 4 columns makes a total of 16.

(7) 2 rows and 1 columns makes a total of 2.

(8) 2 rows and 3 columns makes a total of 6.

(9) 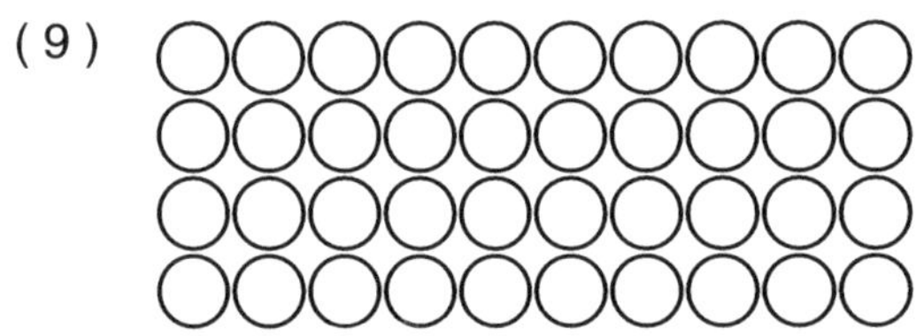
4 rows and 10 columns makes a total of 40.

(10) 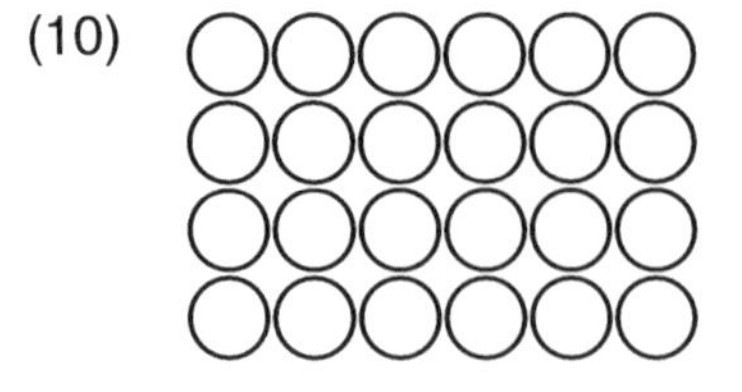
4 rows and 6 columns makes a total of 24.

(11) 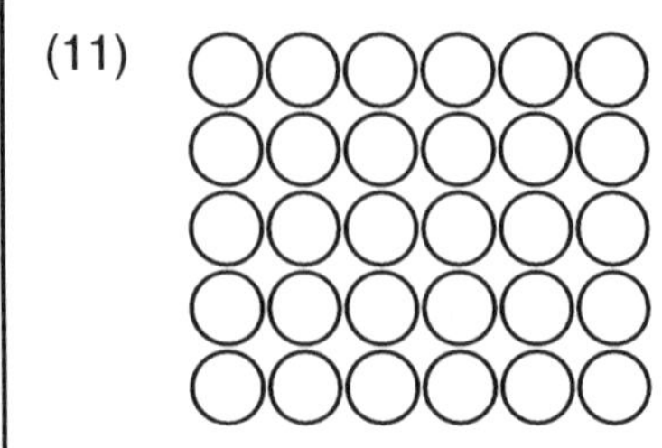
5 rows and 6 columns makes a total of 30.

Visual Multiplication
ANSWER KEY

 Use the dots to help you fill in the blanks to each of the multiplication problems.

(1) 

_2_ rows and _9_ columns makes a total of _18_.

(2) 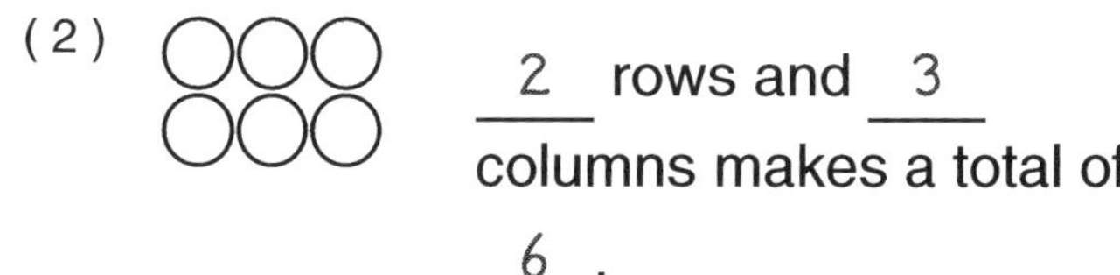

_2_ rows and _3_ columns makes a total of _6_.

(3) 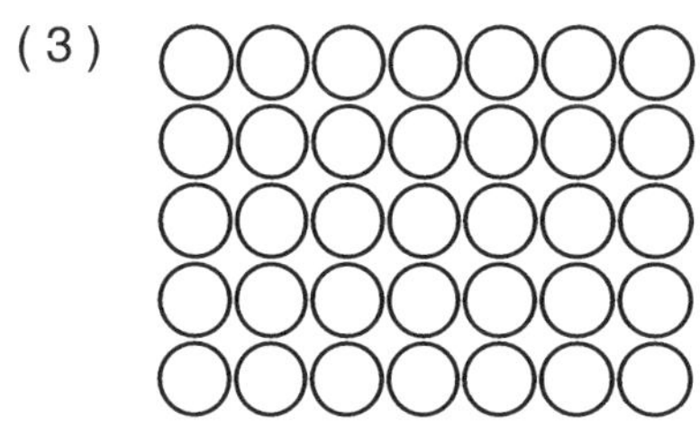

_5_ rows and _7_ columns makes a total of _35_.

(4)

_1_ rows and _3_ columns makes a total of _3_.

(5) 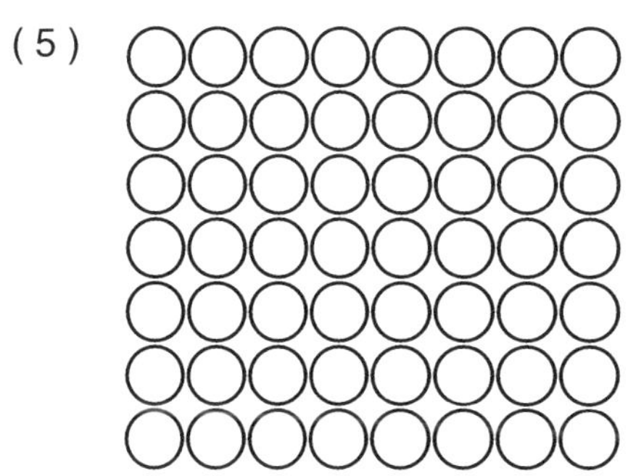

_7_ rows and _8_ columns makes a total of _56_.

(6) 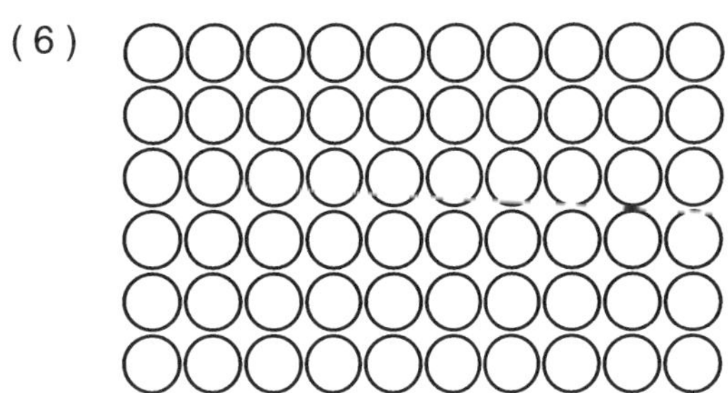

_6_ rows and _10_ columns makes a total of _60_.

(7) 

_2_ rows and _7_ columns makes a total of _14_.

(8) 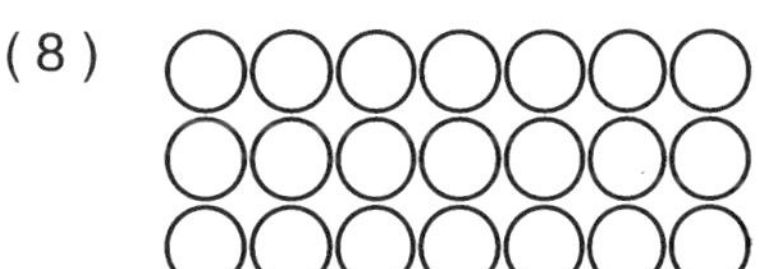

_3_ rows and _7_ columns makes a total of _21_.

(9)

_5_ rows and _4_ columns makes a total of _20_.

(10) 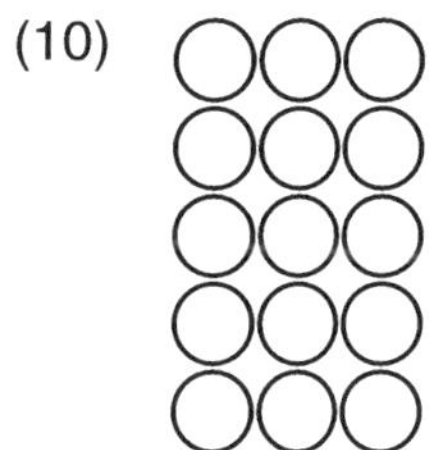

_5_ rows and _3_ columns makes a total of _15_.

Visual Multiplication
ANSWER KEY

 Use the dots to help you fill in the blanks to each of the multiplication problems.

(1) 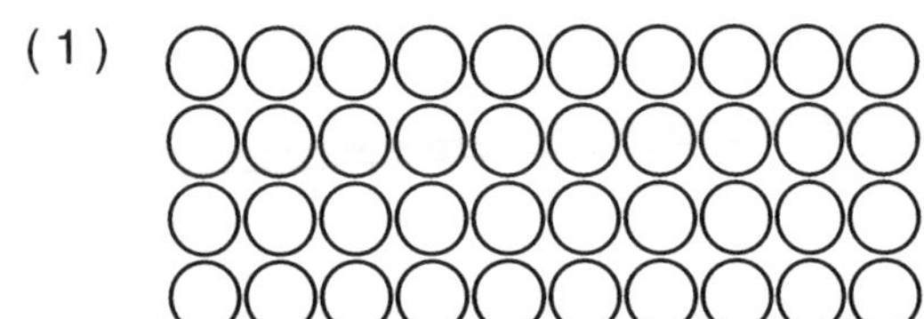

4 rows and 10 columns makes a total of 40.

(2) 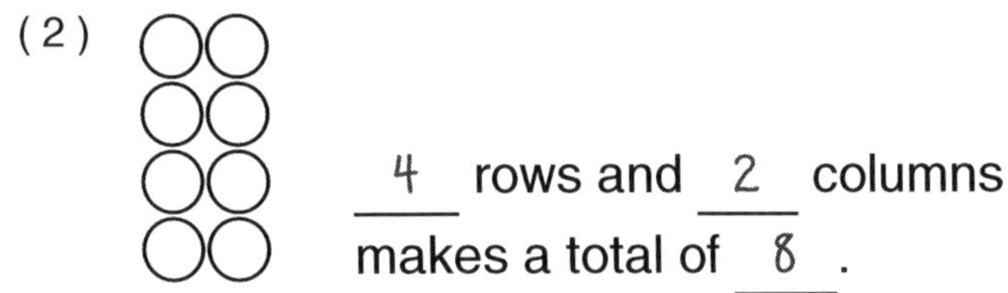

4 rows and 2 columns makes a total of 8.

(3)

1 rows and 6 columns makes a total of 6.

(4)

4 rows and 6 columns makes a total of 24.

(5)

5 rows and 5 columns makes a total of 25.

(6)

1 rows and 10 columns makes a total of 10.

(7)

5 rows and 2 columns makes a total of 10.

(8) 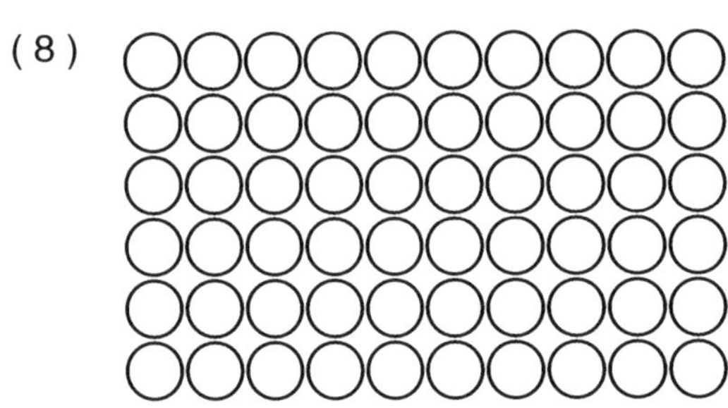

6 rows and 10 columns makes a total of 60.

(9)

1 rows and 8 columns makes a total of 8.

(10)

5 rows and 3 columns makes a total of 15.

Visual Multiplication
ANSWER KEY

Use the dots to help you fill in the blanks to each of the multiplication problems.

(1) 1 rows and 10 columns makes a total of 10.

(2) 3 rows and 8 columns makes a total of 24.

(3) 4 rows and 10 columns makes a total of 40.

(4) 6 rows and 9 columns makes a total of 54.

(5) 1 rows and 2 columns makes a total of 2.

(6) 1 rows and 7 columns makes a total of 7.

(7) 2 rows and 1 columns makes a total of 2.

(8) 5 rows and 7 columns makes a total of 35.

(9) 2 rows and 5 columns makes a total of 10.

(10) 7 rows and 10 columns makes a total of 70.

Visual Multiplication
ANSWER KEY

Use the dots to help you fill in the blanks to each of the multiplication problems.

(1) 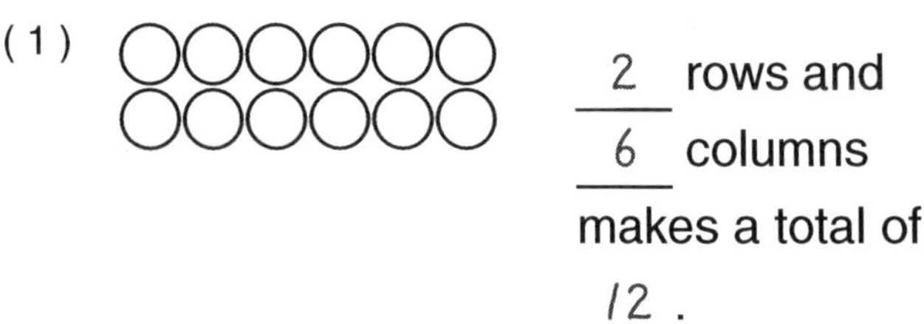

2 rows and 6 columns makes a total of 12.

(2) 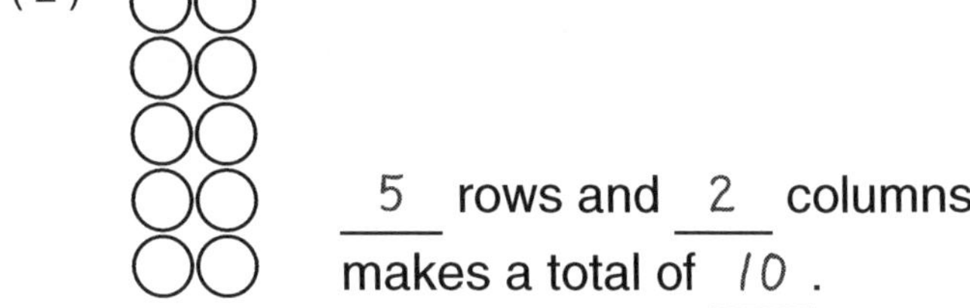

5 rows and 2 columns makes a total of 10.

(3)

1 rows and 9 columns makes a total of 9.

(4) 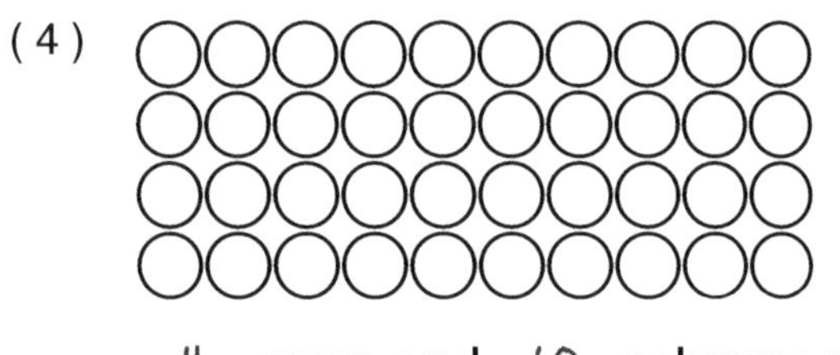

4 rows and 10 columns makes a total of 40.

(5) 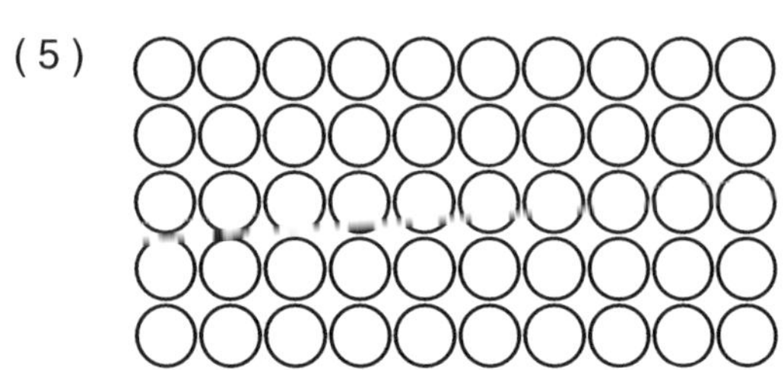

5 rows and 10 columns makes a total of 50.

(6)

3 rows and 6 columns makes a total of 18.

(7) 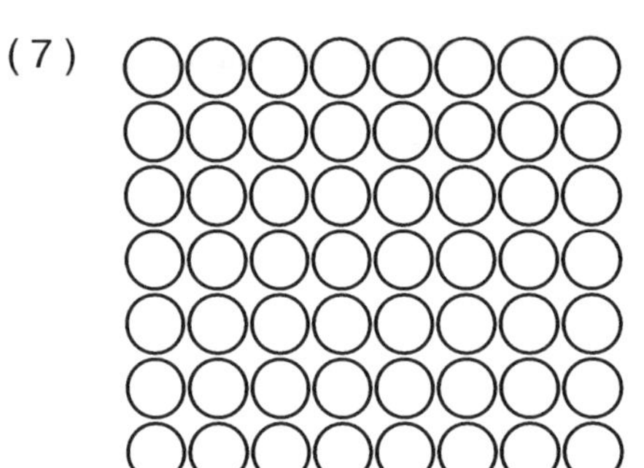

7 rows and 8 columns makes a total of 56.

(8)

1 rows and 2 columns makes a total of 2.

(9) 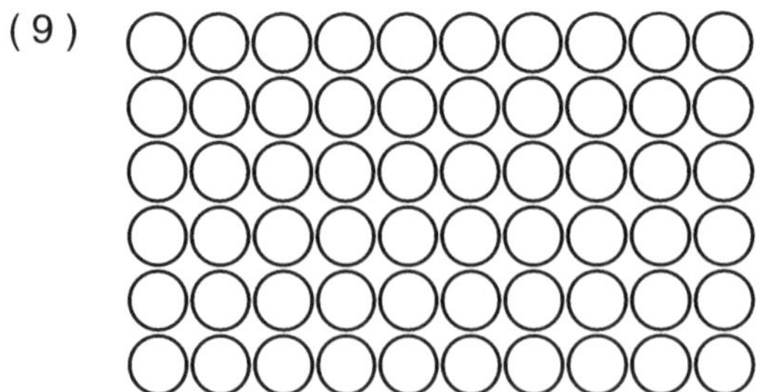

6 rows and 10 columns makes a total of 60.

(10)

3 rows and 1 columns makes a total of 3.

Visual Multiplication
ANSWER KEY

Use the dots to help you fill in the blanks to each of the multiplication problems.

(1)
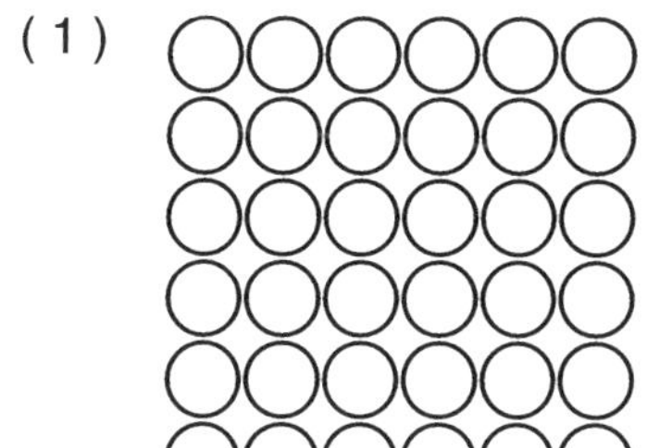
6 rows and 6 columns makes a total of 36.

(2)
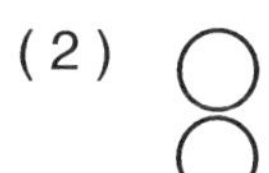
2 rows and 1 columns makes a total of 2.

(3)

3 rows and 4 columns makes a total of 12.

(4)
6 rows and 9 columns makes a total of 54.

(5)

4 rows and 3 columns makes a total of 12.

(6)
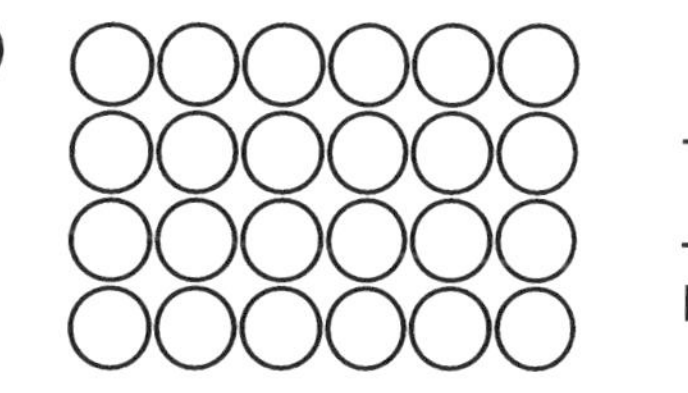
4 rows and 6 columns makes a total of 24.

(7)
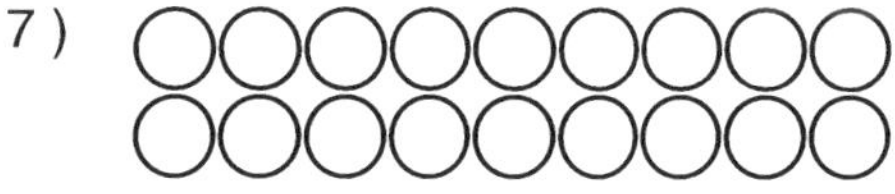
2 rows and 9 columns makes a total of 18.

(8)
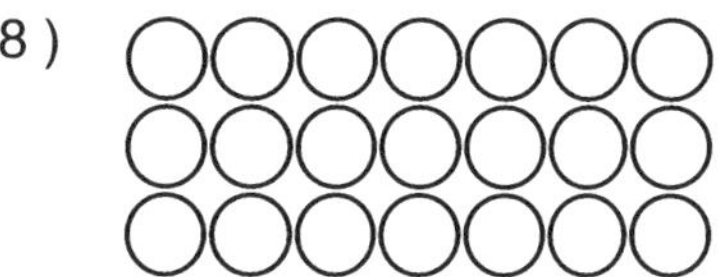
3 rows and 7 columns makes a total of 21.

(9)
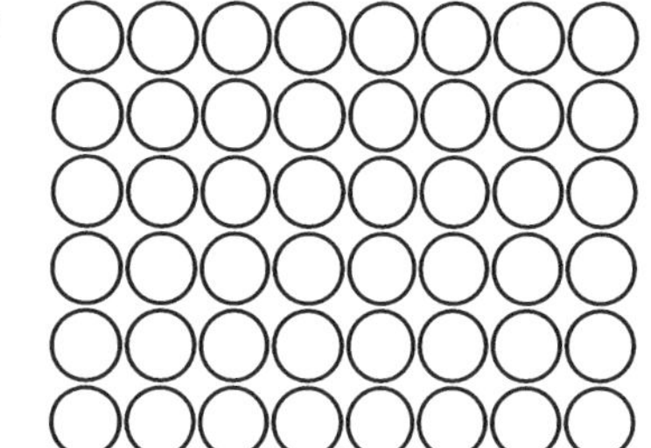
6 rows and 8 columns makes a total of 48.

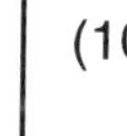
(10)

1 rows and 9 columns makes a total of 9.

Visual Multiplication
ANSWER KEY

 Use the dots to help you fill in the blanks to each of the multiplication problems.

(1) 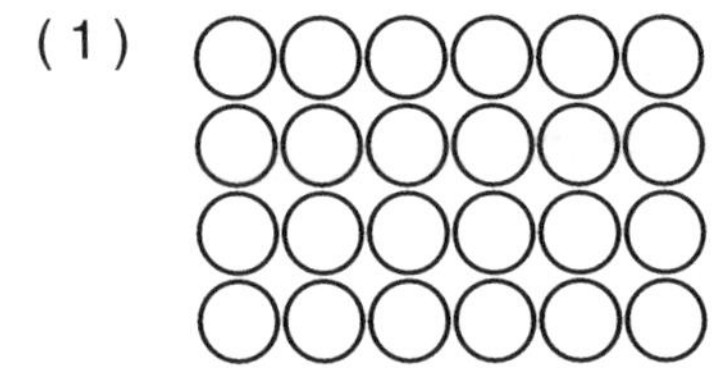

4 rows and 6 columns makes a total of 24.

(2) 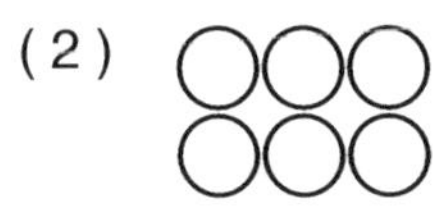

2 rows and 3 columns makes a total of 6.

(3) 

1 rows and 9 columns makes a total of 9.

(4) 

2 rows and 7 columns makes a total of 14.

(5) 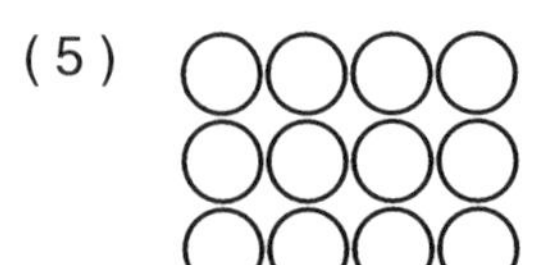

3 rows and 4 columns makes a total of 12.

(6) 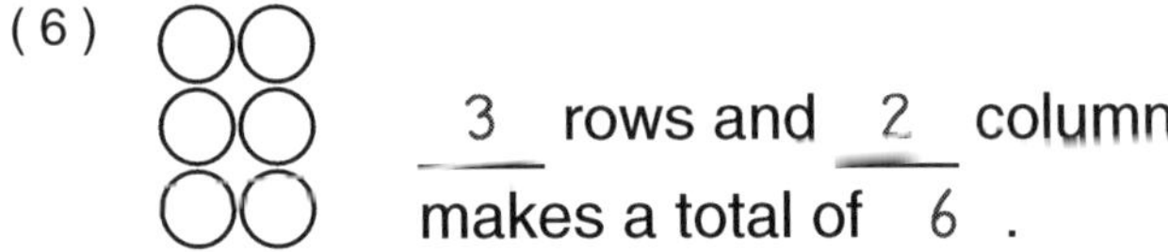

3 rows and 2 columns makes a total of 6.

(7) 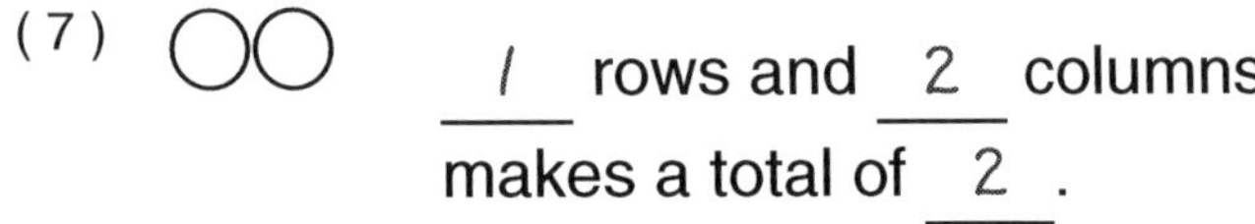

1 rows and 2 columns makes a total of 2.

(8) 2 rows and 1 columns makes a total of 2.

(9) 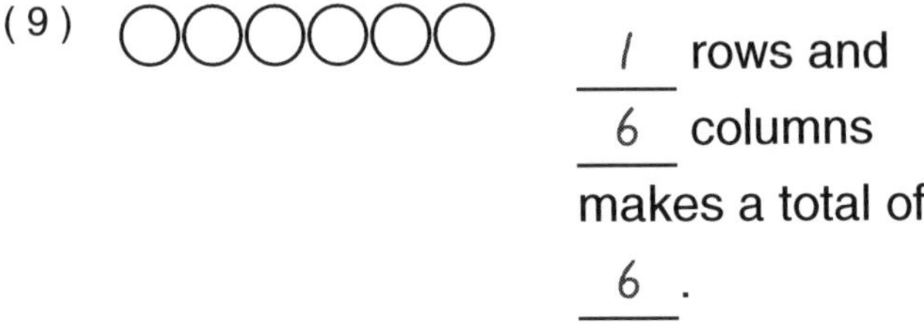

1 rows and 6 columns makes a total of 6.

(10) 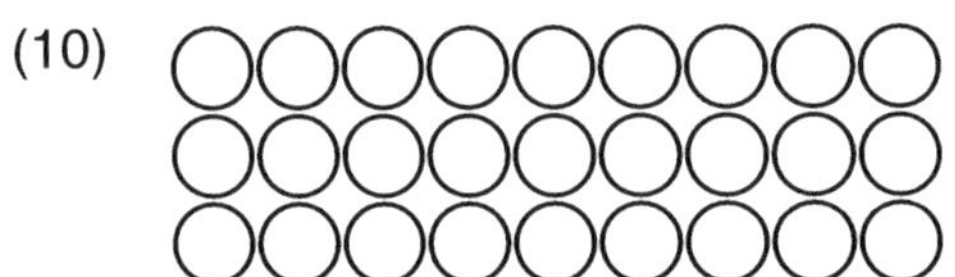

3 rows and 9 columns makes a total of 27.

(11) 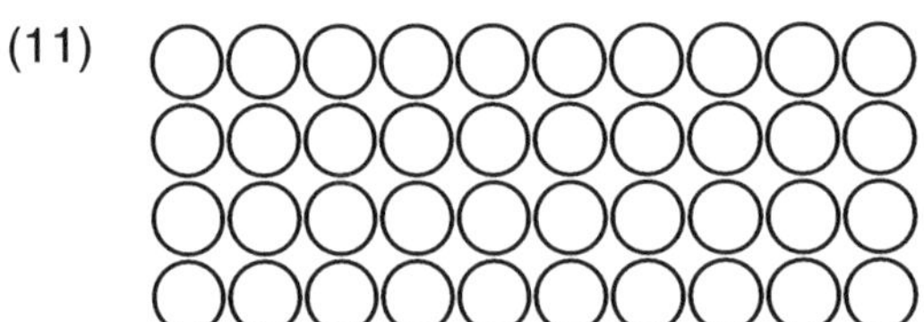

4 rows and 10 columns makes a total of 40.

(12) 

2 rows and 10 columns makes a total of 20.

(13) 1 rows and 7 columns makes a total of 7.

Visual Multiplication
ANSWER KEY

 Use the dots to help you fill in the blanks to each of the multiplication problems.

(1) 

__3__ rows and __9__ columns makes a total of __27__.

(2) __5__ rows and __2__ columns makes a total of __10__.

(3) __3__ rows and __5__ columns makes a total of __15__.

(4) __1__ rows and __7__ columns makes a total of __7__.

(5) __1__ rows and __5__ columns makes a total of __5__.

(6) __2__ rows and __4__ columns makes a total of __8__.

(7) __1__ rows and __3__ columns makes a total of __3__.

(8) __3__ rows and __6__ columns makes a total of __18__.

(9) __1__ rows and __9__ columns makes a total of __9__.

(10) __2__ rows and __9__ columns makes a total of __18__.

(11) __5__ rows and __5__ columns makes a total of __25__.

(12) __2__ rows and __6__ columns makes a total of __12__.

Visual Multiplication
ANSWER KEY

Use the dots to help you fill in the blanks to each of the multiplication problems.

(1)

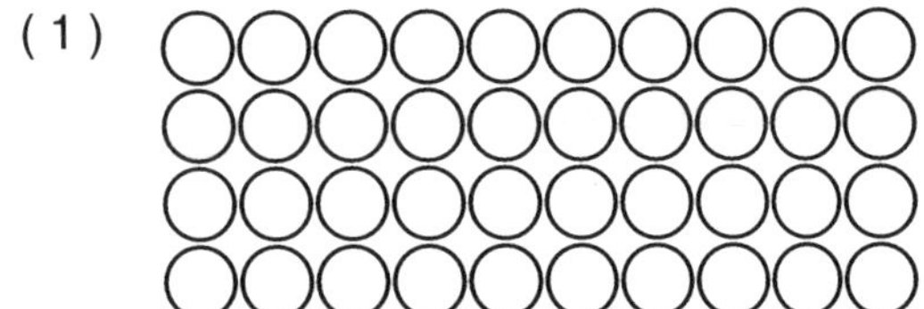

4 rows and 10 columns makes a total of 40.

(2)

7 rows and 9 columns makes a total of 63.

(3)

6 rows and 6 columns makes a total of 36.

(4)

1 rows and 3 columns makes a total of 3.

(5)

3 rows and 2 columns makes a total of 6.

(6)

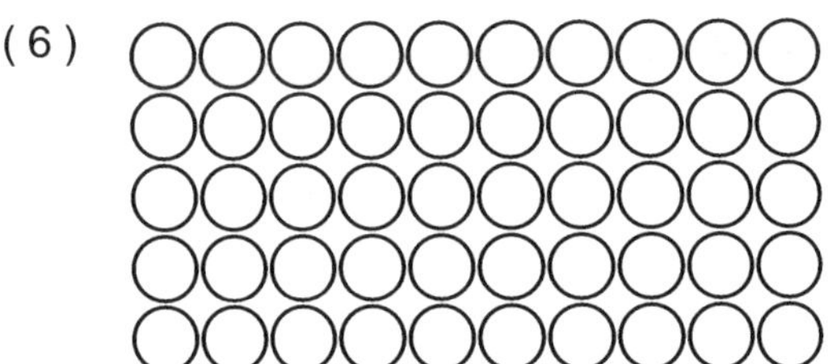

5 rows and 10 columns makes a total of 50.

(7)

1 rows and 5 columns makes a total of 5.

(8)

3 rows and 9 columns makes a total of 27.

(9)

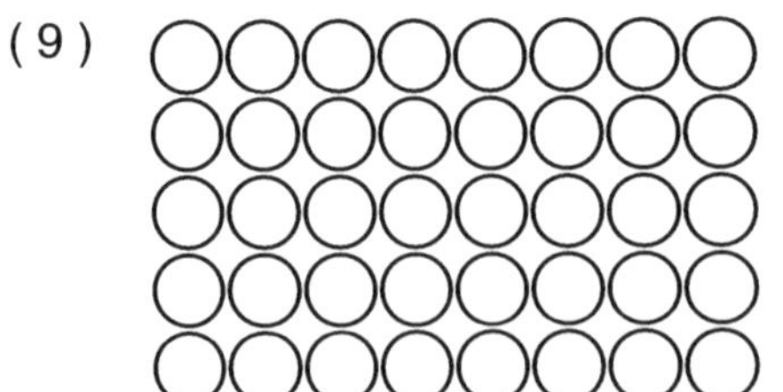

5 rows and 8 columns makes a total of 40.

(10)

2 rows and 10 columns makes a total of 20.

Visual Multiplication
ANSWER KEY

 Use the dots to help you fill in the blanks to each of the multiplication problems.

(1) 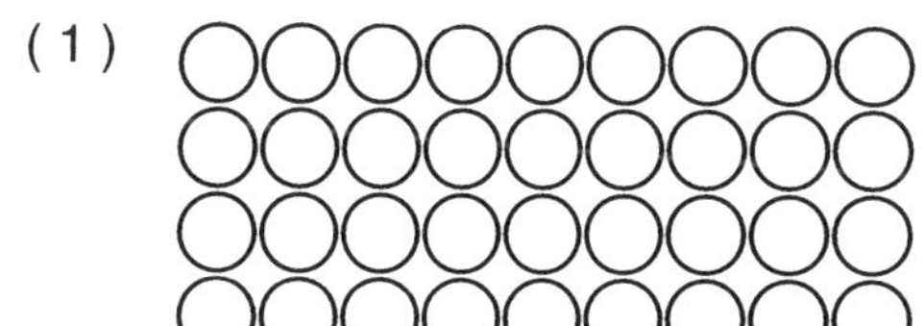

4 rows and 9 columns makes a total of 36.

(2) 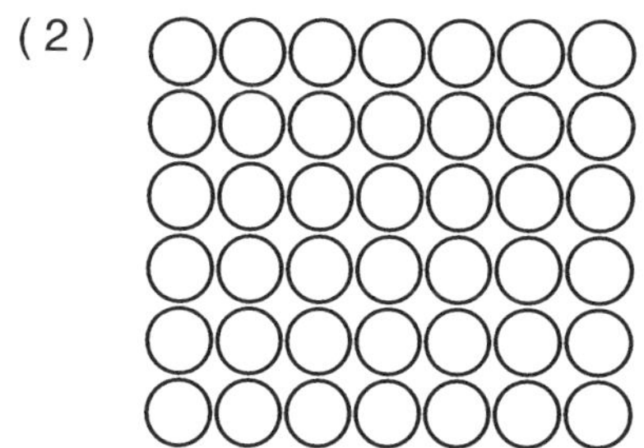

6 rows and 7 columns makes a total of 42.

(3) 

3 rows and 10 columns makes a total of 30.

(4) 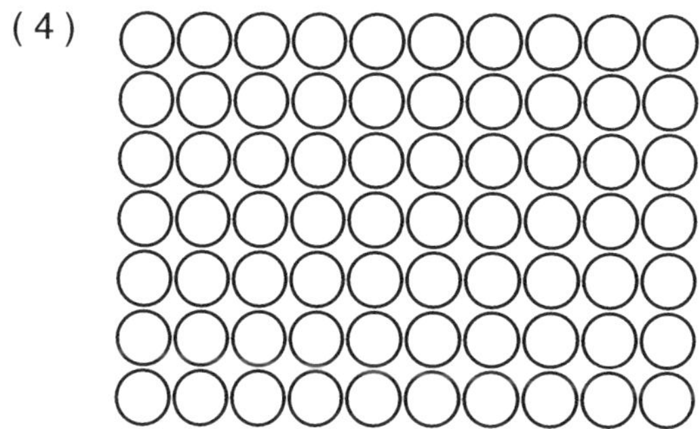

7 rows and 10 columns makes a total of 70.

(5)

2 rows and 6 columns makes a total of 12.

(6) 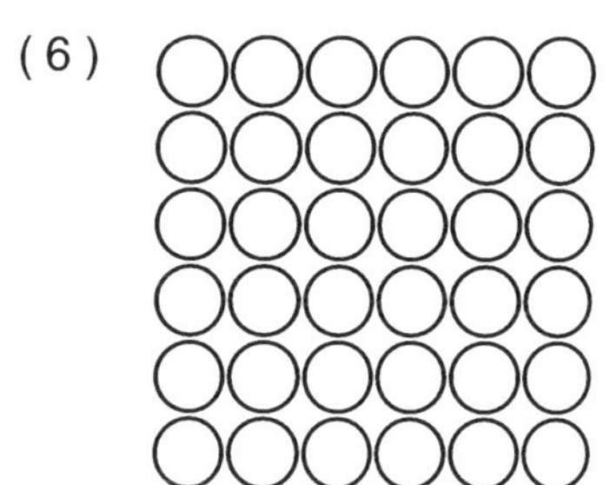

6 rows and 6 columns makes a total of 36.

(7) 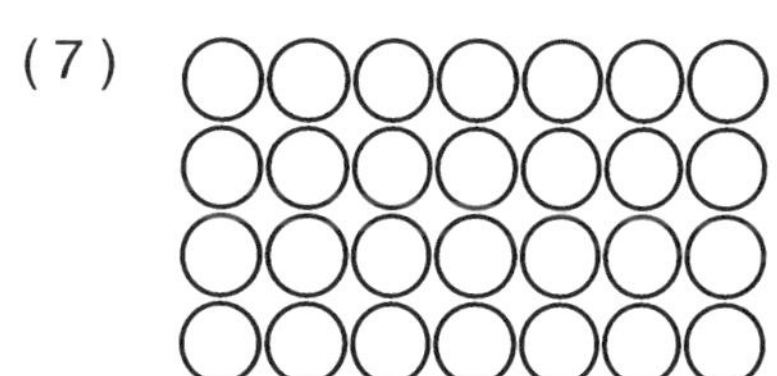

4 rows and 7 columns makes a total of 28.

(8) 

1 rows and 7 columns makes a total of 7.

(9) 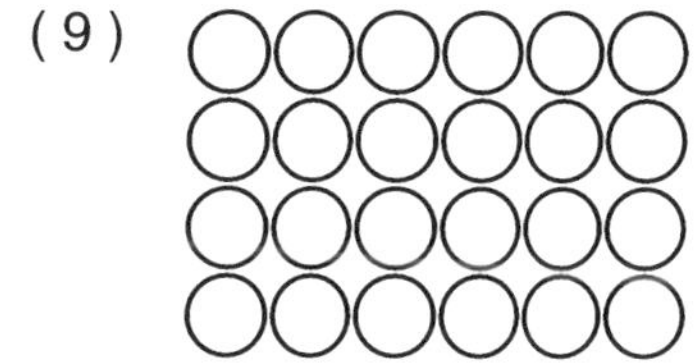

4 rows and 6 columns makes a total of 24.

Visual Multiplication
ANSWER KEY

Use the dots to help you fill in the blanks to each of the multiplication problems.

(1) 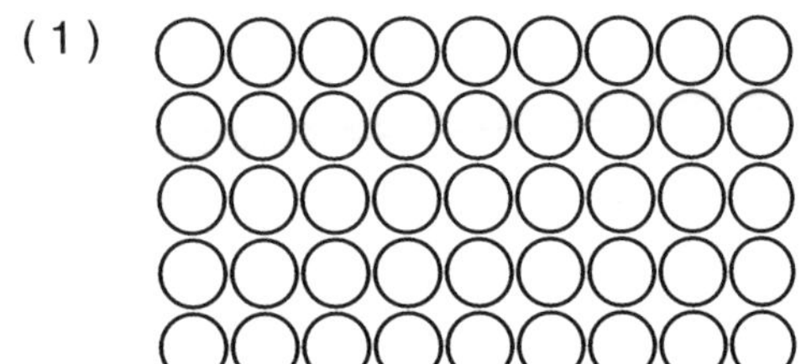

5 rows and 9 columns makes a total of 45.

(2) 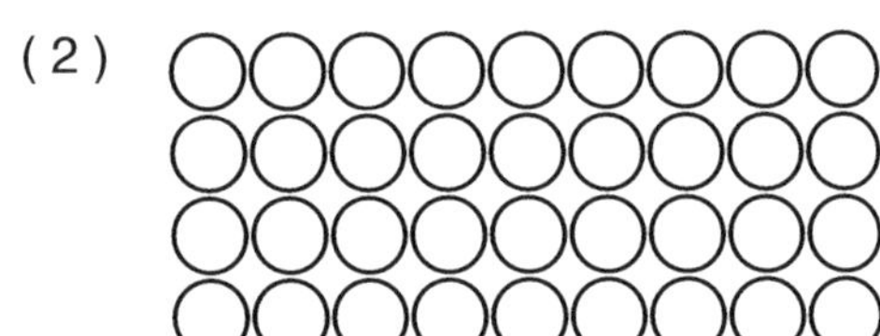

4 rows and 9 columns makes a total of 36.

(3) 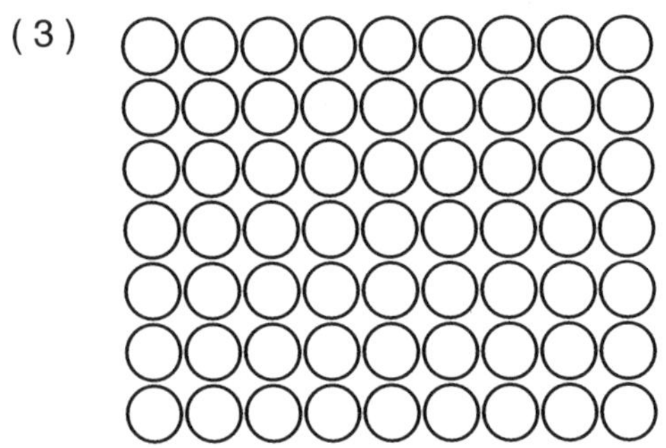

7 rows and 9 columns makes a total of 63.

(4) ○○○○○○○

1 rows and 7 columns makes a total of 7.

(5) ○○○ ○○○

2 rows and 3 columns makes a total of 6.

(6) 

2 rows and 9 columns makes a total of 18.

(7) 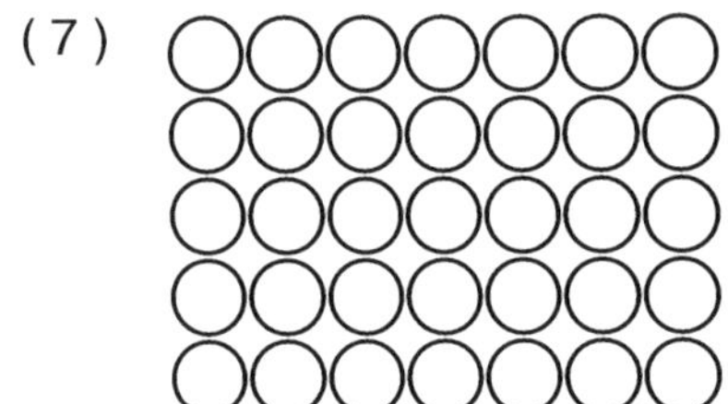

5 rows and 7 columns makes a total of 35.

(8) 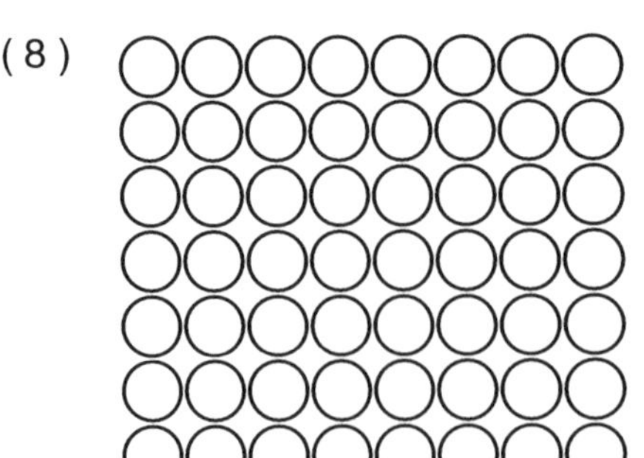

7 rows and 8 columns makes a total of 56.

(9) 

1 rows and 5 columns makes a total of 5.

Made in the USA
San Bernardino, CA
26 February 2019